P9-AGI-359

THE SPIRIT OF SERVICE

THE SPIRIT OF SERVICE

Exploring Faith, Service, and Social Justice in Higher Education

Brian T. Johnson and Carolyn R. O'Grady
Gustavus Adolphus College

EDITORS

ANKER PUBLISHING COMPANY, INC.
Bolton, Massachusetts

The Spirit of Service
Exploring Faith, Service, and Social Justice in Higher Education

Copyright © 2006 by Anker Publishing Company, Inc. All rights reserved. Printed in the United States of America. No part of this publication may be reproduced or distributed in any form or by any means, electronic or mechanical, including photocopying, recording, or by any information storage or retrieval system, without the prior written consent of the publisher.

ISBN 1-933371-01-3

Composition by Jessica Holland
Cover design by Dutton & Sherman Design

Anker Publishing Company, Inc.
563 Main Street
P.O. Box 249
Bolton, MA 01740-0249 USA

www.ankerpub.com

Library of Congress Cataloging-in-Publication Data

The spirit of service : exploring faith, service, and social justice in higher education / [edited by] Brian T. Johnson and Carolyn R. O'Grady.
   p. cm.
Includes bibliographical references and index.
ISBN 1-933371-01-3
1. Student service--United States. 2. Social justice--Study and teaching--United States. 3. Universities and colleges--United States--Religion. I. Johnson, Brian T. II. O'Grady, Carolyn R.

LC220.5.S598 2006
378.1'03--dc22
                            2006009422

This book is dedicated to the faculty, staff, students (current and alumni) of Gustavus Adolphus College.

In the spirit of service, all royalty proceeds from this book will go to the Community Service Center at Gustavus.

TABLE OF CONTENTS

ABOUT THE AUTHORS

The Editors

Brian T. Johnson serves as a chaplain at Gustavus Adolphus College. He is coeditor of *Stories from Christian Neighbors: A Heart for Ecumenism* (Liturgical Press, 2003) and recently completed, in addition to his M.Div. from Luther Northwestern Theological Seminar, a Master's in Sacred Theology from Yale University.

Carolyn R. O'Grady is associate professor of education at Gustavus Adolphus College, and a frequent workshop facilitator for schools and small organizations on issues of diversity, including race, gender, and sexual orientation. Her doctorate is from the University of Massachusetts Amherst in multicultural education. Her research interests include education for social justice, spirituality in education, and K–16 service-learning. She is the editor of *Integrating Service Learning and Multicultural Education in Colleges and Universities* (Lawrence Erlbaum, 2000).

The Contributors

Gastón A. Alzate is associate professor of Spanish in the Department of Modern Languages, Literatures, and Cultures at Gustavus Adolphus College. He is also codirector of the Latin American, Latino, and Caribbean Studies (LALACS) Program. A native of Colombia, Professor Alzate received a Ph.D. from Arizona State University. His research focuses on 20th-century Latin America, Mexican contemporary theater, and Colombian narrative and poetry.

Florence Amamoto is associate professor of English and director of Curriculum II at Gustavus Adolphus College. She has also been active in the Women's Studies Program, church-relatedness initiatives, and the Center for Vocational Reflection. She teaches American literature with a special interest in women and ethnic writers; her research focuses on turn-of-the-century American women writers, especially Willa Cather, and on Japanese-American literature.

Elizabeth R. Baer serves as professor of English at Gustavus Adolphus College. Her most recent book, *Experience and Expression: Women, the Nazis, and the Holocaust* (Wayne State University Press, 2003) is an anthology of essays on gender and the Holocaust, coedited with Dr. Myrna Goldenberg. Dr. Baer is also the coeditor, with Hester Baer, of the first English edition of *The Blessed Abyss: Inmate #6582 in Ravensbrück Concentration Camp for Women* (Wayne State University Press, 2000), a memoir by Nanda Herbermann.

Mark Bjelland is associate professor of geography and also teaches in the environmental studies program at Gustavus Adolphus College. Much of his work focuses on urban and regional planning, water resources, and human-environment interactions.

Leila Brammer is associate professor of communication studies at Gustavus Adolphus College, where she teaches courses in rhetorical and feminist criticism. Her research focuses on social movements, particularly how groups outside of the mainstream construct and adapt their ideology in relation to societal response and conflicts within the group. She is the author of *Excluded from Suffrage History: Matilda Joslyn Gage, Nineteenth-Century American Feminist* (Greenwood, 2000).

Noreen Buhmann is director of the Community Service Center at Gustavus Adolphus College. Formerly, she was the director of the Emma B. Howe YMCA in northeast Minneapolis. She is on the University of St. Thomas advisory board for service-learning.

Loramy Gerstbauer is assistant professor of political science and director of peace studies at Gustavus Adolphus College. She teaches courses in international relations, politics of developing nations, and Latin American politics as well as peace studies. Her research focuses on nongovernmental organization work in peace building and forgiveness in international relations.

Lisa Heldke teaches philosophy and women's studies at Gustavus Adolphus College, where she uses experiential educational methods in several of her courses. A pragmatist feminist philosopher who works on the philosophy of food, she is the author of *Exotic Appetites: Ruminations of a Food Adventurer* (Routledge, 2003), and coeditor of *Cooking, Eating, Thinking: Transformative Philosophies of Food* (Indiana University Press, 1992). She is also coeditor, with Peg O'Connor, of *Oppression, Privilege, and Resistance: Theoretical Readings on Racism, Sexism, and Heterosexism* (McGraw-Hill, 2004).

Callista Brown Isabelle is a 2000 Gustavus graduate. She recently earned her master of divinity degree from Yale Divinity School and the Yale Institute of Sacred Music, with a particular interest in congregational song and liturgical theology. She serves on the board of directors of Holden Village, an ecumenical retreat center in Washington State. She is currently serving as vicar in the chaplains' office at Gustavus Adolphus College.

Chris Johnson is director of the Center for Vocational Reflection and teaches in the Department of Religion at Gustavus Adolphus College. Chris holds a master of arts in theology and ethics from Luther Northwestern Theological Seminary (1989), and a Ph.D. in theology, ethics, and culture from the University of Iowa (1996). Before returning to Gustavus (where he graduated in 1985) to launch the vocation initiative, he was assistant professor of religion and director of service-learning at Buena Vista University.

Peg O'Connor is associate professor of women's studies at Gustavus Adolphus College. She is the author of *Oppression and Responsibility: A Wittgensteinian Approach to Social Practices and Moral Theory* (Penn State University Press, 2002). She is coeditor (with Naomi Scheman) of *Feminist Interpretations of Ludwig Wittgenstein* (Penn State University Press, 2002) and coeditor (with Lisa Heldke) of *Oppression, Privilege and Resistance: Theoretical Readings on Racism, Sexism and Heterosexism* (McGraw-Hill, 2004). She is currently completing a new book, tentatively titled *Morality and Our Complicated Form of Life: Feminist Wittgensteinian Metaethics*. She is also the coeditor and co-publisher (with Lisa Heldke) of *Philosophers on*

Holiday, the only 'zine in the philosophical travel/leisure genre; it can be viewed at http://homepages.gac.edu/~poconnor/

Sharon Daloz Parks is an associate director and member of the faculty at the Whidbey Institute. She has held faculty and senior research positions at Harvard Divinity School, Harvard Business School, the Kennedy School of Government, and the Weston School of Theology. She is coauthor of, among other books, *Common Fire: Leading Lives of Commitment in a Complex World* (Beacon Press, 1996), and the author of *Big Questions, Worthy Dreams: Mentoring Young Adults in Their Search for Meaning, Purpose, and Faith* (Jossey-Bass, 2000).

Nadarajan Sethuraju is the associate dean of diversity initiatives at Gustavus Adolphus College. He is also the director of the diversity center and the Crossroads Program, a dormitory-based initiative with an international and intercultural focus.

Mary M. Solberg, associate professor of religion, teaches courses in various contemporary theologies and ethics and medicine. She earned her Ph.D. from Union Theological Seminary. In past professional incarnations she has edited books, advocated for refugees, and administered international humanitarian aid. She wrote *Compelling Knowledge: A Feminist Proposal for an Epistemology of the Cross* (State University of New York Press, 1997); coedited *Healing by Heart: Clinical and Ethical Case Stories of Hmong Families and Western Providers* (Vanderbilt University Press, 2003); and translated *Luther and Liberation: A Latin American Perspective* (Fortress Press, 1992) by Walter Altmann. She loves to sing Bach's music.

Jenifer K. Ward is associate professor of German and chair of the Department of Modern Languages, Literatures, and Cultures at Gustavus Adolphus College. She serves on the executive committee of the Association of Departments of Foreign Languages and has held fellowships from the Fulbright Commission and the Institute for Ecumenical and Cultural Research. She works in the field of German cinema and literature, and has published numerous articles and book chapters on cinema and adaptation.

Lillian Zumberge is a 2001 graduate of Gustavus Adolphus College. She currently teaches at John Glenn Middle School in Maplewood, Minnesota, and co-coordinates the district's SEED (Seeking Educational Equity and Diversity) program.

FOREWORD

This is an important book because it helps make the unspeakable "speakable." Here, a cadre of highly competent, thoughtful, and courageous professors and administrators, convened and hosted by Brian Johnson and Carolyn O'Grady, have critically reflected on their own moments of awkwardness, discomfort, and subtle and not-so-subtle fear and failure that they have experienced in the classroom, in the college, and in their work as professors and citizens in the wider community.

These moments have occurred when they have found themselves bumping up against the invisible boundaries that have been drawn within academic culture between responsible, rigorous, intellectual competence and those facets of human experience that we describe as faith, spirituality, service, and a commitment to social justice. These boundaries have been drawn by the myth of radical objectivity—a presumption of detachment and compartmentalization—and the corresponding recognition that faith, spirituality, service, and a commitment to social justice necessarily involve one's person. Though contemporary scholarship across all the disciplines challenges the reification of a subject-versus-object distinction, the established norms of the Western academy remain strong.

These authors work within a highly ranked, religiously affiliated school that maintains a working, creative tension between its founding heritage and an unambiguous commitment to open intellectual inquiry. Religiously, they identify themselves variously as, for instance, atheist, Christian, Buddhist, and Jewish, and they represent a broad cross-section of academic disciplines. In their roles as scholars and teachers, they have observed, for example, that when a student expresses a personal, unexamined religious belief in class, it is customary for both fellow students and professors to let the comment (and the awkward moment) pass, rather than engage the student's assumptions as one more easily might in relationship to other subjects. On the other hand, when working with students on an issue of social justice, it is just as likely, they note, that the students' and the professors' (and sometimes even the chaplain's) motivations for working on the issue—motivations and deeply held values that may very well be rooted in spiritual experience and theological perspective (for good or for ill)—will go unacknowledged. They know that sometimes an "A student" writes papers that are acceptable to a professor, although the student maintains beliefs that are diametrically opposed to what appears in the paper. And I, personally, will always remember a conference on service-learning where a dean observed that on his campus the professor who most effectively incorporated community service into his courses was unwilling to provide leadership in encouraging other faculty to do the same for fear of being regarded as "a lesser academic."

This book has come into being because the authors have recognized that it is in the awkward moments and false assumptions that something critically important in their practice of the intellectual life and in their responsibility to their students and to the wider life of our world is at stake. They are recognizing that they are responsible for initiating students into critical thought and also into connective thought. They are coming to terms with what we all know: What is learned in the classroom about the significance of social location, what is experienced in a community ground down by poverty, what is discovered in the chemistry or biology lab, and what is believed or not believed in one's soul may need to be cast into a mutually informing inquiry if truth is to be apprehended as fully as possible. This is especially so if the moral courage, persistence, and bigger vision that is now required to engage the most critical issues of our time is to be manifest in a new generation of citizens and leaders.

In a world where the complexity we now confront tempts all of us simply to carve out a manageable piece and cultivate a narrow expertise, these faculty are wading into big questions: What is the role of higher education in the life of today's commons? What is the purpose of the intellectual life? What is the vocation of a professor? They recognize that the academy is responsible for many things—research and the transmission of knowledge included. The academy also plays a key role as a privileged milieu for the formation of a worthy adulthood. They are coming to terms with the recognition that "whether, what, and how we think about what we believe and value . . . matters—for us as individuals, but especially for us as members of communities, local and global." They are reaching for what one of them describes as "ethical intelligence," which may not be the default option but can become an active choice.

Florence Amamoto writes that in her own college years at Stanford University during the height of the Vietnam War, she learned that college was a time to explore one's values as well as the riches of knowledge:

> It was there that I learned to be concerned about civic issues. It was there that I learned the importance of connecting learning to life. And maybe most importantly, it was there that I learned it all mattered—and that I mattered—that ordinary people could make a difference in the world.

Elizabeth R. Baer quotes Joseph Joubert, a 17th-century French philosopher who said, "To teach is to learn twice." These professors and their colleagues—teaching now in a very different era, and despite the reasonable fears they identify in themselves and in their students, the lack of a common language for this kind of discourse, and the other barriers they describe so well—are generously offering their own experience of teaching and thus learning twice the importance of connecting learning to life. They inform and inspire the professorial imagination, in public and private higher education, by eloquently revealing their honed and emergent practices of teaching, scholarship, and ongoing learning, helping to move all of us further into inadequately charted waters. At a time when whether and how faith should influence the social, cultural, and intellectual milieu is a highly contested question and anti-intellectualism is abroad in the land, they bring a vital and timely gift to the life of the academy.

Sharon Daloz Parks
Director, Leadership for the New Commons
An initiative of the Whidbey Institute

ACKNOWLEDGEMENTS

A substantial grant from the Louisville Institute enabled us to conduct the research that culminated in this book. We thank James W. Lewis, executive director of the institute, for his support of our ideas. Early research efforts were conducted by Sara Pekarna Bisso and Kari Lipke in collaboration with Brian. The Center for Vocational Reflection at Gustavus Adolphus College provided funds for travel, and part of Carolyn's work on this project was supported by a research, scholarship, and creativity grant from the Gustavus Faculty Development Committee. Brian received a sabbatical from the college which contributed to the final stages of this project. A Bush mini-grant from the faculty development program provided essential last-minute funding.

We are grateful for the support and encouragement of colleagues at other institutions of higher education who spent several hours talking with us during our visits to their campuses. These include Victor Kazanjian, dean of religious and spiritual life and codirector of the Peace and Justice Studies Program at Wellesley College; Peter Hocking, director of the Swearer Center for Public Service at Brown University; Rabbi Alan Flam, senior fellow at the Swearer Center; and Keith Morton and the staff of the Feinstein Institute for Public Service at Providence College. Sharon Parks inspired us during an early visit to our college when she asked us, "What are the big questions that should be thought about at Gustavus?" Bruce Thorpe provided us with housing and a vehicle during our time on the East Coast.

Our work would have been impossible without the involvement of those students and faculty who agreed to participate in focus groups with us. We particularly acknowledge the student whose name appears here as Lucy, who really provided the impetus for this entire project.

Our writing efforts were substantially improved through the time we spent at the ARC Retreat Center and Shalom Hill Farm. We thank the staff at these wonderful centers, and particularly acknowledge the assistance of Becky Potter.

We are grateful for the support of several colleagues who read various drafts of this work with a critical eye and in each case provided us with extensive

feedback. We were honored that they felt our work merited so much attention. We especially thank Jim Bonilla, Lisa Heldke, Greg Kaster, Stephen
Kellert, Mariangela Maguire, Mike Reynolds, and Kate Wittenstein. We have
borrowed liberally from the ideas of each of them.

The reference staff at Folke Bernadotte Library were unflagging in their
willingness to track down even the most elusive interlibrary loan material.
Claire Stokes did a masterful job with the index, and we thank her for this
tedious work. The staff of Anker Publishing, particularly Wendy Swanson,
Jennifer Gibson, and Carolyn Dumore, were always responsive and helpful.

The process of this collaboration took several years, and during this time
we learned to appreciate how differently we each approach a task such as
this. Brian brought a deeply rooted understanding of Lutheran tradition to
our work, a substantial sense of humor, the willingness to think about old
ideas in new ways, and a vast degree of patience and perseverance. Carolyn
brought her willingness to ask searching questions, attention to detail, comfort with conflict, and non-Christian perspective. Our friendship has deepened in the course of this project, even as we have learned how to manage
our conflicting views on the subjects we discuss.

Our greatest appreciation goes to our colleagues who contributed to this volume. We are grateful for their willingness to explore uncharted territory with
us. We consider ourselves fortunate to work with scholars who step outside of
their disciplines to wrestle against the academy's isolating and reductionist tendencies. This has been a rich dialogue for all of us.

PART I:
Analyzing the Landscape

1

WHY WE STARTED AND WHY IT MATTERS

Carolyn R. O'Grady and Brian T. Johnson

Two critical events acted as seeds to inspire the development of this book. The first was an interaction Carolyn had with a sophomore student in one of her introductory education classes at Gustavus Adolphus College. It was just after spring break, and Lucy (not her real name) had been in Costa Rica over break building houses. When Carolyn asked class members to tell the group about something worthwhile that had occurred to them over break, Lucy described in detail the work she had done and the pleasure she had taken in it. She realized, she said, that while "those people" were poor, they were still happy, and it taught her a lesson about the role of material possessions in her own life. Further, she said, she had returned from break and "prayed for guidance" about the role of mission work in her future life. She knew, she said, that God wanted her to return and help "those people" in Costa Rica.

This introductory education course had already included a large dose of content about issues of power and oppression in U.S. education. Carolyn and her students had talked about the inequities that exist in classrooms, especially for poor students and students of color. They had looked in particular at the history of Latino education in the U.S. and the discrimination often experienced by Latino students whose first language is not English. Yet here was Lucy reflecting on her experience without any reference to the race and class privilege that enabled her to spend a brief time in Costa Rica helping "those people."[1]

This in itself was not the most difficult thing for Carolyn to manage about this teaching episode; it is common for students at our college to forget at times the ways in which they are members of privileged groups. Rather, it was the religious reference in Lucy's comments that left Carolyn speechless. Lucy was a student who frequently described in class what she had prayed for the prior evening, or how God had answered her prayers in one way or another. These kinds of overt religious references are unusual at our institution, despite the fact that it is a college affiliated with the Evangelical Lutheran Church in America (ELCA). In reflecting on the post–spring break class discussion, Carolyn realized that despite her experience leading class discussions on challenging topics, she was both uncomfortable and silenced by Lucy's use of religious language in describing personal life events. This student had clearly thought about the relationship between faith and service in her life, but had apparently not connected these to the complex relationships and intricacies of cross-cultural immersion.

In the meantime, Brian also experienced a perplexing and eye-opening revelation. As one of the chaplains of the college, Brian has organized students to participate in a sleep-out in front of the chapel during Hunger and Homelessness Week. Some professors have incorporated this activity as part of a service-learning component in their classes. This experiential activity annually draws 20 or more students, and occasionally some faculty and staff. They build temporary shelters out of cardboard boxes, huddle around a trashcan fire to stay warm, beg for food, and attempt to raise awareness about homelessness.

For reflection sessions, Brian invited professors from the political science and philosophy departments to raise questions and share information about the dilemmas presented by a global economy. The conversation centered on students' reactions to participating in the sleep-out, the political, philosophical, and economic issues involved in homelessness, and strategies for working to end poverty. The topic of faith, however, as a motive for engaging in social justice work was never raised, not even by Brian himself. In looking back on this avoidance, Brian realized that while he regularly talks with students about issues of faith or spirituality, he is reluctant to raise faith issues when the event is classroom focused. Since there were faculty present at the reflection sessions, what could have been an intentional examination of the role of faith or religion in social justice work turned into an impersonal discussion.

After Lucy had described her trip to Costa Rica and class had ended, Carolyn immediately sought out Brian to talk about ways to help students develop a more nuanced and critical understanding of the interconnections between the faith they hold, the service they perform, and issues of social justice. Though our individual paths vary, both of us come to this work with a commitment to service, spirituality, and social justice and the desire to help students make these connections. Brian is an ordained Lutheran minister with more than 15 years of experience as a chaplain in higher education. He works closely with students and staff in our Community Service Center, as well as with many student organizations on campus. Carolyn practices *vipassana*, a form of Buddhist meditation, wrote a dissertation on spirituality and multicultural education, and has incorporated service-learning into her courses for several years. Between us, we have a sizeable amount of experience in these issues; yet, as we talked about our experiences with Lucy and the sleepover, we kept asking ourselves how we could have been more effective in those situations.

Over the next three years, we continued this conversation by visiting other institutions that had programs we hoped would give us insight into best practices for making connections between faith, service, and social justice.[2] We also talked with students and faculty at our own campus through focus groups in which we asked specific questions about how commonly (or whether) faculty or students engage in discussions exploring the links between service, spirituality, and social justice.[3]

What we discovered through our campus visits and subsequent literature review is that there is a wealth of material which explores each area separately, but very little that attempts to integrate these issues. What we discovered during our focus groups was that students had few opportunities to talk about the integration of these topics, and faculty had great discomfort with engaging students (or each other) in these kinds of conversations. We have come to learn that Carolyn's reaction to Lucy's comments in class about her faith is not atypical of the sort of discomfort or bemusement that many faculty (and students) on our campus experience. Likewise, Brian's awareness of an avoidance of faith discussion during and after the sleep-out highlights the more general separation between faith and reason, and private and public discourse.

Service, Justice, and Spirituality: Why the Link?

This book explores the intersections of spirituality, service, and social justice in order to probe several essential questions with which we and our colleagues have struggled as educators of undergraduates. How can community service and service-learning be most effective at enhancing justice and equity for all individuals? How can we help college students identify and critique their motives for engaging in service while simultaneously instilling in them the commitment to work for social justice? How can a spiritual perspective enhance an individual's ability to engage effectively in service for social justice and the persistence to stick with it over the long haul?

Many activists who describe themselves as antireligious also admit the importance of a spiritual practice for opening up new ways to work for justice (Thompson, 2001). Tisdell (2003) describes work for social justice as requiring a combination of tools, with the ability to engage the heart as essential as rationality and critical thinking. Paolo Freire, the father of current social justice theory, was a deeply spiritual man whose religious values shaped much of his political and social activism (Stockton, 2001). Since spirituality touches directly on our sense of community (Astin, 2004), a strong sense of spirituality may help maintain commitment to both service and social justice work (Koth, 2003). The combination of inner reflection and outward action can enable social justice workers to live a more integrated life, neither allowing themselves to burn out from the stress of activism nor focusing exclusively and apolitically on their own wellbeing.

It is important that we clarify how we understand the terms we are using. We define *service-learning* as community service that is linked to an individual's academic experience, through related course materials or through reflective activities (Zlotkowski, 1998). Thus, service-learning might be completed as part of a class taught in a school or other educational setting, and it always includes some intentional, guided learning in addition to the service experience itself. On the other hand, *community service* is a process through which individuals are involved in voluntary service activities in their communities but which often does not include any intentionally structured educational component (Minnesota Campus Compact, 1999).

Contributors to this book have their own ideas of what spirituality or faith mean to each of them. As instigators of the project which culminated in this book, both of us tended to use *spirituality* and *faith* somewhat interchangeably (Carolyn being more comfortable with the term *spirituality* to describe her own practice, and Brian being more comfortable with the term *faith* to describe his). In religious terms, the word *faith* connotes the view that there is a God, without the need to scientifically prove God's existence. Often the word *belief* is used in reference to faith, but belief is primarily a cognitive enterprise and does not embody the dynamic realities we would like to ascribe to faith. For instance, faith is concerned with truth, issues of universal concern, the role of doubt and skepticism, action in the world, and meaning making (Parks, 2000). For religious individuals, *faith* can connote adherence to the tenets of a particular religion. We use *spirituality* more broadly to refer to the source of meaning, purpose, and direction in life (Plunkett, 1990). Understood this way, even someone who does not believe in God could be considered a spiritual person, though they may not choose to use that word about themselves (O'Grady, 1992). Burton (2002) asserts that an experience of *spirituality* has varying mixtures of three qualities. It is a way of knowing that is not accessible exclusively through rational thought, it involves a feeling of transcendence or moving beyond the boundaries of the self, and "it is *unitive*, involving a sense of unity with existence and forces underlying its continuing creation" (p. 21). At the same time, we must keep in mind that Western categories to describe faith and spirituality do not always adequately express the complexities of belief in all the world's faith traditions.

Notions of social justice are complex, as Miller (1999) points out in his attempt to assess the many ways in which social justice can be understood in modern society. In a multicultural world such as ours, it can be extremely difficult to build consensus about the ways in which relations of oppression and privilege should be handled. If there is social inequity, then clearly the basic social structure is unjust, but divergent views about what constitutes change for the better can be irreconcilable. Nevertheless, we believe that it is essential to act on behalf of those who suffer, whether or not everyone who acts can agree on a definition of what constitutes either suffering or justice. Therefore, we follow Adams, Bell, and Griffin (1997) in defining *social justice* as:

the full and equal participation of all groups in a society that is mutually shaped to meet their needs. Social justice includes a vision of society in which the distribution of resources is equitable and all members are physically and psychologically safe and secure. . . . Social justice involves social actors who have a sense of their own agency as well as a sense of social responsibility toward and with others and the society as a whole. (p. 3)

Service-Learning for Social Justice

We believe that community service and service-learning are valid pedagogies, and current research indicates they can have great influence on student learning in higher education (Eyler & Giles, 1999; Jacoby & Associates, 1996, 2003; O'Grady, 2000; Rhoades, 1997; Stanton, Giles, & Cruz, 1999; Wade, 1997; Waterman, 1997; Zlotkowski, 1998). Morton (1995) argues for a distinction between "thin" versions and "thick" versions of service. As he describes, "thin" versions are "disempowering and hollow, and can be paternalistic and self-serving" (p. 24) while in contrast "thick" versions are "sustaining and potentially revolutionary, and are grounded in deeply held, internally coherent values" (p. 28). While we recognize that there is a continuum of motivations for engaging in service from thick to thin, or from charity to social change (Morton, 1995), we value most highly the kind of service that is explicitly intended to create changes in the social conditions that perpetuate oppression.

More than 80% of the students at our college voluntarily participate in community service. Some students are involved in one-time volunteer efforts (such as the annual one-day community clean-up effort sponsored by our own campus). Others engage in more sustained service, either short-term (like a spring break service trip) or long-term (service done as part of a course over a semester or year). Sometimes college students participate in service activities because it is required by their fraternity, sorority, or a student organization of which they are a member. But most students engage in service out of a desire to help others, to "give back," or because a service ethic has been instilled by their family or their church. Often, those with whom students work are outside their economic, racial, or social network. Ideally, this provides opportunities for students to develop new lenses for understanding social conditions. However, far too often students' own stereotypes are deepened when they see that those who need help are those who are *not* like the student. Rather than questioning the social order, students complete the service, feel good about themselves, hope they have helped someone else, and go on with their lives.

Maybach (1996) describes the typical service relationship as one in which there is a provider and a recipient, with the person on the receiving end of that relationship seen only by their needs rather than their strengths. This sort of service patronizes individuals or groups that are already marginalized by inequitable social systems. According to Minnesota Campus Compact's (1999) study of model campus-community collaborations, much collaborative work in Minnesota and elsewhere focuses on service activities that ameliorate individual needs (tutoring children, soup kitchens) without addressing systemic problems. While charitable activities certainly can be important work, "they are simply not adequate in and of themselves to create larger social change, i.e. change that addresses tremendous inequalities and fundamental social challenges and creates the structures and conditions that promote equality, autonomy, cooperation and sustainability in communities" (p. 1).

It seems clear to us that the world's great suffering calls for compassionate action. Poverty, racism, and cultural intolerance are pervasive in our culture. In the U.S. alone, almost 13% of the population falls below the poverty line, and almost half of these are children (Wallis, 2000). As Horwitz (2002) notes, "It takes courage to face the world with compassionate attention, to be candid about the injustices we understand, and to probe those we do not" (p. xi). It is easy to feel despair and grief in the face of overwhelming social injustice. Taking individual or collective action on behalf of others who suffer is one way to engender a spirit of optimism about the future (Wuthnow, 1995). As Jones & Maloy (1996) point out, "Ideally, community service learning engages everyone in experiences that raise puzzling contradictions for their taken-for-granted assumptions about the status quo" (p. 38). Unfortunately. this is too often not the case in community service.

For us as educators, students' willingness to embrace service is a foundation upon which we can develop student awareness of social inequities. This process can begin as we ask students to consider several deep questions: "What does it mean to care or to have compassion? How is need manifested? What is helpful or empowering? What is oppressive? How is oppression manifested in society? In me? What is good service? What is the common good? How can we reach a common good cooperatively?" (Maybach, 1996, p. 235).

Clearly, not all service will lead to social change.[4] But service without an analysis of the economic and political conditions that give rise to injustices not only reinforces the status quo, but also colludes with the status quo. Introducing students to social justice issues and asking them to question their motives for engaging in service can create confusion and discomfort for them. Our task as educators is, as Warren (1998) says, to create "a supportive community of learners who can honestly share feelings, speak from a place of authentic experience, and listen compassionately to others who are different from themselves" (p. 135). In particular, we can build on the religious beliefs that some students bring with them into the service experience (Ammerman, 1997).

The Role of Spirituality

In his research on service-learning, Waterman (1997) noted that students involved in volunteer service score higher on measures of intrinsic religiosity than students who do not engage in service. Religious faith or spiritual practice can be an impetus as well as a support for those who engage in service, especially when that work is done with the poor or with others who are targets of social injustice. Religious faith and compassion for others enable believers to hold out and act from the image of what Quakers call "that of God" in others (Bacon, 1985).

But faith-based service also has its risks. It can lead to a paternalistic mentality in which the server patronizes those being served rather than approaching the service experience as a reciprocal endeavor. Service can also be done from a naively "missionary" stance, with those engaged in service attempting to proselytize rather than understand the spiritual or political contexts of those with whom they are working. In either case, the result is oppressive, sometimes racist, and unlikely to result in long-term change in the circumstances of either the server or those being served (O'Grady & Chappell, 1999). As we have discovered, opportunities to raise these kinds of issues related to belief system and practice are often ignored or avoided by educators, usually due to discomfort in discussing religion or out of a desire to avoid the politics of analysis of social inequity. But this avoidance ignores a potent reality about the pervasiveness of religious commitments in American life.

The U.S. is the most religiously diverse nation on earth (Eck, 2001). A 1998 Gallup poll (Lyons, 2003) reported that 82% of those surveyed felt that spiritual growth was a very important part of their lives. The sale of spiritually oriented books has increased eightfold since 1993 (Lantieri, 2002). Yet, religion may be one of the least understood markers of diversity, and is often omitted from texts that focus on multicultural issues. Americans as a whole have a low level of religious literacy, with religious differences often feared, particularly in our post–9/11 world. The separation of church and state has served to protect religious observers of all creeds as well as those who are not religious, but has also had the unfortunate effect of creating a climate in which discussion of religious or spiritual perspectives has become taboo.[5] Few public schools in the United States have adequate programs to help students understand world religions, much less critically examine their own religious beliefs.

Perhaps the most persuasive reason to attend to issues of religion and spirituality is our responsibility to young adults in higher education. Acknowledging the religious or spiritual perspectives our students may hold is as valuable as acknowledging their race or gender, since all of these help shape the way they construct and understand the world (Tisdell, 2003). More than 79% of the 1999 entering undergraduate class at the University of Michigan reported a religious preference and more than 59% said they pray or meditate every week (Walters, 2001). Indeed, 43% of American teens go to church or synagogue regularly (Lyons, 2003). The most recent study of undergraduates and spirituality (Astin, Astin, Lindholm, Bryant, Szelenyi, & Calderone, 2005) took an in-depth look at the religious and spiritual views of college students. While most first-year college students affirm their belief in God, almost half of them describe themselves as "seeking," "doubting," or "conflicted" (Bartlett, 2005). This confirms the work of Cherry, DeBerg, and Porterfield (2001) who, in *Religion on Campus*, explored the meaning religion and spirituality have for young college students and found that the majority of undergraduates preferred to use the term *spirituality* rather than *religion*, believing that spirituality connoted a personal experience or quest rather than fixed, handed-down belief systems.

And it is not only young adults but faculty, too, who seek to live lives of meaning, value, and purpose. As Astin and Astin (1999) claim, academia "has for far too long encouraged us to lead fragmented and inauthentic lives, where we act either as if we are *not* spiritual beings, or as if our spiritual side is irrelevant to our vocation or work" (p. 2).Yet their study of 70 faculty at four California colleges and universities revealed that while some faculty affirmed an overt religious faith or spiritual practice, and others did not see themselves as spiritual beings at all, almost all the interviewees were concerned about "meaning and purpose" in their personal and professional lives (p. 31).

Young adults need opportunities to raise and struggle with questions of meaning and purpose in multiple ways, but too often teachers let them down because of our own nervousness, discomfort, lack of knowledge, or antireligious biases (Nash, 2001). The consequences of this, however, are problematic. As Miller (2001) notes, excluding religious and spiritual perspectives from our discourse in higher education "thwarts the integration necessary for building a wiser world" (p. 300). Institutions of higher education pay a great deal of attention to students' intellectual progress, but too little attention to the development of self-awareness and such affective skills as empathy, compassion, and inspiration (Astin, 2004).[6] In doing so, we not only risk reinforcing the competitive and individualistic mentality so prevalent in the Western world, we also reinforce the notion that the rational and the emotional are entirely separate domains. This is a great danger at a moment in history when the world is in crisis with poverty, illiteracy, hunger, homelessness, and war as the norm for most of the global population.

Those of us who work with young adults must take particular care to help them learn how to participate in activism for a democratic and equitable society. Parks (2000) describes the kind of journey young adults of college age are engaged in and their need for fearless adult mentors to move them into the next phase of adulthood. Many students are seeking a sense of meaning and purpose and desire to do a better job than they think their forebears did in making the world a better place. We believe that service is one way for students to learn the power of activism. Our responsibility as educators is to explore the currents of religious and spiritual practice in our midst, analyze their challenges and benefits, and contribute to the enhancement of the relationships among service, justice, and faith. We can provide meaningful opportunities for individuals to deepen their understandings of spirituality through service activities that build toward a more just world.

The Institutional Context

This text invites authors from our own institution, Gustavus Adolphus College, to describe and reflect on the confluence of service, spirituality, and social justice as those concepts are enacted here. Gustavus offers a rich environment in which to consider the fundamental questions we address in this book. It is a religiously affiliated college with ties to the Evangelical Lutheran Church in America (ELCA). There is a long history of community service and service-learning on our campus, coupled with an explicit commitment in our mission statement to helping students lead lives of leadership in a multicultural and international context. Our college is a kind of laboratory in which the question of how—and whether—religiously or spiritually motivated service can be done in the interests of social justice is explored every day. The lessons we have learned, as well as the successes and failures we have had, can provide guidance for all institutions that work closely with young adults.

The majority of Gustavus students (91%) grew up in the upper Midwest and almost three-quarters of the student body self-report as Lutheran or Roman Catholic.[7] While 20% of these students describe themselves as of another Christian denomination, the remaining students report as Jewish, Buddhist, Muslim, or "no affiliation." But the numbers do not reveal the complexity of our students' dispositions toward faith, service, or justice. Just as there is no single Christian denomination at Gustavus, there is also no one understanding of what it means to be Lutheran.

Not only are the majority of our students Christian, they are also white and middle class. About 1% of our students are international, and another 7% are domestic-born students of color. Our faculty, likewise, is predominantly white (92%), making this an institution that must consciously monitor its own institutionalized racism.

Until about 1960, it was assumed that faculty hired at Gustavus were Lutheran or, at the least, of another Christian denomination. Today there is no formal expectation that staff be Lutheran or even Christian, and though we do not gather statistics on the religious affiliation of our faculty and staff, current faculty's beliefs about God range from atheism to evangelicalism, with most major religious belief systems represented. Although chapel attendance has not been mandatory on our campus since the mid-1960s, faculty interviewees are nonetheless taken to a chapel service during their on-campus interview. This practice enables a job applicant to see how Lutheran *and* ecumenical our chapel program is, and it reinforces the fact that Gustavus is decidedly not a public institution (the first two articles in our bylaws affirm that we are a church of the ELCA[8]). At the same time, the church-relatedness of Gustavus is a contested idea. Some faculty regret what they perceive to be the loss of what they consider a marker of the college's identity, while others struggle with what it means to be a church-related institution.

In inviting participation from our colleagues, we kept in mind several variables. Because we are a relatively small campus with about 2,500 students and about 250 faculty and staff, we tend to know something about each other's dispositions toward issues such as faith, justice, and service. With this in mind, we asked individuals who we assumed were quite religious, as well as those we thought were not religious at all, to consider writing a chapter. We were also intentional in our invitations to those on campus who are involved in social justice work and those who have engaged students in service-learning. Each person we asked to contribute was excited about this project, and even those who declined our invitation were encouraging of this initiative.

Every contributor was given a set of questions (some common to all, others unique to the individual) and asked to write reflectively and from their own experience, keeping in mind that the intended audience for this book is individuals who work with young adults in higher education. The questions were intended to be guides rather than prescriptive directions for authors. Among the common questions were:

- How do you personally define *faith* or *spirituality* and does this influence the way in which you do your work?

- How effective do you think service-learning is as a vehicle for students to become activists for social justice? How do you use service-learning in your own courses and why?

- What role does commitment to social justice play in your work with students or colleagues either in your classes or in other work you do on campus? Why is this important to you?

- In what way(s) do you think the climate at Gustavus *most effectively* helps students or faculty understand links between faith, service, and social justice? How does this climate *least effectively* develop that understanding?

- How would you characterize the climate at Gustavus for conversations about faith, among faculty and/or between faculty and students? What supports do you feel exist for these kinds of conversations? What deterrents do you feel exist?

- What specific programming do you think is valuable for helping faculty or students reflect most effectively on the links between service-learning and social justice?

While we feel this book offers a rich insight into the terrain of Gustavus, some viewpoints are absent. For instance, the voices of students are limited to only two recent graduates. Likewise, the text contains the reflections of many more faculty members than staff, despite the fact that both administrative and secretarial staff work as closely with students and are as important to them—if not more so—than faculty. In addition, since our goal was to explore inter-sections of service, justice, and faith, we chose not to invite contributions from those members of our community who we know are dubious about this work. We cannot claim that our book reflects every aspect of the climate at Gustavus, but we are confident it captures essential elements at this point in the college's history.

Outline of the Book

The book's first part, "Analyzing the Landscape," provides the groundwork by exploring the meaning, practice, and implications of religious or spiritu-ally motivated service as these are done in our context. In Chapter 2, Florence Amamoto writes as a Buddhist about the difficult nature of "faith talk" even at a religiously affiliated institution. She describes some of the ways that spiritual work is done at Gustavus, and she provides an insight into the ways this work may nourish *and* hinder a faculty member's comfort on our campus. Chapter 3 deepens the analysis of our college's landscape by exploring the roles specific programs on our campus play in nurturing stu-dent learning. Noreen Buhmann and Brian Johnson take a close look at the collaborative work of the Community Service Center and the chaplains' office and explore the directional signals that a college's foundational docu-ments can provide.

Part II, "Practicing What We Preach," offers specific examples from facul-ty for integrating faith or spiritual perspectives with service as these have been tested on our campus. In this section, readers will learn about what has worked, as well as what dilemmas remain. Chapter 4 analyzes the ways members of the religion department attempt to extend students' thinking about what it means to be a Christian. Mary Solberg looks particularly at ways to present students with significant opportunities to explore social jus-tice work in the context of Christianity. In Chapter 5, Mark Bjelland exam-ines how he has worked to integrate faith, social justice, and service-learning within his environmental studies classes.

In Chapter 6, Gastón Alzate describes a service-learning project that links Spanish students with our region's growing Latino community and the kinds of ethical and cultural values that are part of this project. In Chapter 7, Mimi Gerstbauer describes the challenge of being an evangelical Christian and an advocate for social justice, and how these two perspectives intersect in her work as a faculty member in political science. The point of view of two atheists is presented in Chapter 8, as Lisa Heldke and Peg O'Connor describe a service-learning course they teach that focuses on the ethics of food production. Their analysis reminds us that "making meaning" is not dependent on holding any religious belief. In Chapter 9, Jenifer Ward describes an international course she has taught in Germany that intentionally blends faith practice, service-learning, and social justice work.

Part III, "Getting to the Heart of the Matter," focuses on specific dilemmas and implications for engaging in service for social justice as these have been manifested for us. In Chapter 10, Leila Brammer takes a close look at the risk faced by faculty who do choose to engage with students (or each other) in conversations about contested topics such as spirituality or justice. Her analysis offers insight into some of the costs and benefits for faculty considering doing this. Chapter 11 describes the opportunities and challenges for Nadarajan Sethuraju as associate dean for diversity development in providing students with campus opportunities to explore religious and racial identities in greater detail. In Chapter 12, Elizabeth Baer describes a faculty development program that assists faculty in teaching with a social justice perspective through the development of service-learning initiatives; more than 25 faculty have participated in this program over the last three years. In Chapter 13, Chris Johnson helps us understand the important role of reflection in enabling students and faculty to explore the ways spirituality, justice, and service can be integrated. This section concludes in Chapter 14 with the reflections of two Gustavus alumni. Callista Brown Isabelle and Lillian Zumberge look back on the time they spent on our campus as undergraduates and the ways in which their experiences here helped—or hindered—their ability to integrate faith, justice, and service.

Our conclusion in Chapter 15 offers a wealth of suggestions and strategies, as well as our reflections as we finish this project.

Last Thoughts

This book represents a conversation in progress, an attempt to tease out how to help undergraduates integrate service and spirituality for the purpose of social justice. We are very grateful to those colleagues who contributed their perspectives to this volume. Academics who discuss spirituality publicly can face ridicule from some of their peers. Several of our contributors are revealing aspects of their innermost landscape that may not be well known to the rest of the college community. In addition, there are sometimes sharply differing views on what role, if any, service-learning, social justice, or faith should play in guiding the work we do on our campus. We ourselves do not agree with everything each of our contributors says, but each chapter offers a unique window through which we can gain a different perspective on the themes explored here. We hope the risks our colleagues have taken will provide the stimulation for wide-ranging conversations about these issues at other colleges and universities as well as our own.

Endnotes

1) Using the words "those people" is an example of how Lucy views Costa Ricans as the "other." This kind of usage serves to reify one's own social position through stigmatization of the "other," even if this is not the speaker's intended meaning. Lucy's language thus reinforces her race and class privilege, and the supposed normativeness of her own experience of the world. In effect, she has "colonized" Costa Ricans through her language.

2) We are grateful to faculty and staff at the following institutions for allowing us access to their good thinking: Providence College, Brown University, and Wellesley College. A grant from the Louisville Institute provided support for this research.

3) Over a two-year period we conducted two student and three faculty focus groups. Participants represented a range of demographics, disciplines, and years at Gustavus.

4) Historian Greg Kaster (personal communication, August 14, 2003) has pointed out that the current popularity of service-learning in higher education seems to have emerged and flourished in tandem with the nation's political turn to the right. While it is unlikely that one has caused the other, it is important to consider whether service-learning has actually been co-opted by conservative elements in order to reduce its effectiveness as a social change movement.

5) Establishment of the White House Office of Faith-Based and Community Initiatives has further politicized discussions of faith and spirituality. We welcome the acknowledgement that service providers do not leave their religious or ethical convictions at the door, and, as Heffner & Beversluis (2002) assert, this initiative provides an opportunity for debate in the public square over the role of faith-based institutions in social service. However, this conflating of church and state has further exacerbated animosity toward rational discussions of the role of spirituality in public life and education, and consequently made our own efforts much more difficult.

6) Hollinger (2002) reminds us that there is a good reason why discussions of faith in modern universities may be viewed as intrusive:

> There was once a time when scholars in the North Atlantic West took for granted a shared Christianity. In that bygone era, the boundaries of the epistemic community and the boundaries of the community of faith were largely coterminous. . . . There are good reasons, too obvious in the intellectual history of the last three hundred years to bear repeating here, why the prevailing epistemic communities now have the boundaries that they do, and why these communities, as a consequence of their relative de-Christianization, no longer count biblical evidence and other religious experience particular to Christianity as relevant to the assessment of a truth-claim or an interpretation. (p. 43)

7) All statistics from Gustavus Adolphus College fact book, April 2005.

8) Specifically,

> Section 1: The College acknowledges the intention of the Evangelical Lutheran Church in America, set forth in its Constitution, to strengthen the College spiritually and academically and to provide oversight and financial assistance. Section 2: The College declares its intention, in pursuing its educational function, to reflect the faith of the Christian Church. (Gustavus Adolphus College, 2004, Constitution section, ¶s 1–2)

References

Adams, M., Bell, L. A., & Griffin, P. (Eds.). (1997). *Teaching for diversity and social justice: A sourcebook.* New York, NY: Routledge.

Ammerman, N. T. (1997). Organized religion in a voluntaristic society. *Sociology of Religion 58*(3), 203–215.

Astin, A. W. (2004, Spring). Why spirituality deserves a central place in liberal education. *Liberal Education, 90*(2), 34–41.

Astin, A. W., & Astin, H. S. (1999) *Meaning and spirituality in the lives of college faculty: A study of values, authenticity, and stress.* Los Angeles, CA: Higher Education Research Institute.

Astin, A. W., Astin, H. S., Lindholm, J. A., Bryant, A. N., Szelenyi, K., & Calderone, S. (2005). *The spiritual life of college students: A national study of college students' search for meaning and purpose.* Los Angeles, CA: Higher Education Research Institute.

Bacon, M. H. (1985). *The quiet rebels: The story of the Quakers in America.* Philadelphia, PA: New Society Publishers.

Bartlett, T. (2005, April 22). Most freshmen say religion guides them. *Chronicle of Higher Education, 51*(33), A1.

Burton, L. (2002). *Worship and wilderness: Culture, religion, and law in public lands management.* Madison, WI: University of Wisconsin Press.

Cherry, C., DeBerg, B. A., & Porterfield, A. (2001). *Religion on campus.* Chapel Hill, NC: The University of North Carolina Press.

Eck, D. L. (2001). *A new religious America: How a "Christian country" has become the world's most religiously diverse nation.* New York, NY: HarperCollins.

Eyler, J., & Giles, D. E., Jr. (1999). *Where's the learning in service-learning?* San Francisco, CA: Jossey-Bass.

Gustavus Adolphus College. (2004). *Amended constitution (bylaws of Gustavus Adolphus College.* Retrieved March 1, 2006, from the Gustavus Adolphus College web site: http://www.gustavus.edu/oncampus/academics/Dean_Faculty/faculty_book/GOVERNING .DOCS.HOME.html

Heffner, G. G., & Beversluis, C. D. (Eds.). (2002). *Commitment and connection: Service-learning and Christian higher education.* Lanham, MD: University Press of America.

Hollinger, D. (2002). Enough already: Universities do not need more Christianity. In A. Sterk (Ed.), *Religion, scholarship and higher education: Perspectives, models, and future prospects* (pp. 40–49). Notre Dame, IN: University of Notre Dame Press.

Horwitz, C. (2002). *The spiritual activist: Practices to transform your life, your work, and your world.* New York, NY: Penguin.

Jacoby, B., & Associates. (1996). *Service-learning in higher education: Concepts and practices.* San Francisco, CA: Jossey-Bass.

Jacoby, B., & Associates. (2003). *Building partnerships for service-learning.* San Francisco, CA: Jossey-Bass.

Jones, B. L., & Maloy, R. W. (1996, September). Learning through community service is political. *Equity and Excellence in Education, 29*(2), 37–45.

Koth, K. (2003, January/February). Deepening the commitment to serve: Spiritual reflection in service-learning. *About Campus 7*(6), 2–7.

Lantieri, L. (Ed.). (2002). *Schools with spirit: Nurturing the inner lives of children and teachers.* Boston, MA: Beacon Press.

Lyons, L. (2003). *Open the doors and see all the—teenagers?* Princeton, NJ: The Gallup Organization.

Maybach, C. W. (1996, February). Investigating urban community needs: Service learning from a social justice perspective. *Education and Urban Society, 28*(2), 224–236.

Miller, D. (1999). *Principles of social justice.* Cambridge, MA: Harvard University Press.

Miller, V. W. (2001). Transforming campus life: Conclusions and other questions. In V. W. Miller & M. M. Ryan (Eds.), *Transforming campus life: Reflections on spirituality and religious pluralism* (pp. 299–312). New York, NY: Peter Lang.

Minnesota Campus Compact. (1999). *From charity to change: Model campus-community collaborations from Minnesota and the nation.* Minneapolis, MN: Author.

Morton, K. (1995, Fall). The irony of service: Charity, project and social change in service-learning. *Michigan Journal of Community Service Learning, 2*(1), 19–32.

Nash, R. J. (2001). *Religious pluralism in the academy: Opening the dialogue.* New York, NY: Peter Lang.

O'Grady, C. R. (1992). *That of God in every person: Multicultural change in a Quaker school.* Unpublished doctoral dissertation, University of Massachusetts Amherst.

O'Grady, C. R. (2000). *Integrating service learning and multicultural education in colleges and universities.* Mahwah, NJ: Lawrence Erlbaum Associates.

O'Grady, C. R., & Chappell, B. (1999). With not for: The politics of service learning in multicultural communities. In C. J. Ovando & P. McLaren (Eds.), *The politics of multiculturalism and bilingual education: Students and teachers in the crossfire* (pp. 209–224). Boston, MA: McGraw-Hill.

Parks, S. D. (2000). *Big questions, worthy dreams: Mentoring young adults in their search for meaning, purpose, and faith.* San Francisco, CA: Jossey-Bass.

Plunkett, D. (1990). *Secular and spiritual values: Grounds for hope in education.* London, England: Routledge.

Rhoades, R. A. (1997). *Community service and higher learning: Explorations of the caring self.* Albany, NY: State University of New York Press.

Stanton, T. K., Giles, D. E., Jr., & Cruz, N. I. (1999). *Service-learning: A movement's pioneers reflect on its origins, practice, and future.* San Francisco, CA: Jossey-Bass.

Stockton, S. (2001). Private conversations about public spirituality. In V. W. Miller & M. M. Ryan (Eds.), *Transforming campus life: Reflections on spirituality and religious pluralism* (pp. 145–160). New York, NY: Peter Lang.

Thompson, B. (2001). *A promise and a way of life: White antiracist activism.* Minneapolis, MN: University of Minnesota Press.

Tisdell, E. J. (2003). *Exploring spirituality and culture in adult and higher education.* San Francisco, CA: Jossey-Bass.

Wade, R. C. (Ed.). (1997). *Community service-learning: A guide to including service in the public school curriculum.* Albany, NY: State University of New York Press.

Wallis, J. (2000). *Faith works: Lessons from the life of an activist preacher.* New York, NY: Random House.

Walters, J. L. (2001). Student religious organizations and the public university. In V. W. Miller & M. M. Ryan (Eds.), *Transforming campus life: Reflections on spirituality and religious pluralism* (pp. 33–55). New York, NY: Peter Lang.

Warren, K. (1998, December). Educating students for social justice in service learning. *The Journal of Experiential Education, 21*(3), 134–139.

Waterman, A. S. (1997). The role of student characteristics in service-learning. In A. S. Waterman (Ed.), *Service-learning: Applications from the research* (pp. 95–105). Mahwah, NJ: Lawrence Erlbaum Associates.

Wuthnow, R. (1995). *Learning to care: Elementary kindness in an age of indifference.* New York, NY: Oxford University Press.

Zlotkowski, E. (1998). Introduction: A new model of excellence. In E. Zlotkowski, (Ed.), *Successful service-learning programs: New models of excellence in higher education* (pp. 1–14). Bolton, MA: Anker.

2

Opportunities and Issues: Talking About Faith at a Church-Related College

Florence Amamoto

Both those inside and those outside of a faith tradition often make assumptions about the promises and challenges of teaching and talking about faith at a church-related college. Those with no knowledge of Lutheranism but extensive media exposure to fundamentalist televangelists or news articles on conservative Christian colleges may assume that talking about faith at Christian colleges is ubiquitous but top-down, oppressive, and constricting, demanding conformity rather than debate or discussion. Those inside the faith tradition, especially one that supports dialogue like Lutheranism and particularly Evangelical Lutheran Church of America (ELCA) institutions, would assume that people talk easily and often about spiritual or religious beliefs and practices. When I started thinking about this issue, I was going to end this paragraph by saying that the assumptions of those insiders and outsiders are wrong—but it's not that simple. Faith-related institutions, especially Lutheran colleges like Gustavus Adolphus College, probably do provide more opportunities to talk about faith, but challenges abound, especially as we try to become more diverse institutions.

Opportunities and Obstacles to Worship

In many ways, Gustavus is lucky. Commentators for the last 20 years have lamented the increasing secularization of formerly church-related colleges in books with titles like *The Dying of the Light* (Burtchaell, 1998). Although Gustavus has not been immune to tensions about its church-relatedness as the faculty has become more diverse and the college more eager to expand beyond its regional reputation, it is not, as many other colleges are, struggling to keep its church-relatedness alive. At gatherings of church-related colleges, people from other institutions often admit to "Gustavus envy"—with good reason.

Gustavus Adolphus College, founded by Swedish Lutheran settlers in 1862, is located in the upper Midwest, an area where Swedish culture and Lutheranism remain strong, so much so that Gustavus still has a majority of students who are Lutheran. This is unusual. Because most small liberal arts colleges draw fairly locally (91% of Gustavus students, for instance, hail from Minnesota, Wisconsin, Iowa, and the Dakotas), many Lutheran colleges, especially on the East and West coasts enroll a minority of Lutherans, which creates its own problems for talking about faith, even at a faith-based institution. Also for these reasons, Gustavus, unlike some of her sister Lutheran colleges that no longer have daily chapel—or that have closed their doors altogether—has retained a vital chapel program. Anyone visiting Gustavus must be struck by how visible its church-relatedness is. Christ Chapel, a big, beautiful, and distinctive building, sits in the center of campus. Although attendance at chapel is no longer mandatory, the college does not schedule classes or meetings between 10:00 and 10:30 a.m. Monday through Friday so that anyone who wishes can attend daily chapel services. Chapel attendance is healthy, drawing between 250 and 400 students, faculty, and staff Monday through Friday.

But even daily chapel is not without tension. Entering Lutheran students are sometimes disconcerted by a daily chapel service that is more traditional *and* more academic and ecumenical than they are used to at home. Not surprisingly, the most popular service is Wednesday's morning praise, an upbeat, contemporary singing service. In fact, almost all of the student-run religious organizations support more familiar, contemporary worship and prayer. The chaplains find they constantly need to instruct incoming students about the *educational* purpose of the chapel program so they are not disappointed that chapel is not "just like home." On the other hand, the only non-Protestants with an institutionalized presence on campus are Catholics, who make up 18% of the student body. This takes the form of the Newman Catholic Center; Catholic students must seek out the Catholic church in town to go to Mass. For non-Christian groups the situation is even bleaker; there are neither student organizations nor worship spaces set aside.

Talking About Faith

This does not mean there are not plenty of opportunities to talk about faith for Christians and non-Christians. I have always felt fortunate to be at a Lutheran college, especially an ELCA college and in particular at Gustavus. Perhaps because university professors, theologians, and philosophers founded it, Lutheranism supports the life of the mind and free critical intellectual inquiry. Acutely aware of individual human limitation, it also supports dialogue, the active exchange of ideas on all topics, including religion. The ELCA is the most liberal branch of the Lutheran church in America, and Gustavus has a particularly liberal and inclusive tradition.

When Christ Chapel was built in the mid-1960s, the college's president, Edgar M. Carlson, instructed its first chaplain, Richard Q. Elvee, that the chapel should be the church of the college. Although a traditional liturgical structure is used, faculty, administrators, staff, and senior students are invited to give the homilies. The chaplains have always issued homily invitations to a wide range of people—not just Lutherans, Catholics, and Episcopalians, but also Jews, Buddhists, and people with no religious affiliation at all. And while each invitation includes the day's Scripture passage, speakers are free to choose their own passage or to ignore it altogether. Some speakers are asked to speak on a particular significant day. Jewish community members have been asked to speak on Yom Kippur, Muslim students now regularly give a homily on Islam during Ramadan, and Mexico's Day of the Dead has become as regular a part of the liturgical calendar at Gustavus as St. Lucia Day. The range of perspectives is only limited by the range of people in the college.

The invitation to speak in chapel reflects not only the idea of the chapel being the church of the whole community rather than the property of one denomination, but also the idea that the chapel program is part of the educational mission of the college. The mission statement of the college states that it "seeks to promote the open exchange of ideas, aspires to be a diverse community that respects and affirms the dignity of all people," and nurtures "a mature understanding of the Christian faith." The chapel program understands that the first two of those ideals help nurture the last.

I have spent a great deal of time on the chapel program because it is the most institutional, formal, and visible of the ways faculty and staff are invited to share their faith perspective; but there are many more. The Office of Church Relations runs a program called Partners in Education, where faculty are invited to offer talks to church adult education groups. Although the talks cover a wide range of topics, they provide another avenue for talking about faith.

Faculty-initiated events provide another opportunity for faculty to share their knowledge and faith perspectives. Some have been one-time events, like a series of three talks on Buddhist perspectives on globalization sponsored by the Sponberg Chair of Ethics. Others are ongoing, like Tuesday Conversations on Religion and Society (sponsored by the Department of Religion), Church and College Retreats for faculty and administrators, and invited guest lectures by people of various faiths in classes and student retreats.

Considering this discussion of the way faculty share their faith perspectives, however, I am struck by several things. One is the sheer number of avenues for bringing one's faith perspectives into one's work here at Gustavus. I suspect most of these avenues would not exist, at least not in these numbers, at a college that was not faith-related. But the number and shape of these opportunities to share faith perspectives depend on people— and thus are fragile. Tuesday Conversations and the Church and College Retreats disappeared when the faculty member most interested in organizing them left the college, although both have been sporadically revived. Being at a faith-based institution does not in itself guarantee people will be talking about faith, especially outside the chapel.

My Story: A Case Study in Diversity, Opportunities, and Challenges

I have wanted to teach since I was in the first grade. I was the first person in my family to go to college and although I went to large research universities for all of my schooling, a small, liberal arts college was exactly the kind of place where I wanted to end up. With my lifelong interest in religion and values, getting a job at a church-related school was a wonderful bonus. I go to daily chapel, give one or two homilies every year, and have been very active in the chapel program and church-related programs more generally, including being one of two faculty on the chapel review in 2000 and giving talks on Gustavus' church-relatedness at new faculty orientation meetings. The college has been very supportive of my interest, giving me opportunities off campus by selecting me as one of its representatives to the first ELCA Vocation of the Lutheran College conference and as its representative to the Rhodes Regional Consultation on the Future of Church-Related Colleges. I have also been asked to speak on my religion not only in classes on campus but also to church groups off campus. I was invited to speak at the fifth ELCA Vocations Conference, which focused on diversity, and to contribute a chapter to a study guide for adult education groups at Lutheran churches. All of this might be unexceptional—except that I am Buddhist.

Small wonder then that when the editors of this volume asked me if I feel I have permission to be who I am here, my answer is a resounding, "Yes!" I know that being at Gustavus has prompted other non-Lutherans to explore their religions as well. One Jewish woman who worked in academic advising credited being at Gustavus for her decision to spend a year studying at a yeshiva in Israel before continuing her professional education. Still, I am well aware of the singularities about my experience that make it easier for me to feel supported in my faith life than others who also do not come from a Christian tradition. Most forms of Buddhism, including my own, are extremely inclusive. My particular form of Buddhism, Jodo Shin Shu Buddhism, is theologically remarkably similar to Lutheranism. Early leaders of the Buddhist Churches of America patterned the church services after Protestant worship. I have spent a lifetime thinking about the many similarities between Christianity and Buddhism, so I am perhaps even more comfortable with our daily chapel services than some people who come from Christian traditions with different kinds of worship practices. Furthermore, students are often particularly interested in Buddhism, and Gustavus has had a longtime exchange with Kansai Gaidai, a university in Japan, which has also nurtured a particularly strong interest in things Japanese on campus. Not surprisingly, those of us with a background in Buddhism are often asked to speak.

Before this sounds too idyllic, I need to point out that I am constantly
aware of needing to bridge the gap in knowledge about my religion. I have
also had to contend with the shock—and sometimes disapproval—of more
conservative Christian students and faculty at my participation in chapel
events. Because of this I constantly have to make decisions about the level of
my participation in a way that my Christian colleagues do not—despite
Christ Chapel being "my church" and my being unusually active in church-
related activities at Gustavus. Being a kind of "inside outsider" means that as
welcome as I've often been, there have inevitably been times when I've felt
more like the outsider. I am also very aware that my experience has depend-
ed greatly on the support of an important handful of people in the chaplains'
office, the dean's office, and the college community, as well as Gustavus's
unusually wide-ranging tradition of inclusiveness.

I also realize that my particular religious tradition and background enables
me to assimilate into the already existing worship structure, which is not the
case for other non-Christians. In the wake of 9/11, Muslim students in particular have been encouraged by the chaplains' office and the diversity center to share their faith formally through homilies in chapel and presentations
in classrooms, and also more informally through conversations and meals
sponsored by the diversity center, especially during Ramadan, when all community members are invited to participate in the fasts and meals of this
sacred season with the Muslim students. Despite this support, there continues to be no place on campus set aside for Muslim students and faculty to
gather for daily prayers.

Muslim students have appreciated the support of the college and the interest other students have shown in their religion, but this example points to two
issues for me. The first is how much our students of color and international
students contribute to the community. In a country where racism continues,
and in an increasingly interrelated world, greater exposure to people of different ethnicities, nationalities, and faiths grows ever more crucial, especially at
institutions like ours with sizeable numbers of students who have had little
exposure to people different from themselves. What is less well noted, however, is how large a personal cost these students often pay. Things that majority
students take for granted—the comfort of familiar surroundings, customs, and

holidays; the possibility of dates and a wide network of potentially lifelong friends—may be harder to achieve for students of color and international students. It is not surprising that a small, residential college can provide speaking opportunities and meals but has a harder time finding space. It is important for institutions to do what they can to support these minority populations and to recognize the personal sacrifices they confront—including overt and covert acts of racism—and the great contributions they make.

Beyond "Talking To": Faith Conversations

It is important to note that almost all the avenues for bringing one's faith perspectives into work discussed earlier involve presentations rather than conversations. Listening to homilies from speakers from a range of faith backgrounds has been enlightening and interesting, but it has been informal discussions with faculty friends and personal reading that have most contributed to deepening my understanding of the Bible, various Christian denominations, and especially Buddhism.

I have been fortunate to have been in two faith discussion groups. The first was a heterogeneous group of five, including two Lutherans, a Catholic, an ex-Catholic who did Vipassana meditation, and me. This group formed, in fact, because of a discussion initiated with me by one of the editors of this book about the difficulties of talking about faith, even at a church-related college. The second group grew out of the Japan seminar, a course development initiative sponsored by the Association of American Colleges and Universities that required schools to put together three-person teams. Those of us chosen for the team were already friends, and after the year-long seminar ended, we decided to continue pursuing our mutual interest in learning about Japanese religion. I know that other faith-related book discussion groups have also existed. Not surprisingly, all of these groups have been relatively small and informal, because real conversations about faith are deeply personal and require an atmosphere of trust.

It might be easier to find others interested in exploring faith at a faith-based institution, but even here there are obstacles. An ever-smaller core of faculty who identify strongly with a faith tradition or even to a church-related college has led to a decrease in the number of faculty who go to daily chapel or organize or participate in church-related activities on campus—places where people who might be interested in discussing faith might find each other and the opening to discuss faith issues. An even greater factor, however, may be increased research and publication expectations on the part of the college and greater focus on research and career advancement on the part of newer faculty. The lack of time may be the greatest deterrent to faith conversations. With teaching, committee work, advising, and research expectations, family and personal time get squeezed. Not surprisingly, faith conversations, especially intensive, ongoing ones, tend to take place mainly among a relatively small group of very interested people.

Similarly, there are many avenues for students to hear about faculty faith perspectives if they are interested, but few institutionalized opportunities to discuss them. Most of my discussions about religion have been with students who already knew me or were in the context of an annual retreat to Blue Cloud Abbey, a small Benedictine monastery, sponsored by Curriculum II—Gustavus' alternative general education program that focuses on an exploration of values. Even in this context where it would seem natural to talk about faith and belief, I usually have to raise the topic for students to feel comfortable asking questions, perhaps because of natural student deference and reticence. "Get to know your professor" nights in the dorms can also provide the opportunity for students to talk to their professors about religion, although, again, it is often the faculty person who has to raise the issue even when the students are interested.

The power differential between student and teacher can make students reluctant to raise controversial topics, but greater hindrances are the view of religion as personal and private and the separation between the professional and the personal in academia (a topic Leila Brammer explores in Chapter 10). Still, breaching these boundaries may be more possible at small church-related residential colleges because of the opportunities for presentations on religious beliefs and for getting to know one's professors on a deeper level than is less likely at a larger, non-church-related institution.

For this reason among others, it is important to support a wide range of people in sharing their faith and talking about their values—not only faculty and chaplains, but also residential life staff, coaches, and secretaries who oversee student workers. These latter groups of people often develop close relationships with students and work in situations that allow them to impart life lessons, but they are overlooked as an important source of values discussion.

Chapel- and student-run groups provide students with a place to discuss issues of faith and belief with their peers, but individual groups often draw like-minded students, and these groups do not necessarily communicate with each other. Since a number of these groups meet to have an alternative worship experience, their gatherings may not be about faith *discussion* at all. Student groups have also sponsored conversations between groups with very different views like Christian and GLBT (Gay, Lesbian, Bisexual, Transgender) groups. These meetings, however, depend on student initiative and active support from the chaplains' office, student life, and the diversity center and have thus been sporadic.

One of the most ambitious projects for encouraging faith discussion was organized in 2002 by a student named Ryan Hanson. Impressed by the documentary film *Questioning Faith: Confessions of a Seminarian* (Alston, 2002), Ryan arranged to have Alston come to campus to show and discuss the documentary, in which the filmmaker, prompted by the loss of a dear seminary friend to AIDS, interviewed people of various faiths on their views and responses to the tragic events in their own lives. But Ryan didn't stop there. He recruited faculty, staff, and students to facilitate small discussion groups for college and high school students on a wide range of topics connected to the theme of the film. Ryan's youth conference, Questioning Faith: God and the Tough Stuff, was a great success and a moving experience for those involved; like the film itself, it was a testament to what the passion, energy, and vision of one person could do.

It is not an accident that these student-run activities have increased in the last few years, as this period has seen the addition of a second chaplain and a part-time staff person shared with the community service office, the hiring of a new director for the diversity center who has been active in expanding the center's activities, and the opening of the Center for Vocational Reflection.

A large campus with a critical mass of various faiths and plenty of physical space can more easily provide the services needed by diverse faith populations. This is much more difficult at smaller institutions where resources—both human and physical—are already stretched to the limit.

Beyond "God Talk": Breaking the Silo Effect

Up to this point, I have focused on opportunities and obstacles to practicing and talking about one's religion—but what are we trying to accomplish by talking about faith in a college setting? Non-Christian students at Gustavus are often concerned that the required religion class, which must be "substantially in the Christian tradition," to quote the college catalog, pushes Christianity while conservative Christian students complain that the class tries to rob them of their faith. Neither is true; the purpose of the course is to put Christianity into historical context and to challenge students to think more deeply about faith issues (Mary Solberg explores this topic in Chapter 4). Faith can be explored in this course and in the chapel programs, but there are other ways to examine questions of faith and values. The college's most prestigious event, the annual Nobel Conference, has always included a consideration of the ethical issues raised by the scientific advances discussed at the conference.[1] The First-Term Seminar, the introductory course taken by all first-year students in Curriculum I, must include an examination of values issues.[2] Two of Gustavus' unique programs, the study abroad program in India and the college's alternative general education program, Curriculum II, revolve around an examination of values and life choices.[3] The Center for Vocational Reflection, founded in 2001 through a generous Lilly grant, reflects the college's desire to make the examination of one's life and values characteristic of these smaller programs available to all students at Gustavus.

The Center for Vocational Reflection was the result of the recognition that Gustavus already supported many initiatives and programs that fostered spiritual development and civic awareness and engagement with our strong chapel and community service programs. What was missing were time and frameworks that encouraged reflection on those experiences. One of the things I love about Gustavus students is that they are so well rounded—the political science major who is a peer assistant also sings in the choir. But this often means they are so overscheduled with activities that they are constantly running from one meeting to the next. What was needed, the planning committee decided, was more *intentional reflection* on the academic, faith, and service-learning experiences available to the students. The opportunity to reflect not only deepens students' learning from their experiences but also encourages the crossover conversation among the students' faith, service, and academic experiences. Busy-ness too often leads to a silo effect: For instance, such experiences as exploring one's faith as a personal issue focusing on one's relationship to God, "doing" community service, and learning about social inequalities in classes become compartmentalized due to the lack of time to think about the connections among them. Encouraging students to explore these connections increases the chances that faith exploration might move to service and service to a sustained and sustainable commitment to social activism.

Why This Matters

Talking about faith has mattered to me personally, because it has enriched not only my knowledge but also my understanding of other faiths in addition to my own. It has prompted me to think more deeply about the faith tradition in which I was brought up in ways that I would not have done without being here and in ways that have been profoundly transformative. A case in point: At the beginning of the Japan Seminar, the ex-Jesuit asked the two Buddhists if we believed in a benevolent universe. Both of us immediately responded, "No! The universe just is."—the standard answer I had been taught in Sunday school years ago. But Buddhism admonishes its adherents to accept nothing on authority, to test teachings against one's own experiences. My friend's question prompted me to think about my life, and what I came to realize is that I *did* believe in a benevolent universe, because my life, especially in the aftermath of a divorce, had taught me that although suffering and loss are inevitable, beauty and possibility also constantly surround us. Indeed, hardship can help us grow and see more deeply. The benevolence and compassion of the universe are in its richness and complexity.

My friend's question did more than enrich my understanding of my faith and of reality, and it did more than provide comfort in hard times. By prompting me to explore more deeply and articulate more clearly beliefs rooted in my lived experience, the question provided me with ideas that I have shared with colleagues and students through homilies and classes. Responses from both have reminded me how much difference talking about faith can make for others.

My faith affects my life as a teacher at Gustavus in less-direct ways as well. Buddhism reinforces certain ideas that shape my attitude and practice, especially because my form of Buddhism focuses not on worship practices, or even matters of belief or salvation, but instead on how one sees and acts in this life. People ask me if I practice Buddhism, but particularly in my form of Buddhism, my life *is* my practice. And what does my religion call me to do? Buddhism affirms the intrinsic value and interdependence of all beings and calls me to be a conduit for the compassion of the universe, to work as egolessly and wisely as I can to help others. Although my central value of service to others and my lifelong desire to teach were multiply determined, my religion has certainly shaped both—and the way I teach. As much as I love teaching American literature, I see my role as more than conveying knowledge about my subject but also as encouraging students' development in all areas of their lives. This can mean challenging their ideas or convincing them they have the "right stuff" to go to graduate school. It can mean going to their concerts or supporting them through dealing with the traumatic loss of a sibling or the aftermath of date rape. In affirming the intrinsic value of each person, the interdependence of life, service, compassion, and gratitude, Buddhism is not different from other religious traditions. This emphasis on community and service, however, does run counter to American cultural and even professional values, which encourage a focus on the self and individual development, assertion, achievement, and advancement. For this reason, I think talking about faith and values with our students provides an important counterpoint to society's messages, but it can also sustain *us* in our vocations and help us think more deeply about what we hope our students will learn and what kind of campus climate we want to create.

The importance of creating a campus climate that encourages an exploration of values and meaning cannot be overstated. Attitudes and values developed in college can have lifelong repercussions, as I can attest from personal experience. The grandchild of poor Japanese farmer immigrants, I was thrilled by the academic challenges presented to me as an undergraduate at Stanford University. But I've come to realize that my sense of vocation and my values as a teacher of American literature were as much shaped by my college experiences as by my classes. In the wake of the assassination of Martin Luther King, Jr., the last quarter of the required first-year Western civilization sequence was transformed from a course on 20th-century history to one focused on racism. During the height of the Vietnam War protests, led by the eloquent dean of the chapel, B. Davie Napier, the chapel played host to William Sloan Coffin, teach-ins, and protest meetings, as well as medieval mystery plays. I learned that the college years should be a time to explore one's values and the riches of knowledge. It was in college that I learned to be concerned about civic issues. It was there that I learned the importance of connecting learning to life. And maybe most importantly, it was there that I learned it all mattered—and that I mattered—that ordinary people could make a difference in the world.

What are our times teaching our students? American ideals of individualism and material measures of success make it tempting to focus on oneself, especially in an era of Enrons and Halliburtons. Students decry the problems facing our nation and the world—global warming and environmental degradation, racism and the widening gap between rich and poor—but feel helpless in the face of the immensity and complexity of the issues and end up throwing up their hands, saying, "But what can one person do?" But it is precisely because so many of the issues facing our society *are* huge and complex, because they take a bigger vision, moral courage, and persistence to solve, that we need a citizenry and a leadership with a thoughtful and well-developed moral sense—people who can see beyond the material, beyond themselves, beyond our borders, and beyond their lifetimes.

Talking about faith can be especially important at small, liberal arts, faith-based institutions, and it can make a difference in students' lives and in the lives of those they will touch. For example, one of the students on the chapel review committee, a conservative Lutheran "preacher's kid," was shocked to find herself sitting next to a Buddhist on the committee; but in her junior year she chose to go to India for her study abroad experience, and in her senior year she asked me to oversee an independent study with her so she could fulfill the creative writing requirement for her English secondary education license by thinking about that experience and her faith journey. I know how much this student grew intellectually, emotionally, and, yes, spiritually, in her time here and how much richer and deeper is the education she can now give to the next generation.

Talking about faith and values is important because one lives one's values whether they have been examined or not. A liberal arts education should free us from the narrow perspectives of our immediate surroundings: our family, our neighborhood, and even our country. It should give us a wider and deeper vision. It should prepare us for our vocation—not only developing our unique talents and gifts, but also opening us to hear the call to develop the wisdom and compassion to be the best agents we can be for the betterment of the world. The most important issues facing our nation and our world are huge and complex. They will not be solved easily, painlessly, or quickly. They will demand moral vision but also persistence in the face of often glacial change and discouraging odds. They are less impossible when sustained by community and faith. Talking about faith, exploring values, can better prepare students *and* teachers for these vital tasks.

Endnotes

1)   Past topics at the Nobel Conference have included The Science of Aging, Genetics in the New Millennium, Unlocking the Brain: Progress in Neuroscience, The Future of the Market Economy, and The Destiny of Women. Each conference includes one or more Nobel laureates as speakers and an ethicist or similar speaker who helps participants consider the moral and societal impact of the year's topic. More information can be found about the College's Nobel Conference at http://www.gustavus.edu/events/nobelconference/

2)   All first-term seminars share several goals:
    • To cultivate the ability to engage in thoughtful group discussion
    • To increase fluency and sophistication in writing

- To develop habits of thinking critically
- To reflect on questions of value

3) The India program began more than a decade ago as a way for students to explore rural and urban issues in India. Students study the socioeconomic, political, and cultural/religious conditions which underlie current issues. Curriculum II is an alternative to the general education curriculum and usually enrolls about 60 students per entering class. The mission of Curriculum II is to introduce students, through an integrated sequence of courses, to the development of the Western tradition with comparisons to non-Western cultures, the examination of values, and the theme of the individual and community.

References

Alston, M. (Producer/Director). (2002). *Questioning faith: Confessions of a seminarian* [Motion picture]. United States: Vagrant Films.

Burtchaell, J. T. (1998). *The dying of the light: The disengagement of colleges and universities from their Christian churches.* Grand Rapids, MI: Wm. B. Eerdmans Publishing.

3

THE ROLE OF INSTITUTIONAL NARRATIVES, FOUNDATIONAL DOCUMENTS, AND PROGRAM COLLABORATION

Brian T. Johnson and Noreen Buhmann

One of the ways to begin conversations about faith, service, and social justice on college campuses is to uncover and claim stories that are part of the historic fabric of the institutional narrative and at the same time are inspirational and motivational for future change and vision. If you were to visit Gustavus Adolphus College and ask about the important narratives of the college, many people could recount these stories. In addition, they could tell you that a large number of our graduates join the Peace Corps, Lutheran Volunteer or Jesuit Corps, or they have interned at the Lutheran Peace Fellowship or Lutheran World Relief offices. They would also probably mention the place and the influence of Christ Chapel in the lives of many of our students. Finally, they'd often speak about the high commitment to exploring the intellectual and philosophical issues relating to justice and peace.

There are connections between the history of our institution, the work many of our graduates pursue, and the kinds of programs we have on campus. This chapter seeks to expose this terrain by recounting the stories of the college, exploring how defining documents and institutional structures support the interpreting of them, and suggesting ways in which collaboration among different college departments has furthered the dynamic tensions inherent in a conversation about service, faith, and social justice.

Institutional Stories

Service

The first story that has significantly shaped the college comes from the founder of the college, Pastor Eric Norelius (1833–1916). Born in Sweden and educated in the United States, he established congregations in Minnesota and

Illinois, founded the Augustana Synod (a cooperative body of congregations which now is part of the Evangelical Lutheran Church in America), and was an avid publisher/writer.

Norelius writes,

> In the fall 1865, when [I] made a visit to St. Paul, I was noti-fied that a family from Dalarna, Mikola Erik Erikson and his wife, had recently come from Sweden, and both had died and left four children in a destitute and defenseless position. Asked if I had any advice regarding these children, it was as if a voice said to me: take them home with you. And I took them home to Red Wing, where I lived then. The following Sunday, I took the children with me to church service . . . and told the congregation how I found these children, and that it was obvious that they needed care, clothes, and food. The congregation was immediately ready to take up a collec-tion for this purpose. The next step was to find a caretaker for the children and a place to live. The latter was found in the space under the church in Vasa, and the former found in Mrs. Brita Nilson . . . a devout and religious woman who came from Stockholm, Wisconsin, where she used to have a small children's school. (Norelius, 1905/2004, p. 247)

Such was the beginning of what would ultimately become Lutheran Social Service of Minnesota (LSS). The story goes on to describe how the home expanded to serve many orphaned children from southern Minnesota. This ministry grew over the years and was rebuilt after tornados and fires demol-ished the buildings. In 1926, the Vasa Children's Home moved to a new location, north of Red Wing, where it continues to serve children and young people with developmental disabilities.

From the four orphaned siblings whom the Vasa congregation cared for in the late 1860s, LSS has grown to become the state's largest social service organization. Owned by the six Minnesota synods of the Evangelical Lutheran Church in America, LSS's mission is to express the love of Christ to all people through acts of service.

Faith

Edgar Carlson, president of Gustavus from 1942–1969, was instrumental in the commitment to build a chapel/church for the campus. As part of that commitment, Carlson believed that a Swedish folk-church model would best serve a campus community. In this model, the campus church is defined by its denominational understandings and by its geographic location, which welcomes all to its common life. As a result, even though the members of the campus community are from differing ecumenical and faith traditions, the chapel is intended for all. In practice, this means there are differing hymnals in the pews of Christ Chapel; preachers (faculty, staff, students, and chaplains) represent a variety of Christian and non-Christian perspectives; and Christ Chapel becomes the center of dialogues and conversations between "Athens and Jerusalem," faith and learning, and the Church and the academy. Anchored in the Lutheran tradition, tethered to ecumenical (Christian) traditions, and open to interfaith dialogue, the college continues to explore how to retain its identity in the midst of diversity in faith and belief.

Justice

In the 1930s Archbishop of Sweden Nathan Söderblom (1866–1931) visited the college. As Haberman (1972) notes in his biography of the 1930 Nobel Peace Prize laureate, Söderblom had an international reputation as an architect of the ecumenical movement of the 20th century. His efforts at ecumenism were hampered by resistance on almost all sides. As Haberman describes, "The French, German, and American church officials were conservative, the Archbishop of Canterbury cautious, the patriarchs of the Eastern Orthodox churches just emerging from isolation, the Roman Catholic Church decidedly opposed, and the proponents usually men without power." Because Söderblom was the head of a national church and a scholar, however, he was able to organize the Stockholm Conference in 1925, which brought together Anglican, Protestant, and Orthodox Christians (Roman Catholics chose not to participate). This conference laid the foundation for future ecumenical efforts; additionally, it brought participating groups together in appealing for world peace.

In 1938, future Gustavus president Edgar Carlson had written "If War Comes," a defense of Christian pacifism that was influenced by Söderblom's earlier efforts. This document helped to focus these peace and justice concerns at the college during his presidency (Schroeder, 1993). This article is considered to mark the beginning of the Lutheran Peace Fellowship, a pan-Lutheran, international effort to keep peace and justice issues at the forefront of church and society (Lutheran Peace Fellowship, 2002).

Guiding Documents

The power inherent in these stories continues to influence how the college goes about its work. And even though colleges struggle with, have ambivalence toward, and regularly rework mission statements and staffing plans, the mission statements and staffing that support these larger institutional visions help to establish priorities, define limits, and create opportunities for collaboration and mutual support.

Mission Statement and Core Values

The Gustavus Mission Statement outlines the goals to which we aspire as a community of educators. It articulates the core values and beliefs of the institution and, ideally, all college work derives its purpose from this source. The mission statement also provides the vision for the college and includes specific statements related to faith, justice, and service:

> Gustavus Adolphus College is a church-related, residential liberal arts college firmly rooted in its Swedish and Lutheran heritage.
>
> The College offers students of high aspiration and promise a liberal arts education of recognized excellence provided by faculty who embody the highest standards of teaching and scholarship. The Gustavus curriculum is designed to bring students to mastery of a particular area of study within a general framework that is both interdisciplinary and international in perspective.

> The College strives to balance educational tradition with innovation and to foster the development of values as an integral part of intellectual growth. It seeks to promote the open exchange of ideas and the independent pursuit of learning.
>
> The College aspires to be a community of persons from diverse backgrounds who respect and affirm the dignity of all people. It is a community where a mature understanding of the Christian faith and lives of service are nurtured and students are encouraged to work toward a just and peaceful world.
>
> The purpose of a Gustavus education is to help its students attain their full potential as persons, to develop in them a capacity and passion for lifelong learning, and to prepare them for fulfilling lives of leadership and service in society. (Gustavus Adolphus College, 2006b, ¶s 1–5)

Nearly everyone on campus is familiar with the language of our mission statement. Reference to it is explicit when faculty prepare documentation prior to tenure or promotion reviews. It is often used to support development of campus-wide programs or policies. Many faculty include it in their syllabi, particularly with first-year students, and ask students to reflect on how the mission statement is relevant for their aspirations at Gustavus. It is indeed a foundational document that helps to define our community.

Embedded in the mission statement are what current college president Jim Peterson calls *core values*. These are articulated on our web site and promotional materials as those institutional values which guide decision-making, shape the curricular work of the college, and help define institutional priorities. The five core values are expressed as follows:

1. **Excellence** — First among our shared values is a commitment to high quality, even to excellence, in all that we do. In the words of Eric Norelius, founder of the College, "Whatever we do, let us do it well." Given our other values, it should be clear that this commitment to

excellence is neither a code word for elitism nor a rejection of the best in Gustavus' heritage. Indeed, our distinctive heritage demands nothing less than excellence.

2. **Community** — Gustavus has always prized community and has been marked by a pervasive sense of concern for every member of the College community. Civility, mutual respect, cooperation, shared governance, and caring have long been hallmarks of the College. Freedom to express a broad range of ideas is central to our sense of community, and resolution of conflicts in the broader society has long been a fundamental concern for us.

3. **Justice** — The Swedish and biblical heritage of Gustavus, its specifically Lutheran roots and bonds, have ensured that justice and fairness are primary institutional values. The College strives to be a just community in all of its actions and to educate its students for morally responsible lives. Relations within the College community are guided by high moral principles, and persons graduating from Gustavus are expected to understand the full moral implications of their actions. "Education for the common good" would well describe what we strive for, and integrity must be one of our defining characteristics.

4. **Service** — The College highly values service as an objective of life and of education. We embrace the biblical notion that true leadership expresses itself in service to others, and affirm the classical ideal of a liberating education, an education that frees one to serve God and humanity to the best of one's ability.

5. **Faith** — The conviction that religious faith enriches and completes learning, is the bedrock of community,

ethics, and service, and compels one to excellence in a divinely ordered world informs our whole enterprise. Without expecting conformity to a specific religious tradition, we encourage an honest exploration of religious faith and seek to foster a mature understanding of Christian perspectives on life. (Gustavus Adolphus College, 2006b, ¶s 7–11)

These values have become an important shorthand for the campus community to define its work and common commitments. In addition to the academic program, several other core programs on campus provide essential ways for students to encounter these values and specifically consider the interaction between service, faith, and justice.

Essential Programs

The Community Service Center

The Community Service Center (CSC) is an umbrella for two kinds of approaches to service. The first focuses specifically on community service endeavors, volunteerism, and leadership development through service. Programs include Big Partner/Little Partner, Junior Great Books, Habitat for Humanity, and Study Buddies. The programs are staffed by students who coordinate the direction and implementation of more than 900 students each year. In those situations where programs do not provide a match for the potential volunteer, students are placed in one of the many community agencies with which the college has formal relationships. For instance, the athletic department recently adopted an area YMCA youth sports program, and increasing numbers of students work with senior center initiatives.

A second strand of the office's work relates to service-learning as pedagogy. The CSC works in collaboration with faculty members who wish to create an experience as part of their class that enhances learning through observation and experience. For example, a faculty member in nursing who teaches a course on violence against women includes a service-learning project at the local battered women's shelter. An education professor has students in one class work in collaboration with high school staff and students to improve learning for ESL students, and another faculty member has students working with the local school district to develop and implement a curriculum that addresses bullying. One of the economics professors asks students to develop business plans for local small business owners as part of a class on that subject, and accounting students recently developed a revolving loan program for upgrading septic systems in a rural county. Anything is possible and opportunities exist for all academic disciplines,

An important aspect of the work of the CSC is its increasing emphasis on rural issues. Students may engage in community service or service-learning experiences in urban areas including internationally, but Gustavus is located in a rural area, and there is an expectation that our college's service efforts should enhance our own region. In addition, many of our students come from rural communities, and most of them return to this rural landscape and economy. Helping them understand more deeply the issues that rural communities face is one way to help them develop goals for future community-based work as alumni. Big-city issues often capture our attention, in part because that is where the media usually focuses its attention, but rural communities have their own struggles with domestic abuse, integration of refugees or immigrants, poverty, and drug abuse. Limited public transportation in rural areas makes it difficult to access social services, including medical care. Even after-school programs for children in rural areas often cannot be sustained because of the challenge of traveling great distances. A current project with Centro Campesino, a migrant farm worker's advocacy group in southern Minnesota, immerses students in the world of labor and human rights, immigration policy, and public education initiatives.

Because the professional and student staff in the Community Service Center works so closely with student volunteers and service-learning workers in academic classes, there are frequent opportunities to engage in conversations about issues of justice and politics. More senior students are coordinators of specific programs, and these students in particular act as role models and mentors for deeper reflection on service experiences. Students' religious or spiritual perspectives often emerge during these conversations, and occasionally office staff witness something akin to spiritual epiphanies, where a particular experience in service radically changes how a student understands the nature of reciprocal relationships or how stereotypes have affected him or her. Service-learning is a wonderful partner in academic learning, because the impressions left with the student after being engaged in a community can be deep and long lasting. Many students remark that the courses that best helped them grasp the intellectual material were the courses that asked them to deepen their learning through service projects.

The Office of the Chaplains

The chaplains' office seeks to serve the entire Gustavus community—students, staff, faculty, alumni, and friends. It is intended to be a nurturing and challenging presence in the academic community. The center of the office's ministry is the worship of God rooted in the Lutheran Christian tradition, yet it values and supports ecumenical cooperation and interfaith dialogue. These key commitments are historically significant in the Lutheran tradition, as our institutional stories demonstrate. (Gustavus Adolphus College, 2006a, ¶1)

These areas of religious focus mean that in daily chapel it is possible during one week to hear from a rabbi-in-residence, a Buddhist faculty member from the English department, a Roman Catholic service of morning prayer sung with choir leadership, a senior student, and a member of the biology department. Chapel is the only public forum on campus in which speakers often reference earlier speakers or their comments, and this creates a kind of recursive public, interdisciplinary conversation. Chapel attendance is not mandatory, but those faculty, staff, and students who attend interact as one community, and often dynamic tensions surface about what it means to be religious, spiritual, or Lutheran, or about the relationship between Christianity and other world religions.

Christ Chapel is also a place of learning where the Gustavus community can experience daily chapel music from around the world, listen to homilies from a variety of perspectives, encounter an expansive expression of art and liturgy, and gather together during significant personal and institutional life passages. A Center for Liturgy and the Arts is in its initial stages of development and will include composers and poets-in-residence.

The ministry of Christ Chapel extends far beyond its walls. Office staff engage in pastoral conversation with people regarding vocation, faith questions, relationship struggles, crisis situations, and the daily joys and sorrows of life. These conversations happen in classrooms, on retreats, after worship, in the cafeteria, on walks in the arboretum, in Bible studies, during service in the St. Peter community, and in many other ways and places.

In the last few years, a series of retreats have been offered for students to reflect on vocation, ministry, Sabbath, privilege, and a variety of related issues. In addition, a group of "apprentices of the chapel" (45 students who are sophomores through seniors) commit to encouraging, listening, enhancing, and assisting with programming that attends to the faith and spiritual life of the campus. These students have been leaders for the Building Bridges Conference, a diversity conference with faith issues as part of the program; they brought the Stoles Project, a visual protest of stoles given by gay and lesbian clergy and their allies; and they assist in leading reflection retreats, book studies, and other events. Many of these students are also involved with student-led groups on campus, including Gustavus Youth Outreach (teams of students who are resources to congregations for retreats, study, fellowship, and music), Fellowship of Christian Athletes, Proclaim (contemporary music and worship), Bible studies, spring break mission and work trips, and other groups that change each year depending on interest and experience.

While Christ Chapel welcomes those from ecumenical Christian traditions, the chaplains' office has been working for several years on locating and creating a hospitable place for people of other faiths to worship as well. A council for interfaith dialogue is in process, and additional continuing educational opportunities for study of world religions outside of the religion department are being sought.

One of the ways the Community Service Center and the chaplains' office work collaboratively is in regard to students who participate in mission trips, such as the one Lucy did in Costa Rica. These students often bring an interest in or commitment to social justice or service in addition to their religious faith, but they seldom have the opportunity to reflect critically about their mission experience, just as Lucy had not. The CSC and the chaplains' office can collaboratively design ways to prepare students before they leave, create reflection opportunities upon their return, and involve them with local projects that can further hone their skills and understandings.

Other Foundational Programs
The Community Service Center and the Office of the Chaplains are essential resources for helping students learn to grapple with issues of service, faith or spirituality, and justice. Other programs on our campus also play a pivotal role in this work. The Office of International Education and the Office of Diversity Development and Multicultural Programs contribute to developing a community that enacts our core institutional values. All these offices work in partnership to ensure that we do the best job we can with our ultimate purpose as a college: educating students.

A distinct aspect of Gustavus is its Center for Vocational Reflection (CVR) which provides opportunities and resources for the entire Gustavus community to explore questions related to purpose, meaning, and value. Established with the help of an initial planning grant from the Lilly Foundation, the CVR builds on the best of the heritage and commitment of Gustavus to help students identify and understand their own sense of calling and develop the skills to live out this calling in a meaningful life of leadership.

Intersections and Collaborations

In helping students explore service, faith or spirituality, and justice, collaboration between offices and programs can enhance the depth of student learning. Our campus is small enough (2,500 students, 600 staff and faculty) that conversations between people working in diverse programs is relatively easy. Because almost all faculty and staff are conversant with the college's mission statement and core values, there is a sense that, for the most part, everyone is on the same page about institutional goals (although there is frequent disagreement about the best way to meet those goals). There is a high degree of communication between program staff and usually a desire to work in tandem rather than at odds. Some other campuses have chaplain's offices and service programs isolated from each other, at times with much antagonism and hostility. When students experience this kind of separation between offices, it tends to foster compartmentalization and lack of integration.

Intentional bridge building at Gustavus has meant the development of a shared staff position between the chaplains' office and the Community Service Center. This staff person acts as a communication link so that the work of each office is complementary. Having a staff member aware of the two programs also ensures that access to service opportunities is widely advertised. This staff person can help students process international experiences, discuss global issues of justice and religion, and reflect on interfaith questions that can arise during a service project. This shared position also offers the opportunity to inform Christian students about the service, justice, and faith work of Christian organizations such as Lutheran Social Services, which assists in refugee resettlement in the U.S., or Lutheran World Relief, which offers disaster response and development efforts. Many students who studied abroad are working with the Colombian Mennonite peace-building organization, Justa Paz, and Lutheran World Relief to address American foreign policy in Colombia. The presence of a person of faith in a shared position between two offices acts as a visual reminder of the kind of integration that can occur when service, faith, and justice work are in dialogue with each other.

Traveling the Institution's Geography

Our historical institutional narratives influence our present-day institutional circumstances in subtle and explicit ways. As a college affiliated with the Evangelical Lutheran Church in America and with a chapel in our midst, we continue the tradition begun by Eric Norelius. We also continue his example of integrating values of faith and spirituality with those of service and justice. Through our guiding documents, we attempt to articulate just what we mean by these core values and how they influence our educational purposes.

A mission statement is always intended as an institution's ideal vision of itself and its purpose. In reality, we struggle, just as any college does, to continually live up to the promise of our mission and our core values. We grapple with what it means to help students live lives of service when occasionally that service can be unintentionally oppressive to others if it is not critically analyzed.

We struggle with what it means to be a college embedded in the Lutheran tradition while also wanting to support ecumenism and nontraditional spiritual perspectives. We argue internally over what it means to be a college committed to justice, when we also must be a college that is financially stable. In some ways we are just like any other business, but in most ways we are not, primarily because we have education as our purpose for existence.

The academic, "seat time" learning that students engage in here is important, but the ancillary features of college life often matter as much or more to the students themselves. A majority of our students participate in international study and/or engage in service opportunities of one kind or another. All students are actively seeking to understand their individual vocations, and they are confronted with opportunities to understand their racial and cultural identities and those of others different from themselves. Significant collaboration between the programs and offices with which students interact most closely enhances their ability to make sense of their college years. Partnerships such as that between the Community Service Center and the Office of the Chaplains invite students to integrate their learning in more profound ways than when such experiences are disconnected from each other.

This collaborative work is not easy. Typically, lines of authority are hierarchical, and who is accountable for what in a collaboration is sometimes blurry. But the benefits for students far outweigh any disadvantages for staff. Students bring 18 years of opinions, beliefs, and judgments with them when they walk onto campus. It takes the efforts of all those with whom they will interact during their undergraduate years to help them make effective links between faith, service, and social justice. If we as adults cannot model how to do this in our language and our institutional structures, how can we expect our students to do it?

References

Gustavus Adolphus College. (2006a). *Chaplains' offices*. Retrieved January 31, 2006, from the Gustavus Adolphus College web site: http://www.gustavus.edu/oncampus/chaplain/

Gustavus Adolphus College. (2006b). *Mission and core values*. Retrieved January 31, 2006, from the Gustavus Adolphus College web site: http://www.gustavus.edu/oncampus/president/vision.cfm

Haberman, F. W. (Ed.). (1972). *Nobel lectures, Peace, 1926–1950.* Amsterdam, Netherlands: Elsevier. Retrieved March 3, 2006, from http://nobelprize.org/peace/laureates/1930/soderblom-bio.html

Lutheran Peace Fellowship. (2002). *Sixty years of witness and struggle.* Retrieved February 27, 2006, from http://members.tripod.com/~lutheran_peace/timeline_60years.html

Norelius, E. (1905). The children's home in Vasa. In *Vasa Illustrata: A civil and church cultural picture.* Rock Island, IL: Augustana Book Concern. (Republished in English, 2004, with translation by members of the church and Vasa Museum. Hastings, MN: Graphic Design, Inc.)

Schroeder, S. (1993). *A community and a perspective: Lutheran Peace Fellowship and the edge of the church, 1941–1991.* Lanham, MD: University Press of America.

PART II:
Practicing What We Preach

4

TEACHING TOWARD SOCIAL JUSTICE: NOTES FROM A RELIGION CLASSROOM

Mary M. Solberg

*A human being who is content with the world will not have
the least interest in unmasking the mechanisms that conceal
the authentic reality.*

—Juan Luis Segundo[1]

Every semester I teach at least one, but usually two, sections of a course called Studies in Religion, one of a number of courses Gustavus Adolphus College students can take to fulfill the one-course religion requirement for graduation. Within a few broad rubrics—in particular, that it be "substantially in the Christian tradition"—individual instructors have considerable latitude in designing their own approach.

Most students resist this requirement, partly in principle, partly because few of them have had any experience studying religion critically. They are skeptical that it can be done, or that they can do it. Teaching Studies in Religion is therefore a challenge. It is also consistently one of the courses I most enjoy teaching. According to student evaluations and informal feedback at the end of the semester, most students say that while they would not have taken it if they had not been required to, they are glad they did.

Why? In some measure, I believe it is because I present the course from the first day, and I teach it all semester, as something of great practical value. The questions we take up, I observe, will almost certainly turn up with some frequency as their lives unfold. Some of them, I suggest, have already had life experiences in which easy answers were worse than no answers at all. Some have already discovered that their parents' values and beliefs will not work for them—at least, not without significant adaptations. Life is not likely to become simpler for them from here on out. In any case, I observe, they will all be better equipped to engage what is coming if they take the time now to examine what they really believe and value. As it turns out, I suggest, these things are at the heart of what religion is all about.

Underlying my approach to teaching religion are two key factors: my passion for what I teach and my conviction that whether, what, and how we think about what we believe and value (including our religious beliefs and values) matters—for us as individuals, but especially for us as members of communities, local and global. A brief excursus into my own history may help set up my observations about what I call "teaching toward social justice."

I was born into a very church-centered family with a long Lutheran lineage, distinguished by generations of faithful laypeople and a handful of ordained clergy, including my father and both grandfathers. By late adolescence, I could have counted on the fingers of one hand the number of times in my life my family and I had not made it to Sunday morning church services. What I remember most vividly about going to church, however—besides singing wonderful music in a first-class church choir—were the talks I had with my father afterward. Toward the end of Sunday dinner, sometimes using the morning's sermon or the sermon text as a stepping-stone, he and I would launch into our own theological discussion. Fidgeting siblings would ask to be excused as Dad and I sat talking. During those years, we talked about lots of things, among them, what "the church" was—really; who Jesus was—really; what made something a miracle; whether or not politicians should talk about religion.

I did not realize just how meaningful those Sunday-dinner conversations were for me until a few years ago, during a conversation with one of my senior advisees, a brilliant double major in science and religion. This student considered herself "religious" but "definitely not Christian." She remarked, with great thoughtfulness, that she might have been more inclined to give church a serious try if she had ever felt that church was a place "where questions were welcome." But she never had. As her advisor—a Christian theologian teaching religion at a Lutheran liberal arts college—I was deeply chagrined. Reflecting on our exchange over the ensuing weeks, I realized that I had also had this experience years earlier. It was at this point that those open-ended conversations with my father came to consciousness again.

When I went off to college—at a highly selective, small, residential liberal arts college associated with the Quaker tradition—I stopped going to church. For the next 20 years, I could count on the fingers of both hands the number of times I went to Sunday church services on my own initiative. From time to time I felt vaguely guilty, but I think it had more to do with breaking a long-established routine than with thinking I was doing something wrong. Had someone asked about my religious self-identification—I cannot recall that anyone ever did—I would have told them I was a Lutheran Christian with a long-standing but (very) dormant relationship with the institutional church.

During the nearly two decades between my entering college and my return to church, the world I lived in and I were shaken and shaped by a multitude of movements and events. Among them were the war in Vietnam; the U.S. civil rights movement; the assassinations of dynamic and idealistic leaders Malcolm X, Martin Luther King, Jr., and Robert F. Kennedy; worldwide student unrest; the second wave of the women's rights movement; gay activism; the Watergate hearings and the resignation of a U.S. president; overt and covert U.S. military interventions in Latin America and the Caribbean.

In fact, it was the last of these that brought me back to church—and eventually, into theology and college teaching. At the end of 1983, the Lutheran World Federation, an international nongovernmental organization with a relief and development arm, asked me to represent them in Central America, with the Lutheran church in El Salvador as my home base. The Lutheran church, numerically quite insignificant in this overwhelmingly Roman Catholic country, needed a protective international presence. Shortly after the Salvadoran civil war broke out in 1980, the church had begun its work with and on behalf of the poor, always those most victimized in war as in peacetime. Not long thereafter, the church began to be terrorized by the Salvadoran government, which interpreted the church's work as Communist subversion, in league with the rebel army. A key part of my job was simply to be a visible physical presence in church. My presence as a citizen of the country whose government was financing the Salvadoran government's war effort, the theory went, might restrain their harassment of the church and its work.

A host of exquisite ironies challenged me as a citizen of the United States. Among them, one haunted me especially: Each morning I heard and watched helicopters that my tax dollars had helped pay for coming and going from the garrison a couple blocks from my home. These gunships ferried soldiers to nearby war zones, bombing guerilla forces and causing considerable "collateral damage" in rural villages and fields. Each morning I then drove to the church to accompany those who were literally risking their lives to help those who had fled to survive. They offered food, medicine, shelter, and, perhaps as important, the knowledge that there was a place of refuge. How in the world, I kept asking myself, had I become part of that place?

Years later, a wonderful professor of Christian ethics taught me a phrase that helped me articulate more precisely my experience of this irony and very many others like it, before and since: "lived contradiction." You grow up learning and believing that various people and things are this way or that. It may, quite literally, never have occurred to you that some of these things might not be so. Lived contradiction is what happens when you have an experience—you live through something—that utterly destabilizes what you believe, that contradicts what you had learned was true.

One overrules one's lived experience, especially of such contradictions, only at one's peril. This is particularly true for those who hope to teach and learn from others anything of real and lasting value. Experiencing a lived contradiction is potentially the most effective entry into openmindedness, that quality of cognition that we exercise when we begin to be able to imagine another way of seeing, hearing, interpreting, and experiencing a common reality. Lived contradictions, when taken at face value, do not require us to throw out what we believed or thought we knew before, but they do require us to reexamine previously held beliefs and assumptions. They persuade us that whatever our assumptions—we do have them—they are all questionable. They compel us to acknowledge the possibility of different perspectives, dispositions, and standpoints arising within ourselves, especially when we encounter others. Often we do not recognize this elementary fact of life without an impetus to do so.

When I teach a course "substantially in the Christian tradition" to undergraduates at a Lutheran liberal arts college, I may very well be that impetus.

I did not recognize that right away, or consider it a pedagogical strategy. Then, some years into my teaching career, I had to write a self-evaluative statement as part of the tenure process. It was at that point that I began to reflect deeply on how meaningful recognizing and naming lived contradictions had been for my own learning, and how important a part of the teaching and learning process doing so continued to be in my classrooms.

For me as a teacher, the point is not to set up conventional beliefs (about anything) in order to knock them down. Nor is the point to invite students to express their often unexamined and conventional beliefs in order to take them apart in the classroom or in their written work. It is rather—conscientiously, respectfully, and consistently—to invite, even compel, students to imagine another way to look at and understand something that up to that point had never seemed to require another thought.

Learning how to do this requires patience with oneself and lots of practice, at least as much for the teacher as for the students. Unless one is willing to see oneself as a student *and* a teacher—as a learner, and not just an instructor—this sort of pedagogical strategy is likely to backfire, creating a stressful, even intimidating climate in the classroom, rather than a vibrant if potentially disconcerting one. From time to time I point out to my students that I would not be teaching this material if I were not continuously asking the same questions and posing the same dilemmas to myself. No one is under the illusion that I am a neophyte in handling this material; that is, after all, one of the most important reasons I am the teacher. But it is true and reassuring to the students to know—as far as I can persuade them—that I genuinely share the difficulties and sense of adventure with them.

Early in the semester, early in this process of discovering real beliefs and values, the notion of *ethical intelligence* becomes very helpful. Part of its helpfulness lies in the fact that it assists all of us in pointing to, or pointing out, an attitude or a disposition that most of us have some ambivalence about. Ethical intelligence entails asking difficult questions and using our intellectual skills to search for answers. Insofar as we choose this path to learning, "we risk upsetting our belief systems. . . . It ought to make [us] uncomfortable" (Marissen, 1998, p. 7).[2] We rightly associate this discomfort with the diverse views, ambiguities, and uncertainties that we encounter in a wholehearted, openminded quest for knowledge. Hence, a commitment to ethical intelligence tends not to be our default option, but must in fact be an active choice, a choice we must renew again and again if we are to be learners with integrity. Over the course of the semester, many students seem to appropriate this sturdy yet nuanced concept, recognizing that there is potentially much more to learning than figuring out "what the prof wants" or jacking up the grade point average.

Another useful tool as we begin to discuss the relationship between what we believe and value, on the one hand, and how we live, on the other, is a distinction Christian theologian John B. Cobb, Jr. (1993), makes between what he calls *avowed beliefs* and *real beliefs*.[3] Cobb uses these phrases in an explicitly Christian context, but I have found them very useful more generally, and so have my students. Avowed beliefs are those one *supposes* one should have if one is to be a good Christian, for example—or American, or Republican, or football player. Real beliefs are those, Cobb says, "that actually shape our responses to what happens"(p. 39). I prefer to put it this way: Real beliefs are those we hold in our heart of hearts. I think our responses to what happens take shape in the tension between what we think is expected of us (because of our membership in a particular community, say) and what we want to do (for a host of reasons, some of which are not even known to us). When the chips are down, moral behavior, ours and others', is pretty complicated.

Why is this distinction useful as my students and I work on clarifying and articulating beliefs and values? For one thing, it should not be a surprise that many people of all ages may, comfortably or uncomfortably, harbor contradictory avowed and real beliefs about a single kind of behavior or act (think of sexuality or birth control, for example). We may or may not even be aware of these beliefs or the degree to which they are in conflict. As we grow up, the institutions that instruct us morally—family and church often head the list—are no more likely to relativize the basis for their instructions than we are likely to ask them to do so. By the time we begin navigating our own boats through various moral shoals, most of us have a sense, but not much consciousness, of what the communities or groups we belong to expect of us. Their expectations include sharing the avowed beliefs of the group. If we have not critically examined those beliefs—and there is little incentive from the group to do so—we would have scant basis for identifying and questioning any internal contradictions between avowed and real beliefs.

As my Studies in Religion students enter more deeply into the discussion of avowed and real beliefs, they often assume that it is always better—more authentic—to act on one's real beliefs than on one's avowed beliefs. Sometimes, we discover, avowed and real beliefs overlap or even coincide, obviating any danger of "faking it" (and, notably, leaving aside any evaluation of the beliefs themselves). Sometimes, we find that it may actually be far more desirable that people act on the basis of their avowed beliefs than on the basis of their real ones. (Consider, for example, acts that spring from beliefs that are racist, sexist, or homophobic—and of the salutary, preventative influence of, say, the public commitment of the college or the nation to the belief that each person is entitled to respect, a belief codified in civil or human rights laws and protocols.) Again, the unexpected, the unconventional, seems to make more sense than the expected, the conventional.

I have been making the case that notions like *lived contradiction, ethical intelligence, avowed beliefs,* and *real beliefs* can and do serve my students and me as a teacher in a course—a religion course—whose value is, I argue, remarkably practical. These notions are intellectually accessible and personally useful to young people between the ages of 18 and 22, especially if time is taken to work with them in small and full-class discussion groups. Giving students a chance to drive such notions around the block—returning with examples, stories, and questions—demonstrates the versatility and utility of these ideas and equips students to think critically and become acquainted with one another in the process.

For almost half the semester, we use these tools and others as we wrestle with significant questions having to do with authority, conviction, faith, belief, doubt, and truth.[4] As central as these concepts are to the study of religion, their implications for how we live, I reiterate often, extend far beyond it. Or perhaps, I suggest, concerns that we have isolated from how we understand and practice religion are in fact deeply woven into it. Do we count as religion only what we find in institutions, traditions, and doctrines? To what degree do these human phenomena truly express our restless passion to make meaning in and of our lives? I raise such questions frequently, insistently, gently, and in many variations. More than anything, they are intended to inspire a willingness to wonder, to think, to look at matters personal and public from slightly different angles. I am no longer surprised to find that, despite some very healthy discomfort, students begin to discover pleasure in this adventure of ideas.

As you recall, the course I have been discussing, Studies in Religion, is one of a half dozen courses from which students may choose to satisfy the one-course religion requirement at Gustavus. The rubric all these courses have in common is that each must be "substantially in the Christian tradition." One of my most conscientious commitments as I teach Studies in Religion is to maintain and model a critical disposition toward that very tradition. On the first day of class, I make it clear to students that this required course, while it happily conforms to the rubric just mentioned, is not designed explicitly or implicitly for indoctrination. Experience has shown me that it is reason-able to assume that most students at Gustavus are nominally Christian. This is one of the reasons a key goal of our work together will be to come to apprehend that Christianity is only one of many religious traditions and ways of making sense of life, reality, and a host of other matters.

Early on I tell my students that I am a believing Christian—a self-denom-ination I neither could nor would wish to hide or deny—and that one of the reasons I teach these classes is that I too am a student with a passionate inter-est in the truth. I also tell them I believe that the Christian story, rooted in Hebrew tradition, contains profound truthfulness about "how it is with us." If I did not, I would not be a Christian theologian. But, I add, I have by no means exhausted my search for what is truthful, how it is truthful, and how to articulate what is truthful, in and about that story. There is no contradic-tion for me between using my mind rigorously and being a faithful Christian. Parking one's mind at the door of this classroom, I tell them, is not an option for me—or for them.

Directly and indirectly, I invite my students—devoted or nominal Christians, members of other faith traditions, fence-sitters, agnostics, or atheists—to join me as critical searchers for the truth, including whatever truth may be contained in the Christian tradition. I make a commitment to them to clarify when I am speaking as a Christian believer about any issue; I remind them that I do not expect them to share my beliefs, and I promise to respect theirs. I invite their questions and critical observations about what I say (about anything) and how I say it.

At a number of points during the first part of the semester—notably, when we discuss authority, biblical authority, and the relationship between Christians and Jews—I make a particular point of reiterating the importance, perhaps especially for believing Christians, of standing "over against" the Christian tradition (neither condemning nor embracing it, but examining it carefully). I do this to encourage students to practice something most of them, Christian or not, have had little experience doing: challenging their own moral and ethical assumptions. I also do so to reassure and underscore my commitment to establishing a space within which we may all enjoy relative safety from judgmentalism.[5]

This concern becomes even more pressing when we approach the only unit in the course explicitly about the Christian tradition. This is a unit on Christology, or theological reflection on the meaning of Jesus of Nazareth, a first-century Palestinian Jew whose followers came to believe was "the Christ," and later, that he was the "Son of God." Students' first assignment is to read one of the canonical gospels and prepare a "Jesus essay," a creative treatment of the narrative for which only two caveats are crucial: It draws its data only from the gospel the student is assigned to read; it displays a degree of skepticism that we could reasonably expect to have applied to a present-day secular narrative, for instance. The assignment requires students to grapple (for the first time, most acknowledge with some chagrin) with a key primary religious text, the Bible, and the specific questions it raises about authority and interpretation.

Exposure to these texts launches our reflection on the development of the Christian community's beliefs about Jesus. Again, I am concerned to make as transparent as possible the approach I have chosen; students should see how we are doing what we are doing—in part, because there are other ways to do it. Our approach is *phenomenological.* Looking back, I think I have taught Christian thought or doctrine this way from the beginning, although only later did I learn that *phenomenological* was a term that could usefully describe what

I was doing.[6] It took some time for me to learn how to pronounce the word, but as soon as I could, I decided to ask my students to learn it, too. For them this is yet another tool that will be useful not just here and now, but also in venues and matters beyond my classroom and subject.

We approach Christology, a subset of Christian theology, as if entering a house occupied by real people who actually believe certain things and make sense of the world in terms of these beliefs. The goal is not to rule on the truth of Christianity's claims (in this case, about Jesus the Christ), but rather to come to some understanding of why and how reasonably intelligent persons might avow such truths and try to live as if they mattered. The exercise is worthwhile for many reasons, among them that those who have made just these claims have, for better and for worse, had a powerful impact on the world in which we live. Once more we are reminded—this time on a global and historical scale—that what people believe affects how they live. This implies that what people, including us, believe matters.

I consider this assertion to be true and powerful. To many if not most of my students, however, it generally seems oddly self-evident, a truism perhaps, and yet—what?—troublesome? elusive? suspect? Perhaps we are now more willing to concede that beliefs generally do affect behavior. But at this point in the course, on the verge of the unit that is "substantially in the Christian tradition," few students, regardless of their disposition toward this tradition, know what to think about how Christian beliefs, whatever they are, do or should affect the life of one who holds these beliefs.[7] Nor are they sure how or whether someone who holds these beliefs will, should, or even could affect the larger communities—local, national, global—of which he or she is a member.

I return briefly to my own story. One of the experiences that galvanized me in El Salvador was being part of a church community that understood its work explicitly as an expression of its Christian beliefs and values. That its work called forth its own government's persecution made the church's determination to put its beliefs into practice even more impressive, in my judgment. The work the church was doing with those who were being displaced by military operations put the church in harm's way; everyone knew that. The pastor and the young people who carried out that work said that this was what God was calling them, as Jesus' disciples, to do. The pastor often reminded his congregation during Sunday services: Just as Jesus had been misunderstood and persecuted in his ministry, and brought finally to a hideous death on the cross, Jesus' followers were bound to risk threats, disappearance, torture, and death for the sake of those in need of justice.

Whether or not one shared this commitment to the Christian story and what it seemed to entail for those who claimed it, both the confession and the praxis—and the way in which church members bound them together—made a powerful impact on all who heard and saw what they were doing and what they were suffering because of it. Many of those who heard this message—many of those for whom the message was intended—were institutions and individuals who meant and brought the church great harm.

This was a quite different experience of church for me, as well as a different experience of how claiming the Christian story, tradition, and community could and did matter. Of course other reasons existed to do what the Salvadoran church did; many Christians and non-Christians risked their lives, too, in humanitarian service to those battered by the war. But for me as a Christian, this particular "lived experience," practical and gritty, provided a demonstration of what, years later, I would lay before my students. This actually happened. Why and how does this kind of thing happen? Why would people do this sort of thing? How does something like this challenge our understanding of the relationship between what Christians claim to believe and value and what difference it makes in real life?

The unit on Christology relies on our having begun to learn and practice strategies that make room for alternative perspectives on important matters, which are deeply and often unconsciously rooted in students' life stories. We prepare by reading four different accounts of Jesus' life and ministry, death and resurrection, each written by an author or authors who had no intention of being objective about their subject. The evangelists were all fully committed to persuading hearers (and later, readers) that the radical claims they were making about Jesus of Nazareth were true.

My students and I discover differences, even inconsistencies, among the stories; we discover that they were written long after Jesus' death, and for different audiences. We discover that the claims that Jesus was raised from the dead came only from those who had been Jesus' friends and followers during his life. Certainties, assumptions—and perhaps most important, the sense that this is the only story in town—are undermined, questioned, and examined. Questions from earlier in the semester come around again, among them: What then is *faith*—for the original disciples, and for 21st-century Christians?

We notice that a significant portion (between a fifth and a third) of each gospel's narrative is devoted to recounting the events of the last week of Jesus' life, including his horrific death and a resurrection witnessed by women and other disciples. Surely the amount of attention the evangelists pay to Jesus' end requires us to ask who killed him—and why. Again, we reach back into earlier discussions about authority and power, and about the historical relationship between Christians and Jews, among others. We then refine and add to our collective sense of the earlier and the present issues. We also discover that each of us, having read one gospel, can find some evidence to explain how and why Jesus might have come to irritate, even threaten, those in power. At each turn, we remember that these stories and the doctrines that followers of Jesus subsequently hammer out are claims Christians are making and continue to make; they are not The Truth, except insofar as they are taken as such on faith by particular human beings.

Concern about social justice and the desire to act toward its accomplishment do not appear from nowhere. Very likely, even a rudimentary sense of fairness, usually interpreted individualistically, is something we learn. In my life, others (notably my parents) have modeled a concern about and a commitment to justice nurtured in individual relationships and then growing purposefully into something that requires wider vision and broader collaboration for a larger community of persons. But it was the Salvadoran experience—and particularly the fact that those I worked with interpreted in terms of the Christian story their willingness to risk their lives on behalf of the most vulnerable—that compelled me to take a much closer look at the tradition in which I had been raised. Were there in that story compelling reasons to care about justice? Was there in that story an understanding of justice to challenge the conventional definition of justice as "getting what's coming to you?" Might our theological reflection on that story help us clarify our part in bringing justice to life in the world?

For most of my students, these are novel questions. What makes them novel is in large measure the juxtaposition of Jesus and justice.[8] Despite the fact that most of my students come from at least a nominal identification with Christianity, very few have heard or seen this connection made, let alone argued as inescapable. In keeping with our phenomenological approach, I remind my students frequently that, as visitors in that "house" where Christians live, our main project is to find out what, how, and why these folks make the claims they do and live as they do, based on those claims. As visitors, none of us is constrained to believe or do what the residents of the house believe and do; we are simply here to try to make sense of their viewpoint. This reassurance seems to make it somewhat easier for students to entertain, even seriously reflect on, the novelties we discover. Many have told me that they never knew that being a Christian entails caring about injustice—and doing something about it.

For me as a teacher—even as a teacher of a required introductory course that is "substantially in the Christian tradition"—what counts most is to equip students with useful tools. As part of that equipment, teachers need to encourage, even require, students to raise questions, not only about the material they are expected to learn, but also about themselves and their beliefs, convictions, and values. The classroom must come to be perceived by students as a place in which they can safely practice with tools whose use entails some risks, including the discomforts of ambiguity, paradox, complexity, difference, and few simple answers.

Good teachers, Palmer (1998) observes, teach who they are. (Bad ones probably do, too.) There is no more powerful pedagogical strategy for teaching toward social justice than to declare and model one's own concern about it: by enlisting the help of one's students in making the classroom a just place; by drawing the world's life, especially the suffering its injustices cause, into the life of the classroom on a daily basis; and by expecting students to rise to the occasion and respond to it. A Christian theologian teaching a required course "substantially in the Christian tradition" may—perhaps surprisingly—find this strategy more challenging at a liberal arts college than it would be at a seminary, for example. That this may be so is no excuse not to pursue it.

Endnotes

1) Segundo, 1976, p. 10. Segundo (1925–1996), an Uruguayan Jesuit priest, was one of the founders of Latin American liberation theology.

2) In this short essay, Marissen seems to attribute the phrase "ethical intelligence" to Swarthmore's president, Alfred Bloom.

3) Cobb (1993) wrote his short and accessible book *Becoming a Thinking Christian* to challenge and assist Christian laypeople to take responsibility for being the theologians Cobb (and I) believe each of us is. It is a first-rate resource for teaching. I sometimes wish it had an intended audience beyond those who consider themselves Christians—and a title that attracted those who belong to other faith traditions or who believe "thinking Christian" is an oxymoron. In any case, I urge my students, whatever their religious persuasion, to adapt Cobb's arguments to their own frameworks.

4) Each semester for nearly 10 years, for example, I have required students to read portions of Paul Tillich's (1957) small classic, *Dynamics of Faith*. Many students report that thinking through Tillich's insights—about *doubt*, for example, as a necessary, structural dimension of faith; and thinking about the distinction between *faith* and *belief*—has liberated them to think about faith in a new way.

5) From time to time I find myself wanting to point out to students that, despite their extreme discomfort about "judging" others' behavior, we humans must and do judge and make judgments all the time, about all kinds of people and situations. Judgment need not be synonymous with condemnation or the expression of prejudice; however, the term *judgmentalism* does have such connotations, and I use it here in that sense.

6) Phenomenology can de defined as: "Description of experience. Hence, a philosophical method restricted to careful analysis of the intellectual processes of which we are introspectively aware, without making any assumptions about their supposed causal connections to existent external objects" (Kemerling, 1997–2002). Several faculty colleagues who have a firmer grip than I on phenomenology as a philosophical approach have taught me enough to enable me to use the term in good conscience in my Studies in Religion classes. In this connection, I am grateful especially to John Cha. Of course, I take full responsibility for any misuse of the term.

7) When asked what Christians do *because they are Christians*, students who identify themselves as Christians often respond in terms of church-going, praying, reading the Bible, trying to obey the Ten Commandments and the Golden Rule, and so forth. These are behaviors they may engage in, they say, but not as "religiously" as they imagine they should. Few have been equipped to *think through* what Christians may be called to say or do about matters of public, national, or global concern. Many have learned that being a Christian entails obeying authorities (whether textual or clerical), rather than engaging in a process of discernment in which those authorities play a role but do not determine the outcome.

8) Elizabeth A. Johnson's (1990) well-written and accessible book *Consider Jesus: Waves of Renewal in Christology* persuasively connects the gospel texts, the emergence of Christological doctrine, and the implications of Jesus' story for the lives of Christian believers. She also introduces students to liberation and feminist Christologies, whose methodologies begin with a passion for justice and a determination to work toward it.

References

Cobb, J. B., Jr. (1993). *Becoming a thinking Christian.* Nashville, TN: Abingdon Press.

Johnson, E. A. (1990). *Consider Jesus: Waves of renewal in Christology.* New York, NY: Crossroad.

Kemerling, K. (1997–2002). *Philosophy pages.* Retrieved March 3, 2006, from: http://www.philosophypages.com/dy/p2.htm#phny

Marissen, M. (1998, December). Faculty view: Is religious faith incompatible with academic life? *Swarthmore College Bulletin, 96*(3), 7.

Palmer, P. J. (1998). *The courage to teach: Exploring the inner landscape of a teacher's life.* San Francisco, CA: Jossey-Bass.

Segundo, J. L. (1976). *The liberation of theology* (J. Drury, Trans.). Maryknoll, NY: Orbis Books.

Tillich, P. (1957). *Dynamics of Faith.* New York, NY: Harper & Row.

5

FAITH, SOCIAL JUSTICE, AND SERVICE-LEARNING IN ENVIRONMENTAL STUDIES: THE STRUGGLE FOR INTEGRATION

Mark Bjelland

What do faith, justice, and service have to do with undergraduate education in environmental studies? As a geographer interested in social justice and theology and charged with teaching several core environmental studies courses at Gustavus Adolphus College, I have often struggled with that question. Thus, I welcomed the opportunity to reflect on ways that I am trying to integrate faith, social justice, and service-learning into my teaching in environmental studies.[1] There have been times when I was tempted to conclude that the type of students attracted to environmental studies were just not particularly interested in faith, justice, or service. It is a challenge convincing students with strong environmentalist values to pay equal attention to issues of social inequality and human rights. It is a challenge to move students beyond their established points of contact with nature through recreation and/or meditation to knowing nature through hard work, whether with a brush saw, scientific calculator, or gas chromatograph. As Leila Brammer and many others note elsewhere in this volume, in a pluralistic academic setting it is a daunting task to create a classroom environment where students can comfortably discuss and consider issues of religious faith.

Fortunately, in those times of discouragement I was badly mistaken, and I am now convinced that faith, justice, and service truly fit within an environmental studies program and strengthen it in important ways. I am far from satisfied with what I have achieved in the way of integrating faith, service, and justice into my teaching of environmental studies, so what I share here are simply the reflections of a fellow pilgrim. In the paragraphs that follow, I provide some background on the unique challenges and opportunities in teaching at a church-related college, describe some characteristics of environmental studies programs at other colleges and universities, and discuss some tendencies I have observed in Gustavus environmental studies students. I share the importance of faith, social justice, and service-learning for my vocational journey and then present different ways I have worked to incorporate them into my pedagogy.

The Unique Challenges and Opportunities of a Church-Related College

My struggles with integrating justice, service, and faith into my pedagogy have taken place while teaching at Gustavus Adolphus College. Gustavus is affiliated with the Evangelical Lutheran Church in America (ELCA) and has a mission statement that promises to nurture a "mature understanding of the Christian faith" while preparing students for lives of service and "work toward a just and peaceful world." However, at Gustavus, like most ELCA colleges, processes of pluralism and secularization have been underway since at least the 1960s (Solberg, 1985). What Solberg and Strommen wrote about Lutheran colleges in 1980 is probably applicable to Gustavus today—that the majority of the faculty are non-Lutheran and a significant percentage are indifferent to or opposed to religion (Solberg & Strommen, 1980). The secularization process brought new perspectives into what was once a sectarian college, but has meant that, for the most part, the norms of secular academic culture prevail. Still, a majority of the students at Gustavus Adolphus are Lutheran and there remains a vaguely religious ethos to the campus.

Reflecting its religious heritage, Gustavus has a long tradition of service, a Community Service Center, high rates of student participation in volunteer service, and high rates of students entering service-related professions after graduation. Gustavus's emphasis on service to society is reflected in the writings of Edgar M. Carlson, the long-serving president of the college during the mid-20th century. President Carlson chaired a large policy study for the Lutheran Church in America exploring the purpose of Lutheran colleges. The committee's report, bearing Carlson's imprint, redefined the primary mission of the church college as service to society (Burtchaell, 1998).

In short, Gustavus represents a novel type of institution: It enforces neither the norms of secular higher education nor the commonly agreed-upon dogmas of a Christian college. Instead, the church association at Gustavus and the somewhat ambiguous mission statement language regarding a "mature understanding of the Christian faith" make it acceptable to talk about faith, while the pluralist culture makes it difficult to find a common language.

The Field of Environmental Studies

Environmental studies is a relatively new and rapidly expanding field of academic study. Among liberal arts colleges, approximately one third offer a major in environmental studies (Bjelland, 2004). Environmental studies is interdisciplinary, containing a significant element of humanities and social science courses, built around a natural science core. Because it is a new field, often cobbled together from existing departmental course offerings, there is considerable curricular diversity from school to school and considerable room for curricular innovation. Many undergraduate environmental studies programs have incorporated service-learning in significant ways (Ward, 1999). In a way, service-learning—a form of experiential learning that uses community service to enhance academic learning—is a natural fit for environmental studies (Zlotkowski, 1999). Most students enter environmental studies because of an appreciation of the environment gained experientially rather than through book learning. Further, since environmental studies is literally the study of one's surroundings, it is natural to expand this awareness to an engagement in community service. Environmental studies students are attracted by the eloquence of the natural world as an antidote to the hyperreality of postmodernity (Borgmann, 1992). For colleges where values are part of the curriculum, directed learning activities that engage local issues are a natural way to integrate values and practical learning into the curriculum. Various environmental studies programs have incorporated service learning through introductory and advanced courses, consultancy-based courses, internships, and K–12 educational partners (Ward, 1999).

Social justice has found its way into some environmental studies programs, thanks in large part to awareness raised by the environmental justice movement. Of the three—faith, service, and justice—faith is least likely to get sustained attention. Issues of religious belief and practice often receive some coverage in environmental studies curricula. Unfortunately, it is rare for an environmental studies professor with a background in theology, ethics, and social science to explore the full ramifications of such issues. And equally rare is the academic discussion of religion and environment that goes beyond generalizations and abstractions to the more personal level of students' beliefs.

Gustavus Environmental Studies Students

The environmental studies students at Gustavus are a pleasure to teach. They are passionate about the environment. They are lovers of trees, birds, animals, and lakes, and they are hardy idealists ready to give up the comforts of civilization to experience the solace of wild places. Once, in an introduction to environmental studies course, I scheduled a field experience involving zooplankton sampling on a local lake. The weather was unusually cold that mid-April day, with snow and sleet pelting us. A stiff north wind created a fierce chop on the recently thawed waters of Lake Emily. Nonetheless, without hesitation, the students pulled on the hip waders, plunged in, and began dipping their zooplankton sampling nets. It wasn't long before the students discovered that the waders had small leaks and were filling with icy water. Still, they pressed on with the sampling work, undaunted by the cold and eager to explore the natural world. Their passion stems from a combination of formative outdoor experiences in their youth, some knowledge of environmental degradation, and a quasireligious devotion to the natural world. As they become increasingly aware of the extent of global environmental problems, they take quickly to a critique of instrumental attitudes toward nature and the role of technology, capitalism, and neoclassical economic assumptions in environmental degradation. Students also show strong appreciation for the work of nature writers ranging from Thoreau to Edward Abbey.

Despite these strengths, there are reasons for concern. The field of environmental studies sometimes goes little deeper than a celebration of the scenic preferences of a privileged class. Some students seem unconcerned by social inequities, lack a sense of civic engagement, and are content to withdraw to the wilderness. Aware of humanity's destructiveness to the environment but lacking a sense of how their own gifts could be used to work toward a more environmentally sustainable future, some are tempted to join the monkey-wrench gang and sabotage the machinery of a technologically advanced society. All too aware of the ecological failings of various religious traditions, environmental studies students may find themselves spiritually homeless.

Faith, Justice, Service, and My Vocational Journey

Teaching is a second career for me and reflects a somewhat convoluted vocational path shaped by my religious faith, my convictions about social justice, and my service experiences. For me, social justice, service, and faith are inseparable—from each other and from my sense of vocational calling. I cannot do justice to my story without including the central formative role of service experiences that opened my eyes in ways books never could. During high school, summer mission trips with a church youth group exposed me to the ugliness of racism and inequality as I witnessed the stark contrast between white and black neighborhoods in Philadelphia and rural Mississippi. It was a summer volunteer experience during college that shaped my career path. That summer I worked at a faith-based community development organization based in the African-American community in a small town in Mississippi. I was exposed to lawyers, teachers, and doctors who had chosen downward mobility and relocated to a needy community where they were using their skills to serve the poor rather than maximize their earnings. Ten years later as a young urban professional working for a prestigious environmental consulting firm, it was my volunteer activities in an inner-city neighborhood that kept me from being content in climbing the corporate ladder. My Christian convictions about caring for the environment led me to leave the corporate world to work in a struggling, environmental nonprofit organization. So, while the university gave me technical skills, it was faith and service activities that shaped my values and life orientation.

My motivation for going into academe was to work in a people-centered environment while addressing issues of environmental stewardship and social justice in ways not possible in a profit-driven consultancy. I did not plan on teaching at a church-related college, simply because I had had little exposure to that type of school. Given the importance of religious faith in shaping my convictions, it seems natural that once I landed a job at a church-related college, discussions of religious faith would find their way into my classroom. It has not been so easy. I find it much easier to talk about social justice in the classroom as if it were a universally agreed-upon value, rather than explaining why *we* believe social justice is important. I find that Gustavus students take naturally to service-learning projects without having to think about their motivations, religious or otherwise, for performing service. But I struggle with speaking honestly about religious beliefs and creating a safe environment where students feel comfortable revealing their own religious convictions.

There is one language used in most academic settings where secularity is an assumed framework and where revealing religious convictions is to risk censure. I have spent most of my academic life in that type of setting, earning an undergraduate and two graduate degrees from large public research universities. Another language is used in schools with a shared, confessional commitment. I spent two years at a theological school in Canada where I experienced that type of academic setting. I am comfortable in a secular setting and in a confessional setting that fits my beliefs. I can speak both of those languages. Coming to Gustavus meant learning to speak of faith in a new way, in a way that attempts to be open, honest, and yet accommodating to a diversity of perspectives.

The Importance of Justice in the
Environmental Studies Curriculum

The environmental movement has been shaped by Romanticist thinking that treats nature and culture as polar opposites. Thus, environmentalists can easily slip into a simplistic embrace of pristine nature and a rejection of working and urban landscapes (Cronon, 1996). Strong Romanticist tendencies are visible among some Gustavus environmental studies students, leading them to value landscapes for their sublime scenery or recreational values more than for their ability to grow crops or in other ways sustain human lives. Not recognizing their privileged status as children of the American middle and upper-middle classes, students tend to focus on preserving "pristine" wilderness without recognizing the extent to which their own consumer lifestyle requires an extensive support network of working landscapes around the world. Ever confronted with environmental problems seemingly caused by too many people, it is easy for environmental studies students to adopt a neo-Malthusian viewpoint that sees overpopulation rather than inequality or overconsumption as the most important source of environmental problems. Thus, integrating social justice concerns into the environmental studies curriculum is a critical challenge.

The dualism of nature and culture runs deep, and as a consequence students and faculty colleagues are sometimes puzzled by the assortment of classes I teach. The majority of my courses are easily packaged under the title of environmental geography: environmental science, physical geography, water resources, and geographic information systems. However, I also teach and do research in the areas of urban geography and urban planning. People can't figure out how someone interested in environmental issues would also care about cities and social issues. However, I believe that the social and the ecological are inseparable, since every social project has ecological consequences and every ecological project has social consequences (Harvey, 1996). Accordingly, the environmental justice movement has challenged the larger environmental movement to pay more attention to environmental inequities and to shift its focus from pristine wilderness to cities and other places where people live, work, and play (Bullard, 1990).

One of the ways I try to convey to students this inseparability of the social and the ecological is by sharing some of my research and professional experiences. Before entering academe, I worked for six years as an environmental engineering consultant. My last major consulting project was directing the remediation of contaminated soils, groundwater, and ocean sediments at a long-defunct wood treatment plant on Vancouver Island, British Columbia. My company was hired by the Canadian government because of its technical expertise. Ostensibly, my job was to manage the removal of pentachlorophenol-laden soils, sediments, and groundwater from a site on Esquimalt Bay. However, the project was laden with social justice issues. The land was part of the Esquimalt Indian Reservation, and past land leasing decisions made by the Canadian government, without the participation of the Esquimalt Band, had led to pollution that had fouled the band's traditional homelands. The environmental remediation was not merely a technical environmental issue. A truly just environmental restoration was not merely about reducing parts per million levels of chemicals but also about training band members for jobs, preparing the land for a socially beneficial reuse, and restoring environmental quality to the point where it could support a traditional, indigenous lifestyle centered on salmon fishing. My point in sharing this case study with my students is that environmental issues have social consequences and that social justice and the environment need to be considered together.

Another way I have tried to inject social justice concerns into the environmental studies program is through my course in geographic information systems (GIS). GISs combine the power of searchable computer databases with interactive computer mapping and are used to integrate everything from satellite imagery to census data in order to analyze social and environmental problems. While teaching GIS technology, I also attempt to teach important geographical and environmental studies concepts. I deliberately use non-Western locations for several assignments. One lab, ostensibly designed to teach how to geocode point data (automatically putting thousands of points on the map based on street addresses or geographic coordinates), has students mapping the locations of toxic release sites in relationship to the location of minority groups. A lab that teaches methods of spatial analysis also exposes students to racial inequities in access to urban parks. In these labs, students discover environmental inequities firsthand and have a feeling of ownership over their discovery of glaring injustices. I find that this approach is highly effective in getting students to think about social injustices and the possible positive social uses of the GIS technology they are learning to use.

The Importance of Service-Learning in Environmental Studies

The potential exists for environmental studies students to become withdrawn from responsible engagement with society. Students receive a heavy dose of information on the environmental problems caused by population growth, urban development, and industrialization. For some, the bewildering array of problems could lead them to reject urban industrial society altogether and abdicate responsible engagement with society. Rather than engage the tough environmental science debates by doing good science, it is easier to make decisions on emotional grounds. Rather than working to find more environmentally sustainable ways to live within an industrialized, urbanized society, it is easier to grab a backpack or a canoe and retreat to the wilderness. For some students, an environmental studies degree is preparation for a life enjoying recreation and meditation in the wilderness, but not for social and ecological change.

Service-learning is essential to environmental studies because it models responsible engagement with society, gives students practical skills, and helps them develop a sense of place within the local bioregion. One way I attempt to model service and community engagement is by bringing to the classroom issues that emerge through my role as a member of a local planning commission or my volunteer work for a local water quality nonprofit organization. The longest-standing service-learning component in the Gustavus environmental studies program is in the conservation biology course. Students are required to do a fixed number of hours of work on the ecological restoration of the nearby Ottawa Bluffs, an oak savannah restoration project of the Nature Conservancy. Here students learn about local environmental issues and get to put their commitments into practice through physically demanding outdoor work chopping out exotic tree species and restoring native plant communities.

However, if the ecological restoration work at Ottawa Bluffs were the only service-learning element in the environmental studies program, students would have a single model for their service to society—that of erasing the human footprint on the landscape. Balancing that emphasis on the restoration of wild places and native communities should be service-learning components that focus on human-modified landscapes and the environmental impacts inherent in everyday life. An internship requirement and long-established internship programs with local governments and nonprofit environmental organizations offer students a chance to connect with local issues and use their skills in service to the community.

Another way I have attempted to inject service-learning is through the group projects in the course I coteach on sustainable development. Student groups are required to do an empirical, data-intensive research project on sustainability in the areas of water, energy, waste, or building and urban design. Student projects have measured energy usage in dormitories, surveyed commuters, analyzed wind-power potential on campus, measured the components of water consumption on campus, and done preliminary design of a "green" residence hall. One group tested the claims of water-saving appliances and spent the day in a dormitory bathroom measuring actual water use with water-saving and conventional fixtures. Students have presented their results to the campus physical plant director and the campus energy efficiency task force. The results of these projects have informed the design of a new residence hall, energy conservation programs, and plans for installing wind turbines on campus. These projects yielded benefits to the campus, the environment, and the students' education. For the students, there is a sense that science and quantitative problem-solving skills can make a tremendous contribution to environmental sustainability. They gain a sense that they can make a difference in society and that their environmental studies skills can be of practical service to society.

Environmental studies students are drawn to my GIS course because it is a job skill that many environmental jobs require. However, GIS technology has significant social issues. GIS technology creates the illusion of an all-seeing, all-knowing, nonsituated view of the earth. In reality all GIS representations have a social context, data limitations, and rely on simplifying assumptions. Thus, rather than training mere button pushers, one of my pedagogical goals for the GIS course is that students become aware of the social context and social implications of the technology. We discuss the growing digital divide, whereby large companies and prosperous units of government are able to make use of GIS technology while ordinary citizens, small nonprofit groups, and less prosperous units of local government may not have access to GIS technology and expertise. This leaves some members of the public at a distinct disadvantage when environmental planning decisions are made based on GIS analysis. Traditionally, I have taught students about the digital divide and other social issues in GIS through a set of assigned readings. Now that I have begun to use service-learning projects for a final group project, the concerns about social context and social implications of GIS take on real meaning for students. Students are placed in groups that work on projects defined by the needs of community partners that lack access or expertise in GIS technology. The community partners for these projects have included citizens' groups, nonprofit organizations, and local government units with limited GIS staff. Students learn that the technology is not a black box, that it is influenced by social context, and that one can obtain different results depending on the quality of the data and the assumptions used in the analysis.

The Importance of Faith in the Environmental Studies Curriculum

One evening I was the guest speaker at the controversy speaker series at Gustavus. I chose as my topic, "What Does Social Justice Have to Do With Environmentalism?" In attendance was an attentive audience of mostly environmental studies students who seemed to click with the connections I detailed between poverty and the likelihood of exposure to environmental hazards. Ironically, throughout the session, we could hear the amplified sounds of a Christian praise and worship event filtering through the building from the basement lounge. One of the students at our session commented that the crowd at the praise and worship event downstairs wouldn't care about the issues we were talking about—environmental responsibility and social justice. Whether or not that statement was true, it troubled me. When it comes to integrating questions of faith into the environmental studies curriculum, I am haunted by two student outcomes that reflect, in different ways, a lack of integration between the lives of faith, academics, and social justice.

For me the story of Jamie illustrates the compartmentalization of religion within a private sphere of life insulated from social justice and academic challenges.[2] Jamie came from a devout, evangelical Christian home. Soon after arriving on campus she joined and eventually assumed leadership responsibilities within the theologically conservative, evangelical Christian student group that sponsored the praise and worship events on campus. She also proved to be among the brightest and most conscientious students on campus. Jamie came naturally to environmental studies because of a strong love of the outdoors that stemmed from childhood experiences at her family farm and lake cabin. But in her environmental studies courses Jamie found her faith under attack. In biology courses, evolutionary theory was the central organizing theme, and given the way it was presented, she assumed that it was incompatible with her Christian faith. Then, in courses dealing with environmental thought she found Christianity attacked as the root and source of the ecological crisis. Jamie's solution was to adopt a defensive posture and to compartmentalize her faith, keeping it separate from her intellectual life.

She earned straight As in biology classes by reciting back the contours of evolutionary theory, all the while never believing a word of it. She was the primary organizer for a creation science conference on campus. When she came to environmental ethics discussions blaming Christianity as the source of the ecological crisis, she used the same strategy of compartmentalization. On exams and papers she wrote the answers necessary to get an A grade, but inwardly rejected what she was writing. Based on my observations, she never questioned the understanding of the Christian faith that she brought to college and as a consequence missed out on opportunities for maturation of that faith. While Jamie has been successful academically and professionally and managed to preserve her Christian faith through her college years, it came at a high cost.

The second story represents a different sort of divorce of faith and intellect. During one particular course, I got to know my students in ways that went far beyond what typically emerges in the classroom. The class was mostly comprised of senior environmental studies majors who had been in several of my other classes. They were deeply passionate about environmental and social justice issues. They were engaged in service activities. In class discussions, this group of students evinced an air of cultured despisers of religion for whom Christianity was both incompatible with a scientific outlook and responsible for innumerable ecological ills. In fact, it was a member of this group who made the disparaging remark about the social and environmental irrelevance of the Christian groups on campus. Thus, I was shocked when these environmental studies students revealed that almost without exception, they had been raised and deeply formed within the Lutheran church. One was a minister's child and several others had worked as church camp counselors. For these students, college appears to have functioned as a place to sever their ties with their Christian upbringing without finding a new place of spiritual rootedness.

In different ways, these stories raise questions about the place of religious faith within a pluralistic but church-related academic context. What is sad about these two stories is that the divorce of intellect and faith took place at a church-related college where we seek to produce students with a mature understanding of the Christian faith. The first outcome is the result of compartmentalizing faith within the sphere of private religion. In this case, I fear a compartmentalized faith may become narrow and unable to adapt to challenges. The movement away from formal religious involvement seen in the second story is a common outcome in higher education (Bowen, 1980). These post-Christian students had not given up on religion altogether, but had abandoned organized religion in favor of individualized spirituality. Nonetheless, they remained highly attuned to environmental and social issues and were eager to lead lives of service. So does it matter that they were no longer part of a particular faith community?

In thinking about the significance of the secularization process illustrated in the second story, I am influenced by Stanley Hauerwas's writings on ethics. Hauerwas (1984) rejects the universalizing notions of modern ethics and claims that all ethics must have an adjective or qualifier such as *Christian* ethics, *Jewish* ethics, *Buddhist* ethics, and so forth. Ethical convictions, writes Hauerwas, are shaped within communities that share a common narrative. Following Hauerwas' line of thinking, my students had lost more than their faith: They had lost the religious basis for their strongly held ethical convictions. Their altruism and willingness to sacrifice on behalf of a cause stemmed from their Christian upbringing. Their shift from the aesthetic spirituality of Protestantism to a devout environmentalism is a well-worn path trod by John Muir and other influential environmentalists (Worster, 1993). They appeared to be operating on energy and values drawn from past ethical capital provided by their religious upbringing. Without roots in a faith community, Hauerwas would question whether they will be able to sustain and pass on to their children a life of commitment to service and social justice in the face of cultural forces that would mold them in other directions.

Reflecting upon these two stories, both of which occurred in my first years at Gustavus, I wondered whether my colleagues and I had failed our students. I had not revealed my own religious convictions, and I had not created a classroom environment where conservative Christian students felt safe examining their faith. I had not balanced criticisms of Christianity's role in the ecological crisis with my own convictions that Christianity offers a strong environmental stewardship ethic. Humbled and chastened, I have gradually worked to reveal more of myself in my teaching and to bridge the gap between the "hard" sciences and the "soft" realm of religious knowledge. I have struggled to find a common language in which to talk openly and honestly about faith.

The diversity of faith perspectives among students and faculty at Gustavus makes it a challenge to discuss issues of faith in the classroom. Confronted with true religious diversity and openness to religious questions, it is tempting to flee to the safety of either a secular or confessional academic setting; however, secular and confessional settings can breed a complacency wherein religious questions are either removed from the table or settled beforehand. Unless we are deliberate about opening discussions to religious dimensions, a secular ethos will become the default environment. The challenge for me is to gather the courage to bring questions of religious belief into the classroom and to figure out how to guide the conversation so that it is respectful of genuine belief and genuine difference.

My approach has been to broaden the reading list, to continually ask questions, to revel in paradox, and to occasionally reveal my own convictions. I am wary of revealing too much out of sensitivity to students who do not share my beliefs and might be afraid to speak out if they disagree with me.

My goal is to be an encouraging and challenging teacher and advisor to all students who enter my classroom, regardless of whether they agree with me on issues of social justice, politics, faith, or anything else. In an environmental thought course, I broadened the perspectives in my reading list by switching from a single author text on religion and the environment to an edited volume with writings by authors rooted in diverse religious traditions. This allowed students a chance to read what evangelical Christians and Buddhists actually say about the environment. I have worked alongside students to reread Lynn White's (1967) well-known criticisms of Christianity's role in the ecological crisis and to balance them with more recent scholarship showing a more positive role for Christianity in addressing the environmental crisis (Bouma-Prediger, 2001; Oelschlaeger, 1996). In one class in which Jamie was a student, I assigned a reading from the history of science literature that described how many, theologically conservative, evangelical leaders of the 19th century felt comfortable fitting evolutionary theory into historic Christian doctrine (Livingstone, 1992). I felt this perspective was useful for safely challenging my evangelical Christian students to question the either/or polarization that was created by the fundamentalist reaction to evolution (Noll, 1994).

Revealing my own religious convictions, in fairly safe ways, has been the most difficult thing I have done as a teacher. I fear being viewed through the distorted lens of caricatures of religious fundamentalists. I fear that because I am identified as a Christian, students will make assumptions about my views on politics, science, the environment, feminism, and other issues. But, whenever I *have* opened the classroom to a discussion of faith by considering different faith-based perspectives on the topic, sharing some of my own personal experiences or mentioning an issue that came up in chapel, I have found it rewarding experience.

Conclusion

In teaching environmental studies at a church-related college, my greatest challenge has been to channel an incredibly passionate environmentalism into a more mature perspective that is service-oriented, attuned to social justice, and rooted in a sustaining faith tradition. Faith, service, and justice are critical components of an environmental science program and can help students connect their environmentalism with service to society and social justice, and find a rooted faith tradition to sustain their environmental values. If we are to meet our stated pedagogical goals of challenging students to assume positions of maturity and service, I believe we must work to integrate discussions of religious faith and social justice into the environmental studies curriculum, and I believe service-learning is a key element in that integration. Service-learning helps connect students to the local bioregion, gives them a sense that their skills can make a difference, and establishes a pattern for a lifetime of service. Thus, some of my most gratifying moments in teaching have been seeing students combine their passion for the environment with an equal passion for social justice, and putting their convictions into action in service of society.

Endnotes

1)   I am based in the geography department but teach courses in geography and environmental studies. In this essay, I chose to focus on environmental studies because I find it more of a challenge to engage that topic and that particular group of students with questions of faith, justice, and service.

2)   Jamie is a pseudonym/amalgam based on the experiences of several real students at Gustavus Adolphus College.

References

Bjelland, M. D. (2004). A place for geography in the liberal arts college? *The Professional Geographer, 56*(3), 326–336.

Borgmann, A. (1992). *Crossing the postmodern divide.* Chicago, IL: University of Chicago Press.

Bouma-Prediger, S. (2001). *For the beauty of the earth: A Christian vision of earth care.* Grand Rapids, MI: Baker Academic.

Bowen, H. R. (1980). *Investment in learning: The individual and social value of American higher education.* San Francisco, CA: Jossey-Bass.

Bullard, R. D. (1990). *Dumping in Dixie: Race, class, and environmental quality.* Boulder, CO: Westview Press.

Burtchaell, J. T. (1998). *The dying of the light: The disengagement of colleges and universities from their Christian churches.* Grand Rapids, MI: Wm. B. Eerdmans Publishing.

Cronon, W. (Ed.). (1996). *Uncommon ground: Rethinking the human place in nature.* New York, NY: W. W. Norton & Company.

Harvey, D. (1996). *Justice, nature, and the geography of difference.* Malden, MA: Blackwell.

Hauerwas, S. (1984). *The peaceable kingdom: A primer in Christian ethics.* Notre Dame IN: University of Notre Dame Press.

Livingstone, D. N. (1992). *The geographical tradition: Episodes in the history of a contested enterprise.* Malden, MA: Blackwell.

Noll, M. A. (1994). *The scandal of the evangelical mind.* Grand Rapids, MI: Wm. B. Eerdmans Publishing.

Oelschlaeger, M. (1996). *Caring for creation: An ecumenical approach to the environmental crisis.* New Haven, CT: Yale University Press.

Solberg, R. W. (1985). *Lutheran higher education in North America.* Minneapolis, MN: Augsburg Publishing House.

Solberg, R. W., & Strommen, M. P. (1980). *How church-related are church-related colleges?* Philadelphia, PA: Board of Publication, Lutheran Church in America.

Ward, H. (Ed.). (1999). *Acting locally: Concepts and models for service learning in Environmental Studies.* Washington, DC: American Association for Higher Education.

White, L. (1967). Historical roots of our ecological crisis. *Science, 155*(3767), 1203–1207.

Worster, D. (1993). *The wealth of nature: Environmental history and the ecological imagination.* New York, NY: Oxford University Press.

Zlotkowski, E. (1999). About this series. In H. Ward (Ed.), *Acting locally: Concepts and models for service learning in Environmental Studies* (p. vii). Washington, DC: American Association for Higher Education.

6
ARE THERE MEXICANS IN MINNESOTA? COMMENTS ON SERVICE-LEARNING AND LUTHERAN LIBERAL ARTS EDUCATION

Gastón A. Alzate

AMIGOS is a community service organization at Gustavus Adolphus College, initiated and sustained by students, that works with the Mexican and Mexican-American[1] community, the majority of whom live in Green Valley, Minnesota. This neighborhood is one of three trailer parks in the small town of Saint Peter. AMIGOS works mainly with after-school programs providing educational and recreational support for Latino kids, teens, and adults. Our main goal is to accompany and support Mexicans in their adaptation to Minnesotan life and their daily struggle with language and cultural barriers. AMIGOS also participates in Mexican celebrations on campus such as Cinco de Mayo, Day of the Dead, Christmas Carols (Posadas), and other cultural activities that link the college with the Mexican and Mexican-American community of Saint Peter.

Though relatively small (about 2% of the county's population), the Latino community in Saint Peter is a good example of the new sociocultural situation in the U.S. The America Southwest (Arizona, Texas, California, New Mexico, and parts of Utah, Nevada, and Colorado) was part of Mexico before 1848. After the U.S. won the Mexican-American War, most of the inhabitants of these territories were stripped of their lands and became American citizens by default, without crossing any borders and without speaking English. In the past 20 years many Latin American and U.S. sociologists have studied how the border, or *frontera* in Spanish, between the United States and Mexico, has been gradually fading as Latinos have taken up residence throughout the country. Anthropologists call this phenomenon *deterritorialization* (Canclini, 2002; Martín-Barbero, 2000). All the immigration issues and their attendant social and political challenges that have traditionally affected California, Arizona, and Texas, have been steadily spreading throughout the U.S.

Migrant agricultural workers first came to Minnesota between 1910 and 1930, recruited in south Texas as part of the U.S. government's *bracero* (migrant worker) program which brought more than four million Mexican farm laborers to work U.S. fields. Mexican migrant workers helped establish the thriving sugar beet industry in Minnesota's Red River Valley. By 1975 Latinos, primarily Mexicans, comprised the largest minority community in the state. From 1990–2000 the Mexican and Mexican-American populations in Minnesota increased 176%. There are about 143,000 Chicanos/Latinos in Minnesota (U.S. Census Bureau, 2000). In addition, each year approximately 15,000 migrant workers travel to Minnesota to work in various industries (Chicano Latino Affairs Council, 2001). Many Mexican and Mexican American workers still find employment in Minnesota's meatpacking, food service, or agricultural industries.

Seasonal field work is backbreaking and poorly paid, but each summer between 15,000 and 20,000 Mexican and Mexican-American migrant farm workers come here to work and sustain Minnesota's efficient economy (Minneapolis Foundation, 2004). In practical terms that means that most likely a Latino, probably of Mexican origin, has picked all the fresh vegetables we consume in Minnesota. Migrant workers contribute to the state's economy, but without health insurance, minimum wage, or bargaining power.[2] The majority of Mexicans are here legally on work permits, despite the widespread assumption that most are illegal residents. Others are U.S. citizens who have relocated here from other parts of the country. The vast majority of Minnesota's current seasonal workers are U.S. citizens and legal permanent residents. They live in south Texas and have been doing seasonal work throughout the United States for generations.[3] The first visit to Minnesota by a Mexican president, Vicente Fox, occurred in June 2004 as a response to Minnesota's growing immigrant population from Mexico. The Mexican community is now spread throughout Minnesota. In some communities more than 50% of the elementary school population is Latino. In the Twin Cities, the Latino student population is about 15% (Chicano Latino Affairs Council, 2005).

The Development of AMIGOS

As a professor of Spanish and a native of Colombia with a specialization in Mexican popular culture, I found having an immigrant Mexican community so close to the college a unique opportunity. AMIGOS began as an independent study I directed in 2000 for two former students, Christine Weber and Emily Dale, who approached me with the idea of getting credit for their major in Spanish while bridging the gap between Gustavus and the Saint Peter Mexican and Mexican-American community. I provided guidance in structuring the experience and the academic background to help students better comprehend the situation of this community. Christine and Emily were curious about one of the topics we had studied in our Latin American Culture class: the invisibility of a marginal community that shares the geographical area with a different and dominant culture. In my class I use the geometrical term *false invisibility*. Mexicans are *visible* in Saint Peter but not *perceived*—in the same way that a three-dimensional figure loses one dimension when seen in a two dimensional drawing or sketch. Needless to say, the unseen dimension is as important as the visible one. In my classes I connect this geometrical phenomenon with an anthropological concept: When an object or subject is excluded from the symbolical order that regulates social exchange, the object or subject is not physically seen by members of the community (Lévi-Strauss, 1967). Said another way, members of the Mexican community do not count as real and visible phenomena in the eyes of most members of the predominantly white Saint Peter community. People of color can be invisible on many levels. They can be physically invisible by being few in numbers, but they can also be invisible within the academic curriculum. Students might spend their entire college career never learning about issues related to Latinos or other racial or ethnic groups different from their own. Through AMIGOS, our students could learn firsthand about the circumstances under which Mexicans and Mexican Americans in our community live.

In order to understand this false invisibility, my students interviewed around 100 members of the Gustavus community, including faculty, about the Mexicans and Mexican Americans in Saint Peter. Emily and Christine

were shocked with the results of this exercise. Eighty percent of the interviewees, including Spanish majors and many faculty, were not aware of the
presence of Mexicans in town.[4] After this exercise, my students and I visited
Green Valley, one of the poorest trailer parks in town.[5] In 2000 there were
18 Mexican families there. There were also 14 in Summit, another trailer
park north of the city. (Just to show how fast the population is increasing, in
2005 there were between 70 and 80 families, counting both trailer parks.)

For their independent study, Christine and Emily created five programs
under the AMIGOS umbrella. These included an after school program for
elementary children, tutoring of English Language Learners (ELL) at the
intermediate school, English lessons for adults, translation of school materials into Spanish for parents, and Junior Spanish Club. From the beginning,
the challenges of bridging the gaps between the college, the Saint Peter
majority community, and the Saint Peter Mexican/Mexican-American community were more complex than we anticipated. The primary problem was
not simply the language barrier between the two communities, but that
there were many preconceptions in each community about the other. For
example, classroom teachers wanted the Mexican kids to behave in class and
speak English as much as possible. But teachers did not understand issues
like culture shock or social, racial, and economic discrimination. The school
staff expected the Mexican kids to adapt quickly, but cultural understanding
on the part of the Anglos was lacking. Many of the children badly needed a
space that was familiar and safe. For this reason, Emily and Christine decided early on that AMIGOS volunteers had to be able to speak Spanish.

While the U.S. is a country that offers many economic advantages to
immigrants, it is also very self-enclosed. Most people in the U.S. know very
little about the history and culture of other nations, including neighboring
ones like Mexico. For this reason, at the end of the year Christine and Emily
attempted to have shared activities between AMIGOS participants and other
previously existing Community Service Center programs such as Junior
Great Books, Little Gustie Sports, and Big/Little Partner. The goal was to
bring together Anglo and Latino community members.

In its second year, AMIGOS gained a new student coordinator in Lyn Li,
who recognized that the program had become too large for its small struc-

ture. There were too many activities and not enough volunteers. Lyn pruned those parts of the program that were not effective and encouraged me to require AMIGOS involvement as a service project in one of my Spanish classes. This was an ethical problem for me, because I was a firm believer that students involved in AMIGOS should be engaged because of a generous and voluntary commitment. I did not want volunteers to become victims through a course requirement that essentially made the service another kind of homework. Ultimately, however, I recognized that with any class there are some assignments students don't like but which are pedagogically valuable, and that sustaining AMIGOS was an appropriate use of class time. Students would have to use the Spanish they had learned in class while working with the Mexican and Mexican-American community in Saint Peter, an appropriate and educational assignment. In addition, Lyn Li convinced me that students would enjoy the experience even though it was not voluntary. Lyn Li believed that after the first meeting with the Latino children, the college students would be happy to be engaged, and she was right. The majority of students who do community service in Spanish classes think it is a valuable part of a liberal arts education. Most think that the experience awakens them to a new reality, and some say the experience changed their lives forever. Proof of this is the fact that AMIGOS has continuously had student coordinators, all volunteers, for each of its programs. The project's success depends upon its members wanting to continue after their class commitment is complete, and so far we have been successful in this respect.

When Lyn Li graduated we entered our third year. The new program coordinators were both double majors—Micah McDonough in Spanish and education, and July Proehl in Spanish and English. Micah and Julie noticed an influx of Mexican and Mexican-American junior and senior high school students and realized that AMIGOS had no program for this age group. In any culture this age group faces crucial challenges regarding individual and community identity issues. These challenges increase for minority students, particularly those living in a predominantly white community. The coordinators' first step in reaching out to the junior and senior high students was to become actively involved in the English Language Learner (ELL) program at Saint Peter High School. Micah and Julie worked alongside the ELL content teacher, translating and assisting students in her classroom. This class consisted of Mexican, Mexican-American, and Somali students. After developing a relationship with these students, Micah and Julie were able to assess their needs, inside and outside of the classroom. They saw these students were struggling with the English language and failing to realize their potential. This prompted Micah and Julie to start Reach, a new AMIGOS program for students in grades 7–12. They named this after school program Reach because it focuses on helping ELL 7–12th graders set and achieve goals. The program was designed with Mexican and Mexican-American youth in mind, but Somali youth were also involved. The major goals of Reach are enhancing social skills, developing community awareness, and improving English language skills. Micah, Julie, and these students spent time researching future occupations, discussing important life issues, and having fun. Meanwhile, these students began to see the abundance of opportunities Saint Peter and Gustavus have to offer them.

Currently, the AMIGOS program continues to try to meet the needs of the local Latino population and provide opportunities for cultural exchange. Each student director has brought new vision to the position. The latest extension of the AMIGOS program is to assist Green valley residents in establishing a daycare.[6] A daycare would be a great step because most of the parents in the neighborhood work long hours, which negatively impacts the lives of their children. They have no option but to work because they receive low wages compared to Minnesota standards. In terms of AMIGOS, Gustavus students could get involved and make the daycare a significant part of the program. However, there have been many obstacles in developing this aspect of the AMIGOS program.

Challenges Inside the Academy

A daycare project that serves an economically and racially marginal community in a small town faces multiple challenges. The most difficult challenge relates to legal and economic issues, while others relate to elaborate organization and state licensure. Then there is the problem of convincing academic administrators and colleagues to support such a community service project. As my students and I have worked to develop the daycare proposal, we have been challenged by questions demonstrating that even for an institution dedicated to the liberal arts, service, and social justice, it can be difficult to undertake a direction that has never been tried before. There are legitimate legal and financial considerations, but I have been surprised by the amount of resistance this project has met. Some questions have been raised about the appropriateness of supporting initiatives within a particular cultural or ethnic group, focusing too narrowly on the Mexican/Latino community, for instance, and making us look biased if we ignore other ethnic or cultural communities.

When AMIGOS was started five years ago, many of these same criticisms were mentioned, and yet AMIGOS has gained widespread support and legitimacy because those involved worked to make it happen. It takes a lot of energy to implement new ideas in a college that values tradition, even when the new directions could help the college gain a distinctive charisma and identity. Nevertheless, although a long road awaits us, the Mexican community will try to accomplish this project by creating a nonprofit organization. I am optimistic that the college will eventually support and take part in a portion of the project.

Service-Learning: The Perfect Pedagogical Balance

Pedagogically speaking, there is one point that is remarkable about the AMIGOS experience. Almost all universities in the U.S. teach what we call *standard Spanish*. This is due to the impossibility of teaching all of the variants of Spanish spoken in more than 35 Spanish-speaking countries around the world. After students graduate, they often face a challenge because the Spanish they will use when working as nurses, schoolteachers, human resources administrators, managers, and so on, is mostly Mexican. AMIGOS is a great help for them to practice the language most members of the Latino population actually speak. Nevertheless, just as important as the linguistic aspect is the fact that most of the students for the first time have Mexican friends, visit Mexican families, play with Mexican children, or are invited to Mexican family events. This is of extraordinary help to me as a professor when I explain any cultural differences in class. As an instructor, I know I can expect each student to relate to a personal experience they have had or are having through their work in AMIGOS. Even if the point of the class is to emphasize cultural differences among Latin American countries, this experience helps immensely as a point of departure.

Another aspect I consider crucial when teaching Latin American culture involves some complex political issues that produce endless debates in class. For me the most difficult part of being a Latin American professor in the U.S. is explaining the contradictory ways in which various American governments in the 20th and 21st centuries have tried to help the third world. Most of the time statistics illustrate the tragic consequences of this "help" and the real human costs of several of these policies, from U.S. support for Southern Cone dictatorships in the 1970s and 1980s in the name of fighting communism, to NAFTA and Plan Colombia in the 1990s.

Most surprising for my students is that the people most affected by these interventions (military, political, or economic), have been people who are not in power: working class, farm workers, indigenous peoples, and those who have tried to support them, including students, teachers, priests, nuns, and human rights activists. Sometimes whole cultures have been condemned to extinction, which is the case of the indigenous U'wa group in Colombia. The fumigation agreements between the American and the Colombian governments include the use of a poison (gliphosphate) forbidden in the United States since 1980 due to the dangers it poses to human and animal life. Considering that several coca plantations are in the Colombian jungles, where many people live, including women and children, fumigations have serious health consequences. The use of this substance has produced cancer, malformations in babies, and destroyed any possibility of cultivating the land for the next 10 years. This is why another indigenous group, the Embera people, has led protests in major Colombian cities against fumigations and has offered to work on manual eradication of coca and poppy plantations. They have been ignored by the U.S. and the Colombian governments. In Mexico many farmers do not work their lands anymore and have relocated to large cities, increasing the number of unemployed urban poor, because American products have invaded the Mexican market in the wake of NAFTA.

These are just two topics common to my Latin American culture class. When my American students listen to these discussions, they typically react in one of three ways. One, they dislike me for talking badly about their country and question my points until the last day of class, even when I cite documentary evidence. Even after they see declassified CIA documents, books by respected historians and economists, or the official web site of the International Monetary Fund, which recognizes that economic globalization does not benefit poor countries if rich countries protect their farmers with subsidies, many students still avoid hearing what I am trying to teach. As a professor of Latin American studies, I am not only dealing with the students themselves, but going against the grain of mainstream American culture as a whole. The second common type of reaction is that some students decide they will learn what they need to pass the class, without caring much about the topics, and just waiting for the end of the semester. However, a few of these students slowly begin to show interest in the topics they did not care much about at the beginning of the course.

The third and least common reaction is that students feel deceived by what they have been taught in high school or the perspectives they have been shown by the mass media. Many of these students feel depressed, because they cannot understand why nobody has told them about these things. After all, they live in one of the richest countries in the world and have access to the best educational resources. There are also the occasional students who are vocal about deeply caring about social justice issues; they are a big encouragement for a professor, because they offer resistant students a peers' perspective. These students are always an inspiration to me. Nevertheless, I am most eager to educate those who have not had access to this type of information before and to help them cope with the disequilibrium it produces. I do not expect students to think like me, but I do expect them to think critically, to be able to defend their arguments with facts, and to be inspired to do further research, even if they do so just to challenge what was taught in class.

I found in service-learning the perfect pedagogical balance for bringing to life the social and political problems of Latin America and Latinos in the U.S. I consider it very important that my students have an experience that may change their lives. The point of departure for this is when each student establishes a personal and individual friendship with a member of the Mexican community. Once this is established, no matter how difficult the topic is, the student will find a solution for the challenges the topic addresses; some of my students consequently look for ways their chosen professions, whether nursing, teaching, or politics, can respond to the ethical and complex problems they have learned about in the class.

To Believe or Not to Believe? That's Not the Question

I have explained the basics of the pedagogical and sociological background of the AMIGOS program over the last few years in Saint Peter, Minnesota, including some challenges related to larger cultural beliefs. Here, I focus on the connections among religion, faith, and service-learning as part of the students' academic experience.

There is more interest in the U.S. than in Latin American in clear-cut religious distinctions. In Latin America (with the exception of some extremely conservative groups) people do not see religious differences as clearly, nor do they think belonging to a church is an essential identity marker. Latin American societies are the result of the mingling of diverse cultures. Many people consider themselves Catholic but do not go to church regularly; others do not consider themselves Catholic but accept Catholic rituals as part of their social life; and others practice Catholicism along with other indigenous religions without seeing any contradictions or errors in doing so.

In the U.S. diverse races, cultures, and religious views often coexist in the same geographical areas but there is very little dialogue or significant exchange of knowledge between these groups, even if people from different backgrounds work or go to school together. Schools teach very little about the beliefs and ways of life of contemporary cultures different from the Anglo-American one. Because of this, there are significant differences between two cultures such as the Lutheran American and the Catholic Mexican, even though the two emerged from the same field of Western Christian tradition.

The fact that Gustavus is a liberal arts college affiliated with the Lutheran church is an interesting paradox for me as a Latin American scholar. On one hand, I appreciate that promoting the understanding of other religious faiths and cultures is essential for this type of college in present times. Exposure to cultural diversity is considered an important educational goal in our globalized world. Cultural understanding also relates to the principle of social justice embedded in the Christian faith, because respecting human rights implies respecting other religious and cultural beliefs, and you cannot really respect something if you do not understand it. Otherwise, you might act based on biases and not even know it. In other words, good intentions do not guarantee right acts. On the other hand, being a religiously affiliated college is a very specific location from which to explore issues of service and social justice. Several students taking my classes have already experienced service work with their churches, and many of those have been in contact with Mexican communities in the U.S. or Mexico through their churches.

Most of this community service has been done from a charity perspective. While this experience is valuable, it is also limited. As Snarr (2003) notes in *Sojourners* magazine:

> Volunteer activities thus center on charitable activities and/or temporary relationships that ameliorate immediate needs. The goal for student development is to realize the necessity and richness of a character based on giving and caring for the other. While this "personal development" approach to service is worthwhile, the model also misses things. Big things. Absent are historical, economic, and political analyses that help students understand how social issues are structured in a specific community, in a specific place, at a specific time. Absent are social justice lenses that challenge students to understand social arrangements and how social change occurs. (p. 30)

Mission or charity work may also be a point of departure for more critical social justice work; however, these religious social service experiences could be problematic because students tend to work with a dynamic often entailed in charity work. This dynamic sets up the "giver" or "helper" as the one who "knows what is best" for the poor, which could potentially result in an implicit sense of superiority to the people being helped. As soon as I introduce economical and anthropological elements into the AMIGOS experience, most students quickly shift from a charity perspective to a more informed and critical reflection on their commitment to the community without losing their Lutheran beliefs. Still, there are a few that keep a paternalistic perspective, believe that the U.S. is the best country in the world, and find nothing wrong with its political or social system. Since my job as a professor is not to force people to share my viewpoints but to guide them in thinking critically, I ask them for arguments and data to support their ideas during class discussions and in the reflection pieces they turn in. Overall, for most students AMIGOS is a new approach or new step in their understanding or learning process regarding the Mexican community. In this sense the program is a tool for gaining knowledge through which they can find their own ways to develop approaches to issues appropriate for their personal, religious, faith, or social justice concerns.

On a more personal note, as a Latin American scholar working with a community service program at a Lutheran college in the U.S., I always remember that pastors and liberation theologians have worked together in Latin America for a long time. In Latin America, people who believe in social justice (religious or not) greatly respect and continue learning from the liberation theology movement that arose in Latin America in the 1950s and 1960s (Boff & Boff, 1986/1987). Liberation theology emphasized the importance of being aware of the structural in addition to the individual conditions producing poverty and evil, including the social sciences as part of a necessary dialogue with theology. Although AMIGOS is not a religious group, it is my goal that students establish similar connections between structural conditions and the injustice experienced by the Mexican community in Saint Peter.

The Complexity of Intercultural Social Justice Work

In order to avoid a paternalistic perspective, it is very important to me that students understand the cultural limitations of an experience such as AMIGOS, especially as many of these students are Spanish minors or majors. It is important not only to be aware of the different economic backgrounds of the people involved (middle- to upper-class American students and poor and working-class Mexicans), but also that the Mexicans living in Saint Peter do not represent all Mexicans nor all Spanish-speaking Americans. In fact, the specific conditions and context of this community are the basis on which the connection between AMIGOS and the Saint Peter community was established. The programs that have been developed were a response to perceived needs as well as desires articulated by members of the Mexican community in Saint Peter. For example, a mother with three children shared with Christine and Emily her concerns about the challenges her children were facing when attending elementary school in Saint Peter and the need for a culturally safe space. This mother became the door to connect and listen to other members of the community in such a manner that the relationship kept growing. As of today, AMIGOS is a resource people in the community trust, and constant communication ensures that the programs are beneficial for the college students and the Mexican participants.

Regarding ethnic differences, it is also essential to understand that getting to know another culture is a long, complex, never-ending process. I usually give students an example from my own situation: I speak English, obtained my Ph.D. in the U.S., and have been living in Minnesota for seven years. In spite of all of this, there are several aspects of the U.S. I still do not understand entirely. There has to be an element of humility when approaching other cultures, and the first step is to recognize that it is not possible to understand others entirely. Your mind must remain always open.

I know one of the first challenges AMIGOS participants experience is to accept that they may have prejudices even if they sincerely want to help the Mexican community. There are cultural barriers to be overcome, such as the food offered to students when they visit, the smell of the houses in which they need to work, the number of family members around when they are trying to help kids with their homework, the lack of privacy, especially for teenagers, or just a different dynamic regarding physical contact (what to Minnesotan eyes may look like constant hugging, kissing, and touching is just normal behavior among friends and family in Mexico). There are lines that are sometimes difficult to cross, because the culture in which people are educated is limiting and places a restriction on appreciating others. This can be seen in the U.S. due to a generalized disregard of the need to learn about other cultures, especially after it became a world superpower in the post–World War II period.

In the same manner, while a culture helps people define themselves, and find a sense of life, reality, spirituality, and identity, any culture also is a barrier that separates people. For instance, at some point in the process of engaging with the Mexican community, a religious college student might conclude that her or his conception of religion is more understandable, more logical, or just clearer than the Mexican one. The same happens with other aspects of the culture (e.g., family structure, gender roles, the education of children, etc.). In my experience these issues are difficult for Gustavus students to express, because they do not want to offend anyone or because they want to be politically correct. While it is not possible to completely overcome this issue, discussing cultural differences in class greatly helps in making students more comfortable with participating in AMIGOS. This also helps them avoid stereotyping. In fact, this is why I believe all types of community service should ideally start with learning about the culture in which students will be working.

Conclusion

Although Saint Peter is a small town, with only 9,500 inhabitants, we already face many racial and cultural confrontations in our schools related to the Mexican community. Discrimination, misunderstandings, lack of communication, preconceptions, and violence involving American and Mexican students of all ages are already happening in our town. Taking into account the history of other states with large immigration rates, the sometimes tense environment is fertile ground for frustration, anger, depression, and social conflicts. The combination of all these elements usually ends up with the creation of gangas (gangs). Because of globalization and deterritorialization, Minnesota will confront the same challenges other U.S. states more traditionally known for their growing Mexican populations have experienced. This issue is difficult to explain to many Anglo-Lutheran Minnesotans in rural areas who are not familiar with cultural and racial discrimination because of lack of experience with large minority populations. As a consequence, it is not easy for Gustavus to help the Saint Peter community by anticipating problems or working toward preventing tragedies such as shootings and fights related to racial hate at the high school.

Nevertheless, students working in AMIGOS can be a tool to educate the Saint Peter community and make it aware of the need for cultural exchange and collaboration. By supporting Mexican children and teenagers, AMIGOS is providing a space, even if limited, for intercultural understanding. Overall, the AMIGOS experience can be more than just another college experience. It can result in a lifelong desire to contribute to changing the world in which we *all* live.

Endnotes

1)   In this chapter I use the terms *Mexican, Mexican-American,* and *Latino.* Within the Saint Peter community, these terms are often used interchangeably, though in actuality *Mexican* refers to citizens of Mexico only, *Mexican-American* refers to U.S citizens of Mexican ancestry, and *Latino* refers to both groups. Too often members of ethnic groups are not given the privilege of claiming their own group name but have one imposed on them by others. For instance, *Hispanic* is a term that was coined by the federal Office of Management and Budget during the early 1980s when the government needed to find a classification to account for the tremendous increase in Spanish-speaking citizens. However, many so-called Hispanics do not speak Spanish, and those who do are racially diverse (e.g., white, black, indigenous, mixed-blood, of Asian descent, etc.). *Latino* is a term long used by people of Latin American origin to refer to themselves (partially in response to the misuse of *Hispanic*) and has the advantage of being a Spanish word rather than an Anglo-generated one. Some Mexican Americans prefer *Chicano,* a term that grew out of the Brown Power movement of the 1960s and reflects the culture and realities of urban, economically oppressed Mexican Americans in the U.S.

2) In order to demand better salaries and better conditions, Mexicans and Latinos have tried to organize but it has been extremely challenging, especially in the companies for which they work. The last attempt was in August 25, 2004 when Latinos tried to establish the United Workers of the North (UTN) to organize seasonal workers at Lakeside Foods in Owatonna. It would have been the first union of seasonal workers in the northern Midwest, but the company continues to work against the unionization effort by sending individual letters asking workers to turn in their cards and assuring them that workers are happy without unions in all of the company's other plants. Centro Campesino (see http://www.centrocampesino.org/) has been the only organization that has helped Mexican workers in their struggle for work guarantees, health insurance, and a better future for their children. The big challenge for workers in this kind of struggle is that they risk their jobs, stability for their families, and a proud history of work in Minnesota's canned vegetable industry.

3) For more information about this topic, see Contreras, Duran, & Gilje (2001) or visit the Hispanic Advocacy and Community Empowerment through Research (HACER) web site: http://www.hacer-mn.org

4) I still do the same exercise in my Spanish classes. Due to the existence of AMIGOS, the percentage has decreased to 60% as of spring 2005. I use the results as a way of explaining marginal invisibility in a hegemonic environment.

5) The trailer park can be seen from Highway 169 when entering Saint Peter from Minneapolis, yet many people had never taken notice of it.

6) This effort has been undertaken with the assistance of the All Parks Alliance for Change (APAC; see http://www.allparksallianceforchange.org/), a manufactured-home residents' organization based in St. Paul, Minnesota, which works to improve the quality of life in trailer park neighborhoods. APAC does not provide monetary assistance, but guides residents in the process of better recognizing their rights and possibilities for improvement and assists them in requesting financial assistance from the State of Minnesota for specific projects.

References

Boff, L., & Boff, C. (1987). *Introducing liberation theology* (P. Burns, Trans.). Maryknoll, NY: Orbis Books. (Original work published 1986)

Canclini, N. G. (2002, December). Anthropology: Eight approaches to Latin Americanism. *Journal of Latin American Cultural Studies, 11*(3), 265–278.

Chicano Latino Affairs Council. (2001). *Chicanos/Latinos in Minnesota.* Retrieved March 3, 2006, from the Chicano Latino Affairs Council web site: http://www.clac.state.mn.us/chicanos.htm

Chicano Latino Affairs Council. (2005). *Hispanic students in Minnesota school districts: 2003–2004*. St. Paul, MN: Author.

Contreras, V., Duran, J., & Gilje, K. (2001, February). Migrant farmworkers in south-central Minnesota: Farmworker-led research and action for change. *Cura Reporter, 31*(1), 1–8.

Lévi-Strauss, C. (1967). *Structural anthropology* (C. Jacobson & B. Grundfest Schoepf, Trans.). Garden City, NY: Anchor Books.

Martín-Barbero, J. (2000). Globalización y multiculturalidad: Notas para una agenda de investigación. In M. Moraña (Ed.), *Nuevas perspectivas desde/sobre América Latina: El desafío de los estudios culturales* (pp. 17–29). Santiago, Chile: Editorial Cuarto Propio/Instituto Internacional de Literatura Iberoamericana.

Minneapolis Foundation. (2004). *Immigration in Minnesota: Discovering common ground* [Brochure]. Minneapolis, MN: Author.

Snarr, M. (2003, May/June). The University of Social Justice. *Sojourners, 32*(3), 28–30, 32.

U.S. Census Bureau. (2000). Table DP-1: *Profile of General Demographic Characteristics: 2000, Minnesota*. Retrieved March 3, 2006, from: http://factfinder.census.gov/servlet/QTTable?_bm=n&_lang=en&qr_name=DEC_2000_SF1_U_DP1&ds_name=DEC_2000_SF1_U&geo_id=04000US27

7

FAITH, PEACE, AND POLITICS: DWELLING IN DISCOMFORT

Loramy Gerstbauer

When I was a teenager, my life goals began to emerge. I took a mission trip
to India with the West Ohio Conference of the Methodist Church. I had
traveled in developing nations before in the Caribbean and Mediterranean,
but India was intense. Not long after I returned, I saw the film *The Mission*
(Ghia, Putnam, & Joffé, 1986) starring Jeremy Irons and Robert de Niro,
about Jesuit missionaries in South America in the 1700s. The film was so
momentous for me that I wrote about it in a special diary I had purchased
at Colonial Williamsburg the previous year; the cover of the diary was dec-
orated paper that we had watched being made in one of the colonial shops.
I wrote,

> Today my thoughts are special. For months I've been think-
> ing along the lines of getting a medical degree, joining the
> Peace Corps, going to India, Africa, a third world area to
> help others medically, religiously, to HELP them. ...I feel
> my calling to this area. *But* is it GLORY that I'm after?
> Mother Teresa fame? [I had met her on my trip.]
> Martyrdom? I'm not sure. My desires are so unusual. How
> would I tell my guidance counselor: I want to help others
> and bring them to God and live a very devoted life.

I didn't write in that diary again until I was deep in the angst of graduate
school at the University of Notre Dame, pursuing my doctorate in political
science, on a completely different path than I had once envisioned.

In the interim I found myself at Wheaton College in Illinois—a nonde-
nominational Christian liberal arts college, largely from an evangelical tradition. I was not a pre-med major for long, but my passion for developing

countries persisted, as did thoughts of a career as a missionary. I enlisted in Wheaton's Human Needs and Global Resources (HNGR) program, an intense six-month internship in a developing nation; I went to Nicaragua and used my political science major to research postwar reconciliation.

The term *evangelical* requires some definition. Olson (1998) has described four essential characteristics of the evangelical movement. They are: 1) a belief that "the Bible is the supreme norm of truth for Christian belief and practice"; 2) "a worldview that is centered in a transcendent, personal God"; 3) a focus on "the forgiving and transforming grace of God through Jesus Christ in the experience called conversion"; and 4) a belief that the primary task of the church is to bring "God's grace to the whole world through proclamation and service" (p. 40). In my own view, most evangelicals view the Bible as God's word, without error in its original writing, and that a personal relationship with Jesus as Lord and Savior is the way to salvation. Some Christians who do not identify themselves as evangelicals also hold scripture in high regard, believe in a personal relationship with God through Christ's atonement on the cross, and that the church is called to share the gospel (to rephrase some of Olson's points above). Thus, I do not mean to imply that only evangelicals are true Christians. The term *evangelical* is fairly new to Christianity. I personally know several Christians raised as evangelicals who have sought new identities in Roman Catholicism or Orthodox traditions; they have not changed the core tenets of their faith in doing so. I have chosen to use the term *evangelical* because it is how I label myself and it quickly identifies me with some of the core Christian beliefs I name here. It is also a term that carries considerable cultural baggage, in part due to its exclusivist claims that Jesus Christ is the only way to salvation (though evangelicals are not the only Christians who make this claim).

At the evangelical institution of Wheaton College, my senior capstone seminar in political science focused on our pursuit, as Christians, of a political science vocation. We read segments of Noll's (1994) *The Scandal of The Evangelical Mind* in which Noll argues that we need to "take seriously the Lord's command to love him with all of our mind" (McManis as cited in Noll, p. 1), written in response to the problem of evangelical anti-intellectualism in recent decades (he also notes that Lutheran and Catholic traditions

managed to avoid this problem).[1] My education at Wheaton instilled in me
a good sense that my obedience to Christ is comprehensive, involving evan-
gelism, service to my community or communities, the exercise of my mind,
and a life that bears fruit for eternity by impacting people on this earth.

In my half dozen years of teaching in higher education, I have encountered
a handful of students who are living out my college-aged dreams—traveling
to the favelas of the world, hungry to learn about other cultures and peoples,
rejecting the suburban, two-car, salaried existence. Then I look at myself and
wonder how I ended up in such a safe and comfortable place, and yet such
a challenging place to live out my own vocation, with the dauntingly beautiful task of molding and pushing along the discoveries and learning of those
not much younger than myself.

The purposes of this chapter are twofold: to offer reflections from my own
struggles with what it means to be an evangelical Christian in academia, particularly as a yet-untenured faculty member at Gustavus, and to show the
ways in which my identity as an evangelical impact my theory and practice
of teaching, especially as it concerns motivating students in political science
and peace studies courses to be concerned about and act on issues of global
peace and justice.

Finding My Way: Living Out My Faith in Academia

Many have argued that academia is not a friendly environment for evangelical Christians. Living out one's faith with authenticity in the academy is a
constant challenge. However, as others, such as Marsden (1995), Noll
(1994), Plantinga (1990), and Wuthnow (1990), have argued, it is an essential task for Christians (and they often speak specifically to evangelicals) to
pursue.[2] As an evangelical who is also a political scientist, integration of my
faith and discipline is part of discovering and living out my identity in academia; it is part of being authentic as a teacher, scholar, and colleague.[3]

It is a constant struggle to be faithful and to determine what being faithful looks like in a diverse environment where most people probably do not
identify with one's views. Integration of faith and learning works differently

at different institutions. My integration of faith and learning manifested itself in different ways at Wheaton College, the University of Notre Dame, and now Gustavus Adolphus College. In each community, the wisdom of being self-revelatory and the acceptability of particular religious worldviews varied. The degree to which I have privatized my faith has accelerated as I pursued graduate studies and then a faculty position.

When entering a new environment, I suppose one behaves as anyone uncertain of their reception under new norms would. One attempts to discern the realm of acceptable behavior. Where are the boundaries at a place like Gustavus versus Wheaton, where faculty and students sign statements of faith, or at Notre Dame where more than 80% of the student body is Roman Catholic? Are questions about boundaries or acceptability even the right questions to ask? What would happen if I offered to pray with a forlorn student who visited my office? If I boldly stated that Jesus was the only path to salvation in a chapel homily? The chapel program at Gustavus provides space for many religious perspectives. While some individuals have proclaimed Jesus as savior in homilies, it is a pretty rare occurrence and seems to make many chapel attendees uncomfortable. Secondly, one seeks a community of support and shared identity, a task that may take years. It took two years at Notre Dame for me to help build and become involved in an ecumenical Bible study for Christian graduate students. This group provided a space for Biblical reflection on our academic pursuits and intellectual discussion of our Christian walk. It was a supportive place to help us think through what it meant to be faithful in graduate school: through acts of service, through standing apart from some of the worst forms of graduate student culture (e.g., constant complaining), and through our teaching and scholarship.

The point of all this adaptive behavior is to adjust to the possible pitfalls of being an evangelical (or any type of exclusivist Christian) in academia. I can say that I have experienced a few of those perils. I was once told at a peace conference that it is *impossible* to have an exclusive faith identity (i.e., to believe there is one path to God) *and* be a peacemaker. People assume that as a highly educated, peace-loving person you would reject the repugnant prospect of views that may condemn people to hell or associate you with the sordid past of missionary conversions. I can understand the critique, and I expect it. Jesus as the exclusive form of God is offensive and always has been. There have been at least a handful of incidents in my time at Gustavus where evangelicals have been disparaged by faculty. Exclusivist truth claims, particularly those that are religious, are seen as intolerant, closeminded, and fundamentalist, whether they are Christian, Jewish, or Muslim. Ironically, many academic institutions that claim to embody tolerance, diversity, and pluralism are in practice not tolerant of perspectives that are not consistent with their political and cultural agendas.[4]

Yet, I must be very careful here because being true to my faith as an academic is not about my comfort in my identity and my need to be accepted in my community. If I make that the story, then something is wrong. The story is about Jesus, and it is my calling to glorify him through what I do. This happens when I behave as a person of integrity and honesty, offer compassion to others, control my anger, teach truth, explore knowledge, exercise my mind, and challenge the minds of others. I remind myself when I find myself focusing on my own comfort that bearing these fruits is what really matters.

Many times I have realized that others who do not claim any faith allegiance are much better than I am at living out Christ's commands, in terms of showing love and compassion to others, caring for their community, and other acts of service. Therefore, I don't expect to stand out to my students or colleagues as some kind of super-woman of compassion, love, and perfect truth. I have certainly held false hopes that an encounter with a Christian professor would leave me feeling warm and fuzzy, when in fact it did nothing of the sort. As George Marsden (1995) argues, the task of the Christian in academia is not just to be a model of and witness to Christ, but also to be faithful to the calling of a Christian in academia, "to integrate faith with one's academic discipline" (p. 1). It would be extremely prideful of me to think that my role as a Christian was to provide compassion, and too limited to see my role as a witness for Christ, though both of those are part of the equation. The real call is for me to be faithful in my vocational pursuit as an academic—to integrate faith and learning.

Leading Others Along: A Faithful Pedagogy

My faith informs my pedagogy; it is behind why I care about students, why
I have passion for my discipline, and why I feel the questions of my discipline matter. My faith is the source of all meaning and value in my life; however, I do not openly convey this to my students, nor do I expect that the
majority of them share in this inspiration.

Despite this, I do believe that integration of my faith with my discipline
is conducive to good pedagogy and student learning, even in a setting like
Gustavus that celebrates diversity outside of the Christian tradition.
Authentic living-out of my evangelical identity and integrating this identity
with my scholarly work and pedagogy can serve multiple positive ends. It
can offer deep critiques of our culture and promote critical thinking. Most
relevant to this volume, it can explore the meaning behind our pursuit of values such as peace and justice, helping me and my students alike to struggle
through the hardest questions of why we do what we do and how we sustain
it; and it can serve to tear down stereotypical conceptions of evangelicals and
other faith identities.

Deep Critiques of Our Culture and
Promotion of Critical Thinking

I won't go into all the ways to relate Christian faith and culture (as many have
done this elsewhere), but I will say that my faith gives me a strong basis for cri-
tiquing my culture and my academic discipline. Princeton sociologist Robert
Wuthnow (1990) argues that the relationship between Christian conviction
and critical thought is a healthy one, even though many academics see
Christians as closeminded. Wuthnow uses the phrase "living the question,"
because "it seems to me that Christianity does not so much supply the learned
person with answers as it does raise questions" (p. 167), including questions
about the "value of the intellectual life itself" (p. 170). Wuthnow also argues
that the Christian faith is a source of deep passion and meaning for these questions. Of course, Christian faith is by no means the only source of such passion.

I stated earlier that my faith is the source of all meaning and value in my life. Values here are the things that make up my worldview, my understanding of purpose and meaning in life, and my place in this world. My values stem from God's revelation through his Word and through the life of Christ. God's character is unchanging, and thus the values He imparts are outside of time and culture. Thus, these values provide a solid foundation from which to critique and question culture and intellectual disciplines.[5]

My faith calls me (and here I may differ from many evangelicals in the U.S.) to look at social justice issues in relation to global politics. My faith does not give me pat answers about social justice issues and how, as a political scientist, I should teach and work for peace and justice. Rather, I am called to constant questioning and interpreting of competing viewpoints. This is also my goal for my students—to question and weigh competing perspectives and theories. Despite what some may imagine, even at Wheaton we were not taught what to believe; this is counterproductive training. As Wuthnow (1990) acknowledges, my faith does spawn my passion for the questions, and I am aware that in order for the questions to matter for students, they must stir something deep within them.

Why We Care About Peace and Justice and How We Sustain Its Pursuit

The words written in my teenage diary now seem innocent or misguided, even silly. Yet, my journey into political science motivated by my India trip and *The Mission* (Ghia, Putnam, & Joffé, 1986) film headiness came from a growing realization that not only did I love to travel and learn about the world, but that global politics were quite relevant to social justice issues affecting the lives of millions of poor and oppressed. This motivates me, and every course I teach attempts to make those connections: to help students see beyond the U.S.; to see our heap of privilege; to see the responsibilities of this privilege (our impact on others, conscious or not); and though I'm less accomplished at this, to empower students to act on this knowledge. The world I live in is rather safe and comfortable, making me question sometimes whether I am modeling a life of service and justice for my students. How can the students who don't see the world's needs begin to understand them and their connection to them? How can those who do see be called to action, and how can all of us maintain commitment?

My college internship in Nicaragua was extremely influential in deepening a vision that I had already been formed through earlier travel in developing countries. Later, the time spent in inner-city Chicago working at a social service job and living in an intentional community of Christians allowed me ample opportunity to reflect on and intellectually question my work. These experiences helped me see and molded my vision.

It is not easy to bring these experiences into the classroom. In some of my courses I do assign experiential components. For example, in my Politics of Developing Nations course, students are required twice during the semester to visit areas that are culturally or socioeconomically different from their own. On the first visit, they are supposed to focus on the causes of poverty and whether their observations agree with theories and explanations of poverty studied in the course. For example, they might think about the role of outside influences on a community, culture, economy, the extent to which health and basic needs are met, the leadership of the area, and levels of violence in the community. On the second visit, they are to visit an agency working for social change and to think about effective and ineffective strategies for change and the role of institutions, traditions, civil society, human rights, and outside aid in these strategies. The exercise asks that they take on the role of a participant-observer and be as openminded as possible during their visit. I also ask that they share their reactions and feelings and that they try to be honest and aware of their own stereotypes and judgments as they interpret their surroundings. I tell students that the exercise is designed to get them to challenge their assumptions about poverty and social change: to compel them to critically think about it, to try to make connections between poverty in developing nations and poverty in our own midst, and finally, simply to expose them to neighborhoods or issues they may not otherwise encounter. The students' visits and the journals they write about their experiences are debriefed in two class sessions.

I also require students in my Introduction to Peace Studies course to attend five different activities over the semester that relate to course themes. This is a fairly common assignment at Gustavus; particularly in our First Term Seminar classes, many professors require students to attend a certain number of lectures, theater productions, concerts, or other events in order to get them involved in our campus community life. In the peace studies course, two of these activities must *actively* involve the students in social change. I found that students had some difficulty identifying what counted as actively involved in social change. Some attended meetings of an activist group (which could count), and one student even attended a protest over the Iraq war, even though he was a war supporter.

These exercises may or may not change students' hearts and minds. Much more in-depth experiences I've had with students may or may not have a long-term impact in their lives and their vision for social justice. I took a small group of students to Nicaragua to study the legacy of the Nicaraguan revolution and its impact on the struggles of the poor in Nicaragua today. Students were deeply moved when we stayed with families in a poor coffee-growing region of the countryside in primitive accommodations. The struggles of these Nicaraguans and their warm hospitality to us outsiders led the students to express that they would remember this for the rest of their lives and that the experience was life-changing. I hope this is true, but I wonder how long the effect will last.

All of the experiences described here fall short of the ideal service-learning model in which there is partnership between the community and the academy, the partnership entails a long-term commitment, and initiatives are based on community needs and form a mutually beneficial cooperation. This model attempts to avoid a situation where students feel they are coming to help the underprivileged and the community is used for the students' educational experience with little benefit in return. In Nicaragua we did join in acts of service, such as picking coffee with the families and helping them prepare meals, but even though students wanted to do something more for these people after we left, the agency that organized our trip has a policy that such "aid" should not be entered into until after several visits when a partnership has been indeed developed with the Nicaraguan farmers. In my

Politics of Developing Nations course, I make an effort to explain to students that they should be aware of the distinction between service-learning and their short visits. My hope is that students can maintain awareness of their role of power and privilege as they visit a site, and I encourage them to think about making a longer-term investment in the community if they desire.

I am not saying that because these experiences fail to reach the ideal model, they are therefore without value or worse, harmful. Exposing students to our world's problems in experiential ways is a good thing. Students may sometimes have a false sense that they are making a difference by their actions, but usually the refrain is that they learned more than what they gave in return (indicating that they are aware of this dynamic). This may be using others for our own benefit, but I think the value of this learning is that it comes from an unexpected source. It is quite a revelation to discover that one can learn from a Nicaraguan peasant—that Nicaraguan coffee farmer now has new meaning and new value to me as a person of dignity, deserving of respect.

Thus, there is a range of activities in the traditional and extended classroom that helps expose students to issues of peace and justice in memorable ways and encourages critical thinking about these as real issues. I hope that these small movements will feed into and build off of similar experiences students have elsewhere in their college career or later in life. Unfortunately, though, this may all end up nowhere. The pull of this world's temptations and commitments (e.g., house, job, loans, family) is too great to be easily overcome by the exposure to and critical thinking about justice issues that experiential or service-learning entails. To surmount these obstacles we need to ask why it is that we do what we do and urge students to ask the same question. It is not enough just to see the need, to have cognitive knowledge and hands-on observation of the need. It is not enough even to feel the need or act on it (like one of my colleagues who has his students imitate being homeless for a few days, or my students who collected a large donation for Heifer International). We also need to address questions of motivation and identity. We need to address the issue of sustainability and accountability of our commitments and vision. If not, we may end up like an American couple I met in Nicaragua who woke up one day many years after college and realized that they had unintentionally developed "affluenza" and were living the "American dream." That they were able to find "a cure" shows unusual courage; they sold their home and most of their belongings and went to Nicaragua for three years with the Mennonite Central Committee.

Taylor (1989) argues, "modern people generally lack any adequate intellectual ground on which to defend their beliefs about benevolence and justice which they hold most dear" (cited in Marsden, 1995, p. 6). What is grounding the values of students? My values stem from my faith. Yet, my goal is not to give students my set of values. It is valuable for students to see that there are multiple viewpoints and paths of social justice. Not all people who care about social justice care about it in identical ways or care about the same issues. I often find in my conversations with colleagues at Gustavus that if I am presumed to be a person who cares about peace and justice, I am presumed to fall down the line on a certain set of issues—I must vote a certain way, I must believe human nature is a certain quality, I must not be an evangelical. This is a narrow-minded view, and I am also guilty of this stereotyping. While faith may not be the only foundation for values, if we care about engaging students at the level of motivations, conversations about faith (our own faith and how we live it out) should not be ignored or avoided, particularly at a place like Gustavus. Unfortunately, I am guilty of this as well.

The peace studies course I teach is the one in which I have most opportunity to explore the personal values of students. Early in the course we examine sources and causes of violence. We look at sociological, biological, and anthropological perspectives on human nature and group violence. The readings represent a wide range of views, and all of them express a particular belief about human nature and its contribution to violence. Completely absent, however, is the Biblical view of human nature that human beings were created in the image of God but fell into sin and now have a sinful nature. After some time spent in class discussing the readings, one student in a recent semester pointed this omission out and shared her personal religious belief about human nature. I completely agreed with her, and yet didn't feel comfortable revealing my own Christian viewpoint. As none of the other students were interested in exploring this angle, the student who raised the issue may have felt invalidated. In hindsight, it is clear that in my role as an instructor, and particularly since I am sensitive to and aware of the need for faith-based perspectives in intellectual thought, this would have been an opportunity to acknowledge the student's view as one that was clearly missing from our readings, and perhaps explore reasons for this omission. This would not even have required me to reveal my own view or to privilege it.

The main text I chose for this course was a reader compiled and published by Roman Catholics (Fahey & Armstrong, 1992), and sections on nonviolence and social change were heavily laden with readings from the Christian tradition. I purposefully chose this text because others I had looked at portrayed religion in a more negative light, as a source of conflict, for example. I thought students would object to the Christian bias in the text, but in the end I had to voice the concern that other religions also have traditions of nonviolence and social change that our book failed to represent. While we acknowledged that many of the writers found their motivation in their faith, we didn't discuss the sources of our own values. Also, in neither of these conversations about the text would I have dreamed of indicating my own Christian biases. To reveal my biases opens the discussion to topics, which if I were to discuss with integrity and without compromise would, I fear, result in stereotyping and misunderstanding on the part of students, affecting their view of me and their perceptions of how I view them.

In my Politics of Developing Nations course I spend a day of class reviewing our abundance and what it would mean to live a life of voluntary simplicity. I borrow suggestions for lifestyle changes from Ron Sider's books (1982, 1997; he is founder of the group Evangelicals for Social Action). I don't always mention that Ron Sider is a Christian.[6] It is not important that he is a Christian, but it is important to discuss why someone would be motivated to live simply and how they could be held accountable for doing so. While we talk about possible motivations, I do not probe issues of faith, nor do I share with students my own motivations. Maybe this is partly because I am not satisfied with my own progress in living out my values.

Despite my reluctance, I think it is hard to get at the motivational questions of why we care about peace and justice without entering the territory of faith. This is particularly true at a place like Gustavus where many of the students are at least "churched" in some fashion. If I, who deeply identify with a faith tradition, have problems engaging students at this level, does that mean we are all doing a bad job of it? Or does it mean that I feel less free discussing faith because in doing so I may problematically reveal my own identity? It is also easy, as a political scientist, to excuse oneself from dealing with the topic. While none of my courses have religion or faith at their heart (I teach international relations, after all), most of my courses do ask questions about the intersection of religion and politics, and all of my courses reflect a social justice bent.

Without more explicitly addressing students' bases for their values, some of the authenticity of their values is lost. Lip service to social justice is all you get if you do not help people to identify with it based on their own motivations and understandings of truth. It must become their own and mesh with what they know and believe to be true. Appleby (1999) and Gopin (2000) make this argument in relation to their studies of religious fundamentalists. In order to counter religious extremism, particularly violent forms, it is imperative that we speak to religious fundamentalists on their own terms. If we say, "You can't be a peacemaker and believe what you believe," or, "Tolerance requires that you accept that your God is not the only true God," then we alienate all of the fundamentalists, and only the less zealous in the faith will adopt the peaceful, tolerant alternative. As Appleby argues, each religious worldview is rich and diverse enough to offer its own justification for violence or for peacemaking, and thus it is most effective to meet religious fundamentalists on their own terms, encouraging not denial of their faith but mining of its peaceful tenets.

The point here is that we must engage in dialogue with people's authentic identities. If people aren't touched where it matters (such as their own faith), then values won't take on the deeper meaning. In order to create lifelong learners, it is important to address the motivation and sustainability questions. This is something I admittedly do not do very well. While these discussions would not require me to be self-revelatory, the question of how much I should be so certainly becomes part of the pedagogical questioning.

Revealing my own faith identity to my students may not be something I ever choose to do in the classroom. There are valid pedagogical reasons to avoid this, such as avoiding student concern that my view would be privileged over theirs in the classroom power dynamic. A bigger concern of mine is that I would lose credibility. In spite of these reservations there are some reasons why self-exposure might be a positive.

Because of my concerns about losing credibility and being accepted, I vowed a while ago to revisit some Henri Nouwen writings (1974, 1975, 1976, 1983; Nouwen, McNeill, & Morrison, 1982). Nouwen was a Catholic theologian who wrote about compassion, service, humility, and hospitality in the Christian life. Nouwen's work is very honest about the trap of musing on the self as a hindrance to reaching out to others. He deeply and humbly shares his own feelings of longing, inadequacy, and frustration with fellow humans and God. Part of the reason Nouwen was such a good teacher was that he shared of his own life and deep struggles. Of course, he had an advantage over me in that he taught theology. But, that is not a good excuse. After all, what did I learn in that course at Wheaton except that my faith extends to all parts and exercises of my mind and is not restricted to one academic discipline or vocational pursuit? Still, questioning what it means to read poetry, complete chemistry experiments, or study political science as a Christian is a perennially puzzling question at a place like Wheaton. It is even more so at a Gustavus, which, while based in Lutheran traditions, is welcoming and celebratory of diverse religious traditions.[7]

It is important to think about (and we all do as teachers) how much of our own identities we should reveal to our students. Nouwen shares deeply of his own struggles to live out his faith in authentic ways in a flawed world. His own struggles become valuable lessons for his students.

Breaking Down Stereotypes of Evangelicals and Other Faith Identities

I was floored in my second year at Gustavus when a group of students asked me to join their early morning prayer group. I had no idea how they figured out I was a Christian. When I asked, they noted that I had read a Psalm in my class on the day after the terrorist attacks in September 2001. This was one of the most outspokenly Christian things I had done in my course: to read from the Bible. The terrorist attacks were so momentous that a response beyond the ordinary was warranted. Also, I wanted to reach students as human beings in what for me is ultimately a human tragedy, not first to raise a political debate. Thus, reading the Psalm seemed appropriate. It was also fairly safe for me, in that it was not meant to provoke discussion. Rather, it was akin to holding a moment of silence and recognition, though one that undeniably called to God for strength. Still, I was shocked that it would make me stand out as a Christian, the kind of Christian who would be interested in an early morning prayer meeting!

If anything, I go out of my way to hide my identity in the classroom, and if students at Gustavus engage in the same stereotyping of "peace and justice" types that I've encountered elsewhere, then they probably have me pegged as someone I am not. If I did reveal my faith identity, students might have their own stereotypes of evangelicals severely challenged. As Marsden (1995) argues, subtle diversities within evangelicalism are lost in the university, where evangelicals are most often associated with fundamentalists like Pat Robertson, Jerry Falwell, or "anti-abortion, anti-feminist, anti-gay activists" (p. 1).

Of course, I don't necessarily need to tell students my own beliefs in order to challenge those stereotypes of evangelical Christians. For example, there have been many opportunities in the classroom to talk about President Bush's faith identity in relation to the war in Iraq and how some evangelical Christians disagree with Bush about the war. Also, my intense awareness of being lumped in with the bad apples of my own faith tradition makes me conscientious about attending to the nuances of other faith traditions as well. Teaching an international relations course after September 11, I made sure I drove home to students that not all Muslims are terrorists, nor is there anything about Islam that necessitates violence. I later had a student from Pakistan thank me for my handling of the issue, since she felt quite exposed in that class after September 11. Many faculty probably made an effort to say this, but I do think that, generally speaking, followers of faiths (of whatever kind) have special insight into the nuances of faith traditions. Particularly, those who make exclusivist truth claims are more likely to understand an identity that does likewise, even from another faith tradition.

Certainly, conservative Muslims, Jews, and Christians have found some common ground in the culture wars within the U.S.. This hearkens back to Gopin's (2000) and Appleby's (1999) arguments concerning the importance of engaging religious identities on their own terms, rather than asserting that they must deny their exclusivist claims in order to fit into academia, cultural norms, or political correctness.

Gustavus and an Environment That Enables Faithfulness

None of this dialogue can happen in an environment where conversations about faith are stifled. Gustavus is definitely not that place, although the challenges about speaking of faith here are different than at a Wheaton or a Notre Dame. Gustavus has its own set of pitfalls and rewards. The rewards for me at Gustavus include ecumenical fellowship, as in the chapel services. This is something I grew to appreciate greatly at Notre Dame, where I gained a deeper understanding and appreciation of Roman Catholicism. Also, the diversity of religious and nonreligious worldviews at Gustavus requires one not to take one's faith for granted and to know where one stands when confronted with alternative views. The pitfalls for me are that common ground is harder to find than at a place like Wheaton, or even Notre Dame. At Wheaton, faculty and students all had a shared faith, a shared basis from which to discuss a variety of topics. There was plenty of disagreement on how that faith should play out in different issues, but there was a common starting point. Without this common starting point, uncertainties result. Uncertainties about where other faculty and students stand can lead to fears about broaching issues of faith in (or out of) the classroom. Frankly, I have not seen the degree of faith and learning integration at Gustavus that is present at Wheaton (and expected there) or at Notre Dame. Other than in orientation sessions for faculty or in special church-related conferences, I don't see faculty casually talking about faith-learning integration or how Gustavus's Lutheran identity affects their pedagogy—not that it doesn't happen, I just haven't encountered it in my five years here. With very few exceptions, I have not been a party to meaningful conversations with faculty about faith in their private lives. Why don't we talk about this? I have encountered more faculty asserting their lack of faith identity at Gustavus than vice versa. This may reveal that the dominant identity is overtly Christian, so that those of other faiths or the nonreligious feel the need to call attention to their needs. Still, I wonder if in its search for inclusivity, Gustavus has silenced some of its opportunities for conversations about faith.[8]

It seems to me that the "comfort question" is central to this discussion. Is Gustavus making non-Christians feel welcome and comfortable? Do evangelicals feel welcome and comfortable? Do the traditionalist Lutherans still feel comfortable? I cannot speak for all these groups, but I believe the reader will have caught on by now that I have experienced some discomfort at Gustavus. At the same time, I don't want my own comfort or that of others to be of primary concern in the pursuit of this institution's mission. Discomfort may be more of a reward than a pitfall. I see my own concern with my comfort as an evangelical teacher as a stumbling block. If I had followed my childhood dreams to become a medical missionary in a far-off place, I would have been uncomfortable quite a lot. Why then should I not expect the same as I pursue my vocation in the mission field of academia?

Perhaps we should all seek to be more uncomfortable and to worry less about making others uncomfortable. After all, many faculty would promote making students uncomfortable as a learning tool. Perhaps freedom to promote discomfort would promote conversations about faith, not silencing or ignoring it, or just living with it in the background. Perhaps one of the greatest rewards of a place like Gustavus is that no one is perfectly comfortable living out the tensions of a school that is grounded in one faith identity but simultaneously welcomes and celebrates other faith identities (an inclusivist position).

Encouraging conversations about faith, particularly in the classroom, does require Gustavus to emphasize its Lutheran identity.[9] Plenty of liberal arts colleges care about academic excellence, about service and social justice, but what makes Gustavus distinctive is that these values are grounded in a Christian tradition. What difference does this make for students who come here as Lutherans, as other Christians, as Buddhists, or as atheists? Certainly Gustavus offers a myriad of opportunities in the chapel program, Bible studies, and outreach ministries. But, what is happening in the classroom? For the rich opportunities to be realized at Gustavus, we first need to be inquiring and probing more about faith in the classroom. I guess I better get to it.

Endnotes

1) Noll (1994) also refers to Robert Wuthnow's (1990) observation that the major frameworks of academic discourse have largely been set by anti- or non-Christians such as Marx, Weber, Freud, Kuhn, and Derrida. Should Christians be part of staging the frameworks of intellectual discourse?

2) Wuthnow gives vignettes of his conversations with several Christian friends in academia. The conversations at some level relate to how these scholars struggle to live out their faith in authentic ways as academics, struggling to be openly honest about a disparaged identity. (Wuthnow begins his piece by citing Tanya Gazdik's (1989) *Chronicle of Higher Education* article that referred to the dangers from evangelicalism on college campuses.)

3) The phrase "integration of faith and learning," or "faith-learning integration," often refers to scholarship and teaching, though I refer more broadly here to integrating my faith with all aspects of my profession. William Hasker (1992) defines faith-learning integration as "a scholarly project whose goal is to ascertain and to develop integral relationships which exist between the Christian faith and human knowledge, particularly as expressed in the various academic disciplines" (p. 231).

4) Reichenbach (2003) argues that pluralist academic institutions often have their own forms of exclusivism: "Although in theory tolerance is the liberal value of pluralism, in practice tolerance often is offered only to those perspectives deemed consistent with or worthy of liberal recognition" (p. 23).

5) I hope it is clear to the reader that I recognize that faith is only one source of values. Other sources of values might also help in examination of our culture. It might also be true that a transcendent source of values (such as God) is unique in its ability to offer critique from a perspective "outside" of human experience and knowledge.

6) I did not choose this text because Sider is a Christian, though it is why I am familiar with it, as opposed to other texts on living simply.

7) Scholars such as Darrell Jodock (2003) and Bruce Reichenbach (2003) would place Gustavus in an inclusivist category, a third path between exclusivist (or sectarian) and pluralist traditions. An inclusivist institution lives in the tension between maintaining its own nonnegotiable core identity while allowing that core to be expressed and enriched by diverse perspectives.

8) See Reichenbach (2003), p. 24 for more on this danger.

9) Some argue that in order to be inclusive and retain the Lutheran identity, a "critical mass" of faculty and staff must embody this tradition (see Reichenbach, 2003, p. 25).

References

Appleby, R. S. (1999). *The ambivalence of the sacred: Religion, violence, and reconciliation.* Lanham, MD: Rowman & Littlefield.

Fahey, J. J., & Armstrong, R. (Eds.). (1992). *A peace reader: Essential readings on war, justice, non-violence, and world order* (Rev. ed.). Mahwah, NJ: Paulist Press.

Gazdik, T. (1989). Some colleges warn students that cult-like methods are being used by Christian fundamentalist groups. *Chronicle of Higher Education, 36*(2), 1.

Ghia, F., Putnam, D. (Producers), & Joffé, R. (Director). (1986). *The mission* [Motion picture]. United Kingdom: Warner Bros.

Gopin, M. (2000). *Between Eden and Armageddon: the future of world religions, violence, and peacemaking.* New York, NY: Oxford University Press.

Hasker, W. (1992, March). Faith-learning integration: An overview. *Christian Scholar's Review, 21*(3), 231–248.

Jodock, D. (2003, Summer). The third path: Gustavus Adolphus College and the Lutheran tradition. *Gustavus Quarterly, 59*(3), 12–23.

Marsden, G. M. (1995). *The evangelical task in the modern university.* Pittsburgh, PA: Association of Theological Schools.

Noll, M. A. (1994). *The scandal of the evangelical mind.* Grand Rapids, MI: Wm. B. Eerdmans Publishing.

Nouwen, H. J. M. (1974). *Out of solitude: Three meditations on the Christian life.* Notre Dame, IN: Ave Maria Press.

Nouwen, H. J. M. (1975). *Reaching out: The three movements of the spiritual life.* New York, NY: Doubleday.

Nouwen, H. J. M. (1976). *The Genesee diary: Report from a Trappist monastery.* New York, NY: Doubleday.

Nouwen, H. J. M. (1983). *Gracias: A Latin American journal.* New York, NY: Harper & Row.

Nouwen, H. J. M., McNeill, D. P., & Morrison, D. A. (1982). *Compassion: A reflection on the Christian life.* New York, NY: Doubleday.

Olson, R. (1998, February 9). The future of evangelical theology. *Christian Today,* pp. 40–48.

Plantinga, A. (1990). *The twin pillars of Christian scholarship: The Henry Stob lectures.* Grand Rapids, MI: Calvin College and Seminary.

Reichenbach, B. (2003, Summer). Lutheran identity and diversity in education. *Intersections, 17*(16), 23.

Sider. R. J. (1982). *Lifestyle in the eighties: An evangelical commitment to simple lifestyle.* Louisville, KY: Westminster John Knox Press.

Sider, R. J. (1997). *Rich Christians in an age of hunger: Moving from affluence to generosity.* Dallas, TX: Word Publishing.

Taylor, C. (1989). *Sources of the self: The making of the modern identity.* Cambridge, MA: Harvard University Press.

Wuthnow, R. (1990, Summer). Living the question—Evangelical Christianity and critical thought. *Cross Current, 40*(2), 160–175.

8

JUST FOOD

Lisa Heldke and Peg O'Connor

On January 4, 2003, the two of us climbed onto an Amtrak train with nine Gustavus students. A day and a half later, we got off in Boston and entered a lived conversation about food and justice. For three and a half weeks, our course, Just Food, explored the question, "What roles does food play in creating just communities?" We sought answers to that question from a variety of sources: academic texts (including theoretical examinations of community, critiques of the so-called emergency food system, and case studies from the community food security movement); various food-related organizations and businesses that we visited as a class; and emergency food providers for whom students worked during their stay in Boston.

The work in these different contexts was equally important; no sharp line divided *theoretical* work from *practical*—an integration we encouraged by requiring students to write papers that placed reading, class discussion, and work in critical conversation with each other. Coming from the discipline of philosophy, which is notorious for valorizing the theoretical and abstract while denigrating the practical or material, we know well the pedagogical dangers of a one-sided diet of theory. In Just Food, we were very careful not to create unbridgeable gaps between the theories of course texts, our classroom discussions, and the practices of students' work sites. We required students to write four integration papers over the course of the term. These papers afforded students the opportunity to make connections between the texts and their concrete experiences. It was important for students to apply theoretical insights to actual experiences and to have actual experiences interrogate their theoretical concepts. We regard this interactive and integrative approach as the best way for students to learn how to become thoughtful and reflective participants in the classroom and at the work site.[1] Students reported feeling like they were "always learning," that even their mealtimes became opportunities for reflection and synthesis. Their conversations became sprinkled with references to "Janet" (Poppendieck) and "Jane" (Addams), the authors of two of their textbooks (Addams, 2002; Poppendieck, 1999), whose ideas took on an urgency and intensity for students because of the work they were doing.

The nine students in Just Food worked at one of three organizations for their entire stay—a strategy that enabled them to learn about the organization more deeply than if they had moved from site to site. Three worked at Pine Street Inn, the largest privately funded homeless shelter in New England that provides shelter, food, and job training to women and men. Rosie's Place, where two students worked, serves meals and provides various other services for low-income women and their children. Haley House, a Catholic Worker house at which four students worked, serves breakfast to homeless men and afternoon meals to neighborhood elders and provides a launching pad for social change activism.

The three organizations espouse very different philosophies and understand themselves to have very different roles in the food system; as a consequence, students engaged in diverse activities and learned a great deal from each other's experiences. Some spent their time in an industrial kitchen, preparing meals for people who live under overpasses and bridges. Some cooked meals created out of odd assemblages of donated leftovers, while others served planned meals catered by local area restaurants. They regularly used their own experiences, and their theoretical commitments, to interrogate each other—and themselves—about the work they were doing. During their three weeks, each student in the class probably made at least one trip through the cycle of believing "my organization *must* exist; my organization *should not* exist, my organization *does* exist, and that is both a wonderful and a terrible thing."

The Just Food course rests upon a number of moral, political, and pedagogical beliefs. Some of these are specific to the course themes of food and justice, while others represent more general commitments:

• All people have a right to security (with respect to food, shelter, employment, and health).

- Various systemic factors leave people without this security, even in the thinnest sense.

- Students will be better able to comprehend the complexities of social injustice and to envision the possibilities of creating social justice when they learn in multiple contexts.

- It is necessary to teach a course concerned with social justice and with experiential education for social change from an interested, engaged perspective.

- The role of the professor is not to indoctrinate students into his or her own worldview. Rather, it is to help students acquire the critical and analytical tools that will enable them to identify, refine, and put to the test their own theoretical commitments.

Conflicts inevitably arise among these foundational principles. Here, we focus upon the conflicts between the last two. Teaching for us—as for many professors—is a balancing act between developing students' abilities to articulate their existing beliefs, and inviting them to rethink those beliefs by presenting them with our own. The tension is real and live—enacted every day in the classroom and the work sites, and only put to rest (if ever) at the end of the course. In this chapter, we explore two ways this tension plays out in the course Just Food:

1) *The nature of social justice and the meaning of moral activism:* Students in this class must find their own sense of social justice and develop ways to engage it with the world. At the same time, we as professors must advocate for our own sense of social justice. To that end, we call upon students to become what we term moral *activists*.

2) *Atheism:* Students in Just Food must have the opportunity to reflect upon the ways that their spiritual beliefs shape their lives as moral agents in society. Simultaneously, we feel obliged to present atheism as a location from which one may launch a moral, socially engaged life.

In what follows, we elucidate the ways in which our foundational beliefs shape the work we do in Just Food, and how we manage—or fail to manage—these tensions.

Just Food: The Class

In Just Food, part of our job is descriptive. We examine the fact that, through flush economic times in the 1990s, the number of people depending on food banks increased drastically. Our work is also diagnostic: We explore the ways that certain economic or political relations exacerbate existing inequalities. And most importantly, our work is prescriptive: If we have adequately described and diagnosed, then we must strategize about how individuals and collectives can transform the institutions and practices that produce such large-scale insecurity. These normative questions are important, especially for students who want to change the world once they see the depth and gravity of the problems. In short, we help students to see the reasons to be moral and political activists and the ways to do so.

We offer a brief discussion of the core arguments of Just Food in order to elucidate more fully the relationship between our moral, political, and pedagogical approaches to social justice.

In mainstream political discourse and public policy debates, the reality that hundreds of thousands of people cannot afford to buy food to feed themselves or their families is described as "the problem of hunger." According to this hunger model, hunger is an unfortunate but perhaps temporary state of affairs of an individual or a family. Hunger is a consequence of bad luck or poor choices or unfortunate situations. This view lends itself to blaming the hungry for being poor and demanding a certain kind of responsibility on their part to pull themselves out of poverty.

The most common response to "the problem of hunger" is to alleviate the immediate need by providing free meals or deeply discounted or free foodstuffs. Many types of organizations provide these services, ranging from local churches working out of their basements, to local food pantries staffed by volunteers, to large food banks receiving state and federal money and private grant money. Hunger becomes a need that is met by social service agencies or individuals engaged in service.

Many of the students who took the class had in the past participated in some sort of volunteer program for feeding the hungry. Most people can imagine being hungry, and this creates a sense of sympathy, which then serves as the motivation for working in the food bank or in the soup kitchen. For some, there is also the added dimension of doing charitable works for others. Taken together, the sympathy and the charity shore up the hunger model, which keeps attention focused on individuals and their unfortunate plights. Hunger, then, is a problem that some people have while others are in a position to alleviate it.

Our examination of these issues begins with several important facts. The number of food banks in the U.S. has increased dramatically, rising steadily through the 1990s. Food banks such as America's Second Harvest have become enormous, with massive budgets, layers of bureaucracy, and near complete dependency on granting agencies and private donations. These large food banks have started to function in ways that are remarkably similar to companies in a competitive market economy.

Many of the course readings drawing from the community food security movement argue that these large providers of free or deeply discounted food have become too good at what they do. While it is true that these food banks are meeting very real immediate needs, their efficiency and success in meeting these needs provides the justification for governments (state and federal) no longer to provide assurance that people will not starve to death in the U.S. Instead, the Bush administration is arguing that monies formerly provided to federal programs should be directed toward private, charitable, faith-based initiatives. Arguments for privatization rest on the fact that these organizations already do this work so well and that there are thousands of volunteers who are prepared to do it. In the hunger model, charity becomes the vehicle for meeting the demands of justice.

In our critical analysis, we examine the ways in which the charity model is politically and morally suspect. At minimum, it misidentifies the problem as hunger and it locates the causes in the lives of individuals. This model cannot recognize the systemic reasons (oppression, economic injustice, institutionalized racism and sexism) that a significant number of people are so economically marginalized that they cannot secure food for themselves and their families in a regular, stable way.

This move to a charity-based approach implies that U.S. citizens can no longer make a meaningful political claim to a right to food, which some might argue is a basic human right, and therefore a moral right. With this shift the people who are already the most vulnerable and marginalized are losing what little protection and entitlement that right could offer. Charity clearly is not sufficient by itself for social justice.

What does justice demand of us? Perhaps it does demand some charity, but not only does charity not address the systemic nature of oppression, it may actually contribute to its perpetuation. Justice as fair distribution is certainly part of the solution to this situation, especially with respect to economic factors such as employment opportunities, but it is insufficient by itself. Distribution is always within a system, and how can we evaluate the system in which judgments of value, desert, and worth are made? Similarly, justice as the possession of equal rights has a place in the analysis, but rights are also the sorts of things that are exercised within a system. How do we evaluate the fairness or levelness of the playing field upon which rights are exercised? These are vexing questions that might lead to despair or even to a nihilistic conclusion that there is nothing that can be done. This would not be a good place to leave students, and so we begin to generate a more robust conception of social justice that requires people to be moral activists.

Social Justice and Moral Activism

In our view, social justice has a dynamic character. It is never a given, but rather is created and maintained in the context of relationships, both at the micro-level of interpersonal relationships and at the macro-level of social institutions and practices. Social justice is also fundamentally connected to conceptions of responsibility, and not simply in the sense of assigning blame, which often involves backward-looking assessments. Rather, responsibility rests upon recognition of one's obligations and duties, of the rights of others, and most importantly of the humanity of other people. Social justice is forward-looking. It requires that people take responsibility for the shared conditions in which we live and act, and it requires that we work toward making these conditions better so that people can not only survive, but thrive. If we can help students to recognize the ways that their well-being is so connected to others—even or especially others who seem radically different—then we have taken the necessary first step in effecting social change.

We operate with a conception of human nature as social and dynamic. What it means to be human is to be connected with others in all sorts of ways and in different degrees. We are creatures who stand in multiple relations with and through other people, animals, and the natural and social environments. This is what we are, and this is what we do. The well-being of each of us is inextricably connected with the well-being of others around us. This does involve empathy, but it also involves responsibility of a much deeper sort. Each of us, individually and collectively, has a responsibility to be in the world in ways that promote the well-being of others and that enable others to become more fully human by being more connected with others.

In this course, we like to believe we are helping students become *moral activists*. We chose this term rather than *political activists* quite intentionally. In our culture, the expression "political activism" is most often used as a pejorative; it functions as a quick way to dismiss a belief that conflicts with the dominant views. Most people think of political in the narrowest possible sense of "related to the state or government." Political activism becomes synonymous with unhappiness with or disapproval of a government or its policies. In the post 9/11 era, political activism of this sort is vulnerable to charges of being unpatriotic. We sharply disagree with this narrow understanding of "political," because it makes it seem as if the political is its own freestanding domain. We operate with much broader understandings of moral and political categories and the relationships among them. But given that we live in a world where our views about these relationships are not widely shared, we have chosen to use *moral activism* rather than offer lengthy qualifications and justifications for rehabilitating the expression *political activism.*

Moral activism has multiple dimensions and each of them involves a tension. Moral activism requires that people be willing to interrogate their own beliefs and values. All of us in Just Food have had preconceived notions about poor people—how they became poor, what they should do to get out of poverty, and what we could or should do to help. This self-reflection requires that one make a good-faith effort to be open to questions and experiences and to be ready to explain why one holds particular beliefs. This, hopefully, was happening through the course readings, the work in the organizations, and on the field trips. Investigating one's core beliefs can be deeply unsettling, and even while a person is casting off some beliefs, he or she may begin to hold others even more firmly.

Moral activism also requires that one come to develop one's sense of moral justice. We offer certain concepts and frameworks drawing from our training in ethical theory. The work sites and the organizations offer their own definitions and approaches, some of which are in tension with each other. Developing a sense of social justice is an ongoing task, and one's sense of social justice is no more immune to interrogation than other moral beliefs.

In addition, moral activism requires responsible engagement with the world. To anyone except a person trained in ethical theory, this may seem so obvious that it needs no discussion. But one of the points we stress in this class is that everything has moral implications, even the most common and ordinary things. We also offer a systemic analysis of poverty and discuss the ways people are complicit in maintaining systems of oppression, even when they are not doing so intentionally. Even more upsetting is the analysis that people's very well-intentioned efforts to alleviate "the hunger problem" may contribute to the oppressive conditions in which people live. Clearly, we worry that students will be so overwhelmed that they will feel completely defeated.

Throughout the course, students drew inspiration from a metaphor that Janet Poppendieck (1999) offers in *Sweet Charity?* to illuminate the nature of the problem of many people living in poverty and the different ways to respond to it. She asks readers to imagine that they live along a river, down which a baby floats one day. The people take care of this baby and provide excellent care. But then a few more babies come down the river, and then more keep coming at an accelerating rate. Soon many more people are needed to care for these babies. The caregivers are so busy meeting the needs of all these babies that they are unable to go upstream to investigate the causes of the babies coming down the river. This metaphor captivated students and it became a way to identify the ways they could respond to the poverty.

Being a moral activist is being on that river. Our moral beliefs and sense of moral justice will help to identify where each of us wants to be on that river. For some, their place is downstream, meeting emergency needs that have become normal and common. Others are working their way upstream, thinking about public policy issues and other measures. Still others might be at the head of the river, doing what they can to change the conditions that result in so many falling into the river. Each kind of work is vitally necessary and requires good, compassionate, thoughtful people whose lives and works create a more socially just world.

Education for Social Change

In designing this course, we drew our inspiration from models in experiential education and from education for social change. Particular influences include the philosophers John Dewey (1916/1985) and Paolo Freire (1970/1997), and the Higher Education Consortium for Urban Affairs, an organization which provides integrated experiential learning programs with a focus on social justice and civic engagement.

We choose not to describe the course as a service-learning course. The term *service* carries too many connotations with which we are not eager to associate ourselves. In the Christian contexts in which we both grew up, the term tended to invoke the image of the selfless missionary, spreading the Good News (along with medicine and clean water) to the heathen. There is also the notion of a *service provider*, working in a social service organization. A service provider is often portrayed as someone who performs his or her assigned function in the machinery of social work. The service provider does not aim to change the way things are, but rather seeks to ensure that those who are not well served by society are given a leg up. This notion of service is in fact something that we problematize in Just Food; our analysis in the course focuses upon the ways in which hunger has become an institutionalized need that can be filled by creating a set of service organizations. A third connotation may be less dominant in our students' minds, but is there nonetheless: the model of domestic service—being a servant.

Readers may object that an enormous distance separates these images (of missionary, service provider, or servant) from the reality of service-learning. From our perspective, that distance is immaterial; the fact remains that these images hold a powerful influence on our students' imaginations and their understandings of the term *service*. Several decades of careful theoretical work in the field of service-learning—work that has expanded the concept of service far beyond Lady Bountiful—have not counterbalanced the force of these images, which students bring with them into a service-learning course.

There may be a good reason for this; the concept of service may, necessarily, rest upon a nonreciprocal understanding of who provides what for whom. It may, necessarily, presuppose a hierarchical relationship—note that, regardless of whether the dominant or the subordinate person is the server, in all the examples discussed above, there exists a hierarchy. Indeed, one could argue that the concepts of social service and the service of mission work derive from the concept of *domestic* service. Part of the power evoked by the image of missionaries serving the poor, for instance, is precisely that, in the act of service, the missionary willingly assumes a subordinate role.

In contrast, terms like *experiential education, education for social change*, and *civic engagement* may carry no particular associations for students; they may not even know what some of those words mean.[2] We regard this as an advantage; it gives us the opportunity to work *with* students to develop working models of community, of participatory social change, and of democracy and democratic process. In contrast, using the term service-learning tends to require that we work *against* students as we struggle to challenge their preconceptions about "helping the unfortunate."

Our concerns about the connotations of *service* arise particularly strongly in Just Food, a course that places students in the very kinds of organizations for which they may have done service work in a confirmation class, the high school honor society, or the Boy Scouts. These early experiences often imprint students with the idea that their job is to "help" those "poor unfortunates" who can't seem to help themselves. In this view, there is nothing wrong with the system; it's just that some people don't, can't, or won't succeed in it—and that is where people can help, by providing for those who can't, and nudging along those who don't or won't.

In contrast, the philosophy of Just Food challenges the very notion that our food system is a just system working well, and that hungry people are simply individual anomalies who can be "serviced" back into the well-fed mainstream of society. It challenges the legitimacy of social service agencies that focus only on pulling the babies out of the river, never questioning why so many of them are falling in further upstream. It challenges the hierarchies that seem to be inherent in the language of service and works to replace them with models of reciprocity that make clear the ways in which even those most privileged by a system are dependent upon those who are most marginalized by it. And it seeks to move students beyond thinking about social service as the answer to thinking about systematic, institutional social change as necessary for increasing social justice.

Our attempts to embody this moral position as atheists at a religiously affiliated school illuminate a second instance of the foundational tension in the teaching role we describe. This tension sets one's responsibility to espouse one's deeply held views against the responsibility to create a space in which students can develop their own ideas. Religion and spirituality present particularly challenging terrain on which to negotiate this tension, for they are often deeply, emotionally held beliefs—beliefs that students may think it is inappropriate, even immoral to challenge, and to which they are unwilling to consider alternatives.

(Not) Speaking of Faith

Our presence in this volume has a faint whiff of the paradoxical about it, given that we are among the known atheists at this Lutheran college. While we hardly proselytize our position, neither are we particularly quiet about our rejection of the concepts and language of faith and spirituality. The paradox actually runs deeper than our inclusion in this volume, and extends throughout our work at the college. Our commitments to social justice often bring us to make common cause with people of deep spiritual and/or faith convictions, and with departments and programs specifically associated with the faith tradition of the college. Far from finding this an untenable position, however, we believe it affords us an important perspective at the college.

What do we mean when we say that we are atheists? At minimum, that we are uncompelled by the explanatory power of a god; we do not believe that such a being is at work in the universe. Furthermore, we find no role for the concepts and language of spirituality in our life; they, too, offer no explanatory power that is not available via the material and conceptual world we inhabit.

In classroom contexts, we have in the past tended to hide our atheism in plain sight, neither working to obscure it, nor making any particular issue of it. When faith matters arose in class discussion, we neither pursued them nor shut them down, but allowed them to float through a discussion, borne on the shoulders of students who wished to explore them.

Our motivation for doing so was born of our recognition that, in a context in which faith is presumed, making oneself visible as a three-dimensional, human atheist is a full-time job that could have the effect of making one's atheism one's *only* defining characteristic. We chose not to make it so—at least in part *because* we are committed to pursuing a social justice agenda. Because we do not want to be caricatures, we have often attempted to leave our atheism out of the equation—to surrender our commitment to espousing our own views in the interest of giving students the space to develop theirs.

Our experiences in the intense climate of Just Food taught us an important lesson about the dangers and limitations of this approach. A powerful and disturbing episode in the class revealed to us that sometimes, when we believe we are bracketing our views in order to give students the room to discuss their own faith perspectives, students read our reticence as *hostility* to religion and disdain for those who espouse it. When we do not respectfully explain to students the nature of our beliefs, and assure them of our commitment to creating opportunities for student reflection and dialogue about their faith, they not only may assume that such discussions are unwelcome, but may infer that our atheism will lead us to attack and belittle them for their beliefs. We may create a situation in which *any* comment we make about, say, a religious *organization* constitutes an indictment of *faith in gen-*

eral. Far from opening space, our silence about our own beliefs may in fact serve to eliminate the very possibility of space.

About three-fourths of the way through our January term in Boston, we learned that much earlier in the term several students had become convinced that we were disdainful and dismissive of religion and religious people. Their evidence? We had made a critical (and, yes, cynical) comment about the Bush administration's plan to provide government funds to religious organizations doing social service work. This proposal—which we objected to on the grounds of the separation of church and state—has also been opposed by many *religious* groups, a fact which the students dismissed as irrelevant. Whereas we saw ourselves as joining with many progressive religious organizations in criticizing the *government* for what we viewed as an unwise policy, students saw us as bashing religion. As a result of their perception, students selectively "shut down" around us about certain topics—most notably faith. Our twice-weekly reading seminars began to be formulaic and stilted as a result of several students' unwillingness to try out ideas for fear that we would silence them. Their anxieties about speaking of faith seemed to take on a more global quality; they became reluctant to say *anything* that contradicted what they took to be the "party line" (a party line they also thought several other students shared).

We came to know of students' anger when Lisa decided—with considerable misgivings—to look at the class journal that students had been keeping during the month to see if it could explain the undercurrents we sensed in the class, but about which we could not persuade students to be explicit. The matter of whether or not we professors had access to this journal was murky; in our class discussion about the question, people had expressed contrary desires on this point. Because of this conflict, we had decided not to read the journal. However, at least some students were under the impression that we *were* reading the journal, and thus were aware of their feelings and concerns—including their anger over what they perceived as our "religion bashing" comment. Given that we remained silent on the matter, students who assumed we'd read the entries naturally enough concluded that it wasn't okay to talk about this in the classroom. And so they fell silent.

Learning of their anger was devastating for us as professors and mentors. We were dismayed that they had so misunderstood our criticism of the government as a criticism of religion, but more than that, we were disappointed that we had so clearly failed to create a space in which they could say, "What do you mean by that?" in response to a comment with which they disagreed—or with which they at least understood themselves to disagree. While we had believed we were inviting students to enact aspects of their religious beliefs through the class (e.g., by choosing a Catholic Worker house as one of the work sites), and while we were keeping our own beliefs out of the classroom, students interpreted any remarks we made about religion through the lens of their incomplete and inaccurate understanding of what it means for us to be atheists.

This experience has persuaded us to be more explicit about our atheism in the future, to be more inviting of students' questions about our choices, and more inquisitive about their own choices. While we entertain no illusions that this will always happen easily, or that it will result in fewer classroom explosions, we have little doubt that it will be a more effective and respectful way for us to help students develop their faith perspectives than our attempts to hide or minimize our views. We have learned that, ironically enough, talking about our own positions *more* is also a better way to create a space for students to develop their own positions.

Just Food, the course, has revealed to us the limitations of hiding in plain sight and challenged us to become more articulate about our atheism—about the ways in which we can and should embody that atheism in the context of this Lutheran college. Out of this experience we have developed the most genuine role we can presently envision for the atheist professor. It represents the atheist's position not as derivative of, or devolved from, a faith perspective, but as a position with its own internal integrity, its own ethical and political commitments—a live alternative to faith. In this regard, it represents a sharp contrast to the choice to hide in plain sight (a choice that requires one to minimize or erase one's position), or to play the devil's advocate (another common choice that amounts to allowing one's position to be used simply as a convenient foil against which students can develop their own faith). The choice to be explicitly atheist while inviting discussions about faith represents our best current effort to negotiate the tension between developing students' abilities to articulate their existing beliefs, and inviting them to rethink those beliefs by presenting them with our own.

In any given community, the tenability of this alternative depends upon atheists and persons of faith attempting to understand each other's position and resisting the urge to subsume it under their own. This role is—surprise!—very difficult to articulate and to live. Had we consciously worked to embody this perspective in our January-term class, we would have been explicit about the fact that our own commitment to social justice emerges from our fundamental belief in human worth and dignity, a belief that is unconnected to any metaphysical or spiritual views about gods or afterlives. We would also have more intentionally invited students to articulate their spiritual perspectives. Finally, we would have made clear, in words and through our modeling, that we believe that these various faith and nonfaith perspectives would have to converse with each other, challenge each other, and identify the common elements in each other.

Atheists who choose to embody this role choose a position that is tremendously uncomfortable—but then so do persons of faith. Genuinely listening to positions one rejects is tiring, nerve-fraying work. But it is not always exhausting, for not everything is a matter of contention. Sometimes, groups of atheists and persons of faith discover each other as fellow travelers—which frequently happens on matters of social justice, for instance. We and our students were often virtually unanimous in our recognition of the ways that features of the emergency food system either preserved or damaged the dignity of the persons using the system. Where we disagreed, disagreement was not necessarily rooted in faith, but rather was lodged in differing opinions about what constitutes responsibility, or whether and when choice is appropriate.

Reflecting upon our work at the college as a whole, we realize that this is a role we have long occupied *outside* the classroom. We regularly choose to participate with people of faith in community conversations and projects, and we choose to do so in a way that *respects*, even when it does not *understand*, those choices. Therein lies the heart of the matter: Genuine, sincere conversation among atheists and persons of faith is a paradox, a tenuous, fragile, *contradictory* thing. It, itself, is untenable—but also, we believe, necessary for atheists and for persons of faith.

This role is not without its dangers, chief among which is the danger that the atheist will enter conversations in a spirit of (pardon the pun) "bad faith." Presenting atheism as a genuine choice does *not* amount to seeking to destroy others' faith. Choosing the latter betrays our commitment to creating a climate in which students can develop their own positions. It would eliminate the tension that exists between creating such a climate and espousing one's own beliefs—but at the expense of one of our fundamental beliefs. As such, we are clearly not willing to take this route. We *don't* believe that "professing" is the only important thing we do as professors. At the same time, we believe it's important to show others—including our students— that atheism represents a live, *ethically engaged* option, an option they may choose to take.

We find it particularly important to embody this orientation in the context of teaching for social justice—important to challenge the notion that matters of peace and justice belong exclusively to religion and religious people. We want students to understand that atheism and social justice are not mutually exclusive terms—that people may be motivated to seek justice in the world for reasons rooted entirely in a desire to improve the world for those living in it at the moment.

Endnotes

1) The integration papers had a clear structure with two components. The first was that students needed to pose a question, raise an issue, or outline a thought that was forming about their organization. The question or issue may have been about the organization's mission, the particular issues it was addressing, or the means organizations were using to meet the needs of their guests. For example, some students were truly vexed by the question of choice: Should people receiving free food have a choice about what they are eating? Should a person receiving a free sandwich ask for a different one because there were clear indentations from someone else's fingers? Students' ability to form a question or to understand something as an issue was closely tied to the readings in the seminar, and in this case the concern was raised in *Sweet Charity?* (Poppendieck, 1999). The second component of the integration paper was to use a conceptual tool or idea from the reading to reflect upon the issue or question raised. We asked students to reflect on how and why the tool they chose is useful in thinking about the issue, how this tool illuminates something that another tool could not, and how this tool may be limited in

its applications. The most important thing for us was that students thoughtfully discuss what an adequate answer would look like. This opens the door to the possibility of imagining transformation.

These papers were difficult and demanding for students; the papers challenged them to make the connections for themselves. Quite often, these connections were hard to find, and students had to stretch themselves in different ways that they were unaccustomed to doing. We made it very clear that if it seemed to students that they were working really hard on these, they were probably doing something right. Our hope was that these integration papers would provide a forum for theory and concrete experience to continually cross-fertilize each other.

2)   This, of course, will likely change as *civic engagement* becomes a 21st-century buzzword. We make no claims about the staying power of the words we have chosen; we only claim that, at present, they do not present the particular kinds of obstacles represented by the term *service*.

References

Addams, J. (2002). *Democracy and social ethics.* Chicago, IL: University of Illinois Press.

Dewey, J. (1985). *Democracy and education: An introduction to the philosophy of education.* Carbondale, IL: Southern Illinois University Press. (Original work published 1916)

Freire, P. (1997). *Pedagogy of the Oppressed,* (Rev. ed.). New York, NY: Continuum. (Original work published 1970)

Poppendieck, J. (1999). *Sweet charity? Emergency food and the end of entitlement.* New York, NY: Penguin.

9

ORA ET LABORA: PRAYER AND SERVICE IN AN INTERNATIONAL STUDY ABROAD PROGRAM

Jenifer K. Ward

What is the difference between taking a group of students across town to do service-learning and taking them across boundaries of culture, language, and nation? In what follows, I discuss two separate experiences of the latter. The first was in 1999, for one month, and the second was in 2000, for five months. Both were in Germany. In the first, which I discuss only briefly, we learned about issues. In the second, we learned about ourselves and each other. I would like to argue that the latter experience—ironically, the "selfish" one—was the one that helped shape a group of students for a lifelong orientation to service that will bear fruit long after their grades were posted.

Epiphany, 1999

In January 1999, I took six students to Berlin to spend one month learning about the changing multicultural face of German society. It was my first attempt to incorporate the relatively new concept of service-learning into my teaching, and we spent our time visiting various organizations and outreach ministries run by the Lutheran church in Berlin. Some aspects of that month were successful, but in the end, I must confess that the service "learnings" were only accidental. Upon reflection several years later, I can say that the intellectual work was well designed. The emphasis of the course was on the various multicultural communities living in Berlin and their difficulties with integration or acceptance into mainstream German culture. The course was very issues-focused, and the discussions and direct service were designed to highlight questions of language barriers, cultural differences, and legal hurdles faced by immigrant communities. The weakness of the course was the lack of specific links between the issues and the service. The students learned quite a few facts and figures. They also did some service—providing childcare for a weekly tea gathering among German, Turkish, and Kurdish women, for example—but in spite of the fact that I had them journaling about their experiences, I have to confess I had no real sense of what my own goals were for the admittedly short time we had in Germany. In addition, while we had some opportunities for informal processing along the way, I was never really seen (or felt myself to be) an integrated member of the group. After all, I was their professor. After we had returned to the U.S., I gave them feedback all at once in the form of a grade and comments in their journals.

So they did *service*. And they did *learning*. But the two were disconnected. I am certain it was not a bad experience for anyone, including the local communities—in fact, I think everyone benefited. But if I could do it again, I would change quite a bit. My initial contacts were with church workers, but I only asked them to serve as a referral agency. I missed the rich opportunity to discuss, quite specifically, how their own outreach work was informed by their faith, and how their work transformed, strengthened, or tested their faith. I was not comfortable with addressing these questions so overtly in 1999. I would be able to do it today, having pulled off a five-month program in Germany. In this second experience, my own willingness to dive into the complexities of negotiating my own faith issues—even as I walked side by side with students exploring theirs—contributed to a much more coherent experience for the students, but also allowed me a transformative five months.

Maundy Thursday, 2000

On Maundy Thursday in 2000, I sat in my small apartment in Halle, with most of the students on the Term in Germany, a semester-long study abroad experience in the Lutheran centers of Germany. We had come to do academic work in three different cities: Wittenberg, Halle, and Erfurt. By this time, our small group had been in close quarters for more than three months: We were our own social group, our own service project partners, our own classmates—and all this in a country where we were outsiders with a language barrier. We enjoyed the deeply loyal and bitterly combative relationship of a cobbled-together family, but we were at a tense moment in the course of the semester. So we gathered in my living room by candlelight, shared a light meal together in strained silence, and then began what had become a common ritual: the practice of *culpa* (Stewart, 1998). Patterned after centuries of practice in monastic communities, we acknowledged to each other and to ourselves all of the ways in which we had injured or been injured by each other. I admitted to every known interpersonal transgression, and those I neglected to mention were pointed out to me by others, and so on around the circle of people.

Our group had been practicing culpa since January in Wittenberg. I had known that our five-month program would begin in Wittenberg, continue in Halle, and conclude with a month in residence at the *Augustinerkloster* in Erfurt, the monastery where Martin Luther had been a monk. In that last month, we would be wrapping up our five-month stay, and I would be teaching a course on monastic history and contemporary practice. Knowing that we would be joining an existing monastic community, the Sisters of the Casteller Ring, in their daily life and work, I had tried to be intentional in the preceding four months about initiating the students into reflection about living in community, even as they did their ongoing academic work and service projects. Because the sisters lived according to the Rule of St. Benedict (Fry, 1981), and patterned their community life according to the intersection of prayer and work—*ora et labora*, in Latin—my hope was to introduce the students gradually to an orientation toward service that would grow organically out of their community life and responsibilities to each other.

Since we were not studying abroad in the conventional sense—there was no possibility of integrating into the German university system, and the students had no requirement for previous German language proficiency, for example—it was clear from the first days that I, as accompanying professor, would not likely be able to stand above or outside of the group of 12 students from Gustavus Adolphus College and Saint Olaf College, two Minnesota institutions affiliated with the Evangelical Lutheran Church in America.

As an academic trained in the field of Germanic languages and literature, I had no professional resources to draw on in my new role. Indeed, walking with these students through general developmental stations in their journey abroad would have been challenging enough. But in this context, there was the added complexity of accompanying a group of overtly Christian students (with one exception) on a journey that became, for them, as much about faith and spiritual growth as it was about the history of Germany, Luther, and the Reformation. While I am a Christian, I found myself ill-prepared to serve as any kind of pastoral presence—not because I have no pastoral intuition, and not because I shy away from discussing even my most ambivalent feelings about faith. My initial discomfort stemmed from the degree to which my scholarly and professorial self, on the one hand, and my Christian self, on the other hand, did not know how to be in conversation with each other.

Having just completed a sabbatical at the Institute for Ecumenical and Cultural Research, which is affiliated with Saint John's University and Saint John's Abbey in Collegeville, Minnesota, I had had the opportunity to immerse myself in a monastic setting grounded in the Rule of Saint Benedict. My final planning for the Term in Germany had been done while at Saint John's, and my course on monasticism, to be taught in Erfurt the following May, had been shaped by my daily encounters with the monks, the prayers, and the physical setting of the abbey. But even so, the reality of looking my students in the eyes and answering their questions about my own faith perspectives was altogether different from gathering readings on monastic communities, lining up service projects with my contacts in the Lutheran church in Germany, or even talking theoretically about theology.

The first time we performed culpa in Wittenberg, therefore, I had planned it as an exercise for the students in which I myself would not participate. My idea to suggest it came from the tension that had built after three weeks of understandable difficulty in adjusting to a new culture, a new language, each other, and the resulting homesickness. Rather than spend a semester with individual students coming to me to complain about their classmates, I insisted that we start our journey together with a covenant to address tensions as they arose. The flaw in my plan was that I wanted to manage the process from the outside or from above, to remain an impartial facilitator and maintain professorial distance. (And this is the way, I would argue, that many of our students approach the communities in which they intend to do service-learning projects.) I quickly learned that I was asking these students to do something that made them feel enormously vulnerable, and after what seemed like an eternity of painful silence, I realized I would have to go first. What happened through this gesture is that my place in the group changed irrevocably from "above and outside" to "equal and within," at least as far as personal disclosure went. This, in turn, allowed me to grow and be transformed alongside my students during the course of the five months.

By the time we got to Maundy Thursday, the students had lived in two cities, Wittenberg and Halle, had done service projects in various sites, had learned enough German to venture out into the world independently, and had come to some reconciliation with each other about the very different ways in which they thought about faith and worship. They had signaled in the first days that they wanted to have regular evening prayer together. Since most of them were familiar with the sung prayer style of the ecumenical and international monastic community in Taizé, France—many in the group had spent a week in Taizé in February—they took turns planning worship for the group using Taizé chants. They had already wrestled with the fact that all of them came from very different worship traditions and had learned to enact ecumenical hospitality by planning inclusive services. Still, tensions ran high. Our living situation in Halle placed us in daily confrontation with people who had been "left behind" by the unification of Germany. Faced multiple times daily with homelessness, drug abuse, domestic disputes, alcoholism, and poverty—and having just visited the concentration camp at Buchenwald—the students had been taking their tensions and sadness out on each other.

The Maundy Thursday evening prayer, therefore, was a poignant and tender attempt at reconciliation and enacting service in intimate terms. In my living room, the students prepared for that ritual associated with Maundy Thursday: foot washing. Rather than have one symbolic person wash the feet of others, the students set up an elaborate, snaking chain. One student started by kneeling at the feet of the person to her right. As she washed his feet, she told him what she had been feeling toward that person: pain, dislike, frustration, love. She dried his feet and moved to the next person in the circle. The student whose feet had just been washed waited until the person to his right was free and then washed her feet. Every person in the room washed every other person's feet. While this service to each other was only tangentially related to our official work in Germany, I believe it was crucial. By recognizing that interpersonal tensions in the group, as well as exhaustion and sadness, could drain our community of its energy to do our chosen work, we served one another and ourselves for the greater good. By being self-serving in ongoing ways, in other words, we ensured that we would later be sustained for service to others.

Pentecost, 2000

When we finally arrived in Erfurt in May 2000, our notions of service were challenged even further. Much of what we were asked to do revolved around providing hospitality to pilgrims who were on tours of "Luther sites" in the eastern part of Germany. We scrubbed floors in the church, we weeded the courtyard, we mowed the lawn, we staffed the sales table for exhibits, we did whatever odd jobs needed doing to assist the sisters in their work. Because of our preexisting notions that laudable service really only counted when we set aside our privilege to help those less fortunate—a stance I feel is all too prevalent in many service endeavors—our contributions were difficult to measure. These sisters were sturdy and content, and the pilgrims we encountered arrived in air-conditioned buses with cameras dangling from their necks. But in an era of strapped finances and dwindling membership in the church in Germany, and given the cost of maintaining the monastery as a place of pilgrimage, retreat, and historical and cultural heritage, we came to believe that we were providing a valuable service indeed. In this regard, the lesson we learned was that service is rendered when we support an articulated need, even if indirectly. Our tending to the monastery garden, for example, freed the sisters to spend more time operating the café on the monastery grounds, where all were welcome to gather and eat, regardless of ability to pay. Sometimes helping others work for social justice is, itself, working for social justice.

Perhaps the most surprising illustration of the many ways in which service can be understood unconventionally came on our last night in the monastery. As part of their academic course during that month, the students were given the option to participate to varying degrees in the daily liturgy of the community. The sisters gathered four times daily for sung prayer in the Benedictine tradition: at morning, noon, evening, and at the closing of the day. There were seven sisters. There were thirteen of us. For a month, four times daily, at least half of us joined the sisters, and all of us were typically there for the closing prayer of the day. The difference between seven sisters singing a Psalm and seven sisters joined by twelve American students and a professor—several of whom had choral training and lifelong experience in the musical traditions of their American congregations—was compelling. Sister Roswitha (the sister who endeared herself to all of us by asking how to say "Pfingsten," Pentecost in English, and then proceeding to wish us "Happy Petticoat" at every opportunity) would regularly violate her sisterly reverence at prayer by grinning delightedly at the sound of these very un-German, exuberant voices struggling with the liturgy day in and day out. But soon the students began to learn the words, and by the end, were settled into the rhythms and—like the sisters—began to slide silently into their seats and intone the confession: "Ich bekenne Gott, dem Allmächtigen, und euch, Brüder und Schwestern, daß ich gesündigt habe . . . " (I confess to God the Almighty, and to you, brothers and sisters, that I have sinned . . . [Liturgy for Compline, 1996, p. 1394, translated by author])—a full circle return to our culpa of earlier days.

On our last evening in Germany prayer began at 7:30, and the bus was to pick us up later that night for our trip to the Berlin airport. All of us gathered with a strong, bittersweet sense that we had been enriched by our time in Germany, in the monastery, and with the sisters. We sang the liturgy, as always, this time punctuated by quavering voices and moments of silence as some shed tears. After the final blessing by Sister Ruth, the prioress of the community, we stood. Typically, everyone would depart in silence. But Sister Ruth spoke. She asked us to stay and hear a special blessing. The other sisters began passing out candles to each of us as Sister Ruth explained that our presence among them would be missed. She asked each of us to light our candle and place it at the foot of the altar. When they returned to pray early the next morning, she explained, what had become twenty-one voices would be returned to seven. We would be en route to America, and they would be bereft of our presence. But they would find comfort in the candles, representative of the light we had brought into their lives. Sister Ruth explained to the students that she knew that they had been coming to prayer for a variety of reasons: some to fulfill a course requirement; some out of curiosity; some because they loved to sing; some because they valued the rhythm of regular prayer throughout the day. But, she offered, what we had perhaps not considered was that we had provided a valuable service to them. The emotional energy required to sustain a very small community of seven sisters in an urban ministry with scant resources was considerable. They were together constantly: at work, at home, at rest, at prayer. And even they suffered from time to time from "burnout" or fatigue with their vocations. Sister Ruth went on to claim that *their* prayer life had been reinvigorated. Our presence among them, just our presence, our singing, our smiles, joining our voices with theirs in the singing of liturgy of the church—just these seemingly selfish things had changed their community prayer life and they owed us thanks. The students were stunned. Who were the servants and who the served in this scenario?

Lent, 2004

Four years after the semester in Germany, two of the students are in divinity school. One did two years of volunteer work at Holden Village, an ecumenical retreat center in Washington. One student spent a year with the Jesuit Volunteer Corps. Three students spent a year with the Lutheran Volunteer Corps, and one with the VISTA program. Two worked at the ARC Retreat Center in Minnesota, and one continues to work there. And one was diagnosed with ocular melanoma during this Lenten season. I received a distraught e-mail from one of the students, saying that our friend was about to have surgery and needed the prayers of the "Germany group," and could I please spread the word. As we reconnected around this sobering news, including comforting words via email from the sisters in Erfurt, I am struck by how we were all changed by our time together. We did not heal the world during our semester. Hunger was not ended, justice did not replace injustice in obvious ways, global peace was not reached. But 12 students and I learned to make peace with each other on a regular basis; we learned to support and sustain each other—in spite of our differences—when confronted with the feelings of displacement that came from being jolted out of comfort zones in a new culture and new language; the majority of the students ended their college careers by entering into yearlong, faith-based volunteer service organizations.

I went into the experience thinking that our service was to build a bridge between U.S. colleges with a Lutheran heritage and institutions in the so-called new German states—the former East Germany. By foregoing the well-trampled path of taking groups to Munich or Heidelberg, I believed I would be serving the mission of our colleges better (Ward, 2003), and would also give postunification eastern German institutions a boost in their new internationalization efforts. What I learned was that our service was far less measurable than that and far more important for our own progress as individuals dedicated to the project of being outwardly oriented. What I took from the five months was a recognition that the important thing is not to save the world. The important thing is to want the world to be better and to be involved in the process—with others—of saving the world. The former implies a focus on the need to "get credit" for having saved the world, and the emphasis is on *who* has done the saving. The latter carries a recognition that the world, if it is saved, will be saved in communities of individuals. The emphasis is on *the world* that needs saving.

Easter, 2004

In our context at a Lutheran institution, it is hard to separate all this talk of saving from the backdrop of a grander narrative of redemption. For me, and for most of the students, this was the red thread that ran through our experience, if often beneath the surface. And as I write this now, in the season of

Easter, I am humbled by the fact that I was served by 12 students in ways most of them do not even realize. I gained insight into my various selves: the teacher, Christian, scholar, and human being. I accompanied the group to make sure they had a rigorous academic experience, to run interference for them with German agencies, to teach them what I could and to open their eyes to a culture and a history in a part of the world I love. But I came back with a sense that my disparate selves had achieved a kind of integration I had no idea I missed. The need to reconcile *ora* and *labora* within my own work life became clearer to me, and I am unapologetic about my orientation as both scholar and Christian. I have no doubt that the students on this trip will continue to give their time and energy to the pursuit of peace and justice in the world. And while any number of successful models for service-learning exist in our institutions today, my hope is that individual faculty members will feel empowered to think broadly about the nuanced definitions of service and how they might be brought to bear on seemingly humble projects locally and abroad. Finally, I would like to reinforce the notion that service need not be equated with selflessness. Self-care, discernment, spiritual practice, and reflection are fundamental to the development and sustenance of good and healthy *servants*, without which—after all—there is no service.

Postscript: August 2005

And then the 12 were 11. Courtney Walker died last week, and once again our group has reconnected—this time to remember the hospitable spirit of our friend. I dedicate this piece to her memory.

References

Fry, T. (Ed.). (1981). *RB 1980: The rule of St. Benedict in Latin and English with notes*. Collegeville, MN: Liturgical Press.

Liturgy for Compline. (1996). *Evangelisches Gesangbuch*. Stuttgart, Germany: Gesangbuchverlag Stuttgart GmbH.

Stewart, C. (1998). *Prayer and community: The Benedictine tradition.* Maryknoll, NY: Orbis Books.

Ward, J. K. (2003, Spring). Serving the mission: A study-abroad and service-learning case study. *Association of Departments of Foreign Language Bulletin, 34*(3), 25–29.

PART III:
Getting to the Heart of the Matter

10

FEAR OF DISCLOSURE IN THE ACADEMIC MILIEU

Leila Brammer

In the pursuit of an open and authentic classroom, I frequently offer my experiences as examples of concepts or as prompts for class discussion, particularly with issues of social justice. My disclosure often includes issues that are quite significant to me, and I hope that my open discussion and reflection serve as a model for students in thinking about their own position and identity in the world in relation to social justice. My faith is an important part of my life and fundamental to my interest in social justice issues, yet I have never directly shared any personal aspect of my faith in the classroom. I have made general, usually joking, references to being Lutheran, used specific examples I witnessed in a church service to clarify a concept, and am known among students as a supporter of the chapel program. From these examples, my students know in a general sense that faith is a component of my life, but I do not directly share my personal belief system. Certainly other aspects of my life that are important to me do not find their way into the classroom, but it is surprising that I am reluctant to discuss my faith, considering I am at a church-related college where individual conversations with students reveal their desire to discuss such issues and with my own awareness of the importance of these discussions to student growth. And, from my discussions with colleagues, I am not alone. Reflection on this issue reveals critical questions: Should faith, particularly the personal faith of an instructor, be discussed in the college classroom? What deters faculty from such discussions? If we do discuss faith in the classroom, how can it be done in a way that mitigates concerns and creates a comfortable environment for faculty and students?

In endeavoring to respond to these matters, I have specifically reflected on faith in the classroom within the context of courses involving service-learning or social justice at a church-related college. Throughout my years of teaching,

I have had a number of informal conversations about the surrounding issues with colleagues and students at a variety of institutions. When I began to think about this chapter, I more intentionally continued these conversations and sought out the views of other colleagues and students. My reflection and conversations with faculty and students illuminated these issues for me in ways that may be valuable to other faculty as they think about approaching faith in the classroom. This chapter addresses, on the basis of my reflection and conversations with faculty and students, the benefits of such discussions, the concerns of faculty, and some approaches that might mitigate these concerns.

Faith in the Classroom

Numerous studies have shown that teacher immediacy, particularly self-disclosure, in the classroom leads to increased learning and positive perceptions of the learning process (Gill, 1988; Goldstein & Benassi, 1994, 1996, 1997; Hartlep & Forsyth, 2000; Pearce, 2000). These benefits have been shown in subject matter tests, interviews with students, and teaching evaluations. More specifically, instructor self-disclosure plays a significant role in a service-learning environment. Students process their experiences through sharing and listening to others share their experiences. Indeed, in processing service-learning and discussing issues of social justice, personal experience is imperative to understanding the issues and providing students with a comprehensive view. In these situations, instructor experience can serve as an important model of how to live a life of conviction and how to manage the difficulties and complexities of that type of life.

Although books and articles on service-learning emphasize the importance of reflection, even specific reflection on the relationship between identity and service-learning, most do not mention faith as a significant factor. This might grow out of the general societal discomfort and the particular academic resistance to faith. Even those who do mention faith seem to have ambivalent feelings about it. In a book detailing the reflections of service-learning pioneers, faith is spoken of as a motivating factor but is placed last on the list, even though later in the book the pioneers discuss it as a determining factor in helping them cope with obstacles (Stanton, Giles, & Cruz, 1999). But service-learning literature does point to identity as a fundamental component in student growth. DeVitis, Johns, and Simpson (1998) speak of the "crucial lessons for identity formation" in service-learning and contend, "In response to the call of community, the student also learns more about her own strengths and limitations—her own cognitive, affective, and spiritual resources" (p. 15).

Rhoades (1997) in his study of students who engage in community service observes, "We all have a sense of self that we bring to all we do" (p. 13). He specifically notes, "The college students whose lives and experiences I share throughout this book also have social histories and a sense of self that they bring to their community service work" (p. 15), and argues that our work as teachers is to help students see how such activities contribute in fundamental ways to one's sense of self. Rhoades maintains that identity issues must be central to teaching college students, since every decision "pertains in one way or another to issues of identity" (p. 19) and that during college students face more identity challenges than during any other time. In his study, Rhoades found that faith or spirituality is central to these identity issues. He observes, "For a number of students, involvement in community service contributed to their sense of self as a spiritual person. Several students in this study saw strong connections between their faith and their commitment to serving others" (p. 193).

Social justice work also contains an apparent link to faith in its call for "social change aimed at reducing or eliminating social inequality and injustice" (Lisman, 1998, p. 65). If our students bring issues of faith identity to service-learning and social justice, then do we have an obligation to at least help them make sense of their experience? Certainly, I have always felt that way, and most faculty and students with whom I talked identified the connection between service/social justice and faith as an important component of education at a church-related college. My colleagues who teach as part of a women's studies program most clearly spoke of the importance of identity in research and in action, and some noted intentional reflection on issues of identity is essential, particularly in relation to issues of social justice.

Many faculty with whom I spoke thought faith could provide motivation and a significant link to social justice and service among students, and they indicated that many of our students who are engaged in issues of social justice and are actively involved in meeting needs in the community are motivated by their faith commitments. Some believed that integrating faith discussions into service-learning could encourage more students to be involved, make their involvement more meaningful on a personal level, provide a model for living their faith beyond college, and advance personal reflection and growth on faith and action. Some faculty pointed to the Gustavus Adolphus College mission statement, particularly coupling two phrases: "mature understanding of the Christian faith" and "meaningful lives of leadership and service." For those faculty, service-learning, teaching about social justice, and linking both with faith discussions seemed like part of our charge. Similarly, faculty talked about the worth of modeling faith and having faith mentors. A few of my colleagues shared poignant stories of how they still use models of faith from their youth or how as young adults a particular person was important in mentoring their faith. Their models and mentors were family, family friends, or church contacts, and, while they said they felt a need to model or mentor for others, some were unclear about whether they had or should serve in this role for students. Throughout the conversations at different times a theme emerged that faculty themselves need models and mentors for how faith can be explored productively with students.

In fact, though faculty spoke of the potential benefits for students in having teachers who model a life of faith and purposeful reflection on faith, they rarely engaged in such disclosure in the classroom. Reasons for this reticence were many. Despite the identified benefits of personal disclosure, particularly in service-learning or when discussing issues of social justice, limits to disclosure were also identified, and those limits included faith and faith-related issues.

Impediments

Almost universally in my discussions, faculty reported discomfort with discussions of faith. Few faculty had ever engaged in such a discussion with a student, even in a one-on-one situation, and those who had expressed concern about how they handled the situation. Overwhelmingly, regardless of belief in their value, faculty do not make faith discussions or faith mentoring a practice in the classroom or in their lives as educators. Some faculty directly stated that while faith had importance in social justice and service, students need not reflect on or discuss the role of faith in those specific courses, but rather that other courses or organizations could fill that gap. The exceptions to this were faculty in religion departments, who shared that these discussions—academic and personal and large group and interpersonal—were a part of their work as professors at the college. Interestingly, faculty in other departments clearly argued that those with training such as chaplains, those in the religion department, or others should do this work, since it is within their subject matter. Most surprisingly, students seemed to agree. Even the students who identified themselves as very religious were not sure about the place of faith in non-religion courses. These are students with whom I have discussed faith in an interpersonal context, and even they were concerned about the ramifications of a classroom discussion. Students shared the conviction that faith is within the purview of the religion department and identified discomfort with the issue similar to that of faculty members.

Reasons for faculty and students' reluctance to discuss these topics include: the difficulty in integrating such discussions into an academic environment; not wanting to impose beliefs on students; fear of offending students with different faith traditions; concerns about answering challenges or being judged on the basis of such disclosures; and the deeply personal nature of faith, including a general discomfort with discussing issues of faith, particularly with students or acquaintances.

Faith Versus the Academy

Most faculty, even at a private church-related college, have a background in public education. Even those who attended small, private, church-related institutions for their undergraduate degrees completed their graduate work at public institutions, where faith in relation to the coursework or their areas of specialty was not formally examined. In short, faculty have not formally explored their subject matter in relation to faith, and, even if an individual faculty member has reflected personally with family, friends, and colleagues on the connections, they lack models for integrating these reflections into the classroom. Frankly, because of our training and the perception of the academy, the idea has probably never occurred to a number of faculty.

Faculty, students, and society as a whole are conditioned to see the academy as a place for rule-based scientific or academic exploration and not as a place for reflecting on faith or spirituality. Sloan (1994) in his work on Protestant higher education, writes, "The conception of knowing and knowable reality that has come during the past centuries to dominate modern culture and education has left little place for the concerns and affirmations of religion" (p. viii). Marsden (1992) argues that the secularization of higher education has resulted in the secularization of the history of higher education to the extent that very few faculty understand the historic and valuable link between religion and education in American society. As a result, faculty are trained to compartmentalize faith in their scholarly life and so are poor models for living active and engaging lives of faith. Many of my colleagues do live enviable lives of commitment and service that grow out of their faith, but the academy, if not unaccommodating, is certainly not a supportive environment for directly engaging faith. None of my colleagues referred to concerns about direct sanctions from the institution, but they were concerned about how others on campus and particularly in their scholarly communities might react. Further, many felt that integrating faith discussions in their classrooms would be a violation of some academic or disciplinary code, even though they noted that no formal written code existed. Personal beliefs about the position of faith in the academy were extremely strong among faculty and resulted in a great degree of concern about the place of faith in the classroom and their prospects for success if they did attempt it.

Further, the language of the academy does not lend itself to faith discussions. The scientific model, the foundation of inquiry in many fields, is ill suited for reflections on faith. Faith cannot be proved scientifically; if it could, we would not call it "faith." Perhaps our inability to fundamentally define faith—Faith in a creator? Faith as making meaning out of the world? Faith as a belief in something larger than ourselves?—is precisely what hinders us in bringing it into the more objective world of the academy. Bringing faith into a discussion of science can lead to complications, and my colleagues in the sciences often encounter this in teaching evolution. A few students at Gustavus openly, actively, and emotionally resist evolution as being in opposition to their Christian faith. Evolution and Christianity can coexist quite easily, but arguing at once that evolution can be scientifically proven and creationism cannot, while offering that God could have created the world in which evolution proceeded, negates the scientific method as the foundation of knowledge. As such, knowledge and faith are distinct and unrelated, and integrating them becomes extremely difficult. Similarly, in the humanities and the arts, inquiry requires research and evidence, again leaving knowledge and faith not easily reconciled.

The framework of the academy and its language produce obstacles in integrating faith discussions into the classroom and present considerable difficulty for faculty members in publicly and directly asserting their spirituality as foundational in their work. Rhoades (1997) contends that there are personal and scholarly dangers to this perspective. He writes,

> When I started participating actively in community service, my understanding of research was different from what it is now. Research was about being disconnected, objective, and neutral. It did not involve the passion, feeling, and concern I brought to many of my community service activities. The kinds of things I associated with community service had no place in research. (p. 16)

Fear of Proselytizing

Although the academy environment is central to the reluctance to discuss faith, faculty and students were also concerned that discussing faith might lead to proselytizing. I and my colleagues have found that when we talk about politics, students are very sensitive to whether we give fair treatment to both mainstream political parties. My students are very quick to label my affiliation and then filter my comments based on their views. Interestingly, what they believe about my party affiliation is different for individual students, and their sensitivity says much more about their ability to handle critical thought on issues; however, this problem does shed light upon what might happen with a discussion of faith. The concern about a faculty member using the classroom as a pulpit for personal faith directly relates to concerns about the purpose of the academy, but both faculty and students were more concerned about unintentionally imposing beliefs on students, which is exactly the concern students voice about political affiliation in the classroom.

Faculty spoke of the power of their position in the classroom and on campus and feared that they might inadvertently influence students rather than foster a deliberate reflection on faith by individual students. The fear was that if adopting a faculty member's faith became an easy choice for a student, it would be more harmful for the student in the long run. As an example, one colleague related a story about how his talk about tennis in class has led a few of his students over the years to take up the sport. Others spoke of faith as a personal journey and that any shortcut or divergence from the personal path would not be helpful. In fact, in *How College Affects Students*, Pascarella and Terenzini (1991) found that student-faculty contact does result in changes in occupational and other values, and that closer relationships result in greater change. This concern may overvalue faculty influence and minimize student thought, but for vulnerable students or for students who strongly identify with a particular faculty member, this may be a consideration. Students also indicated fear that other students might use the discussion as a forum for proselytizing, and a few students spoke of instances in class and in informal conversations with other students where this had happened.

Fear of Offense

The other side of this equation is the concern that a student might be offended or marginalized by the discussion. Even faculty members who very directly discuss social justice and political issues in class and students who are actively engaged in community action organizations expressed concern that students from other faith traditions might be upset or silenced by discussions of faith in the classroom. Some of these faculty members spoke with pride about how we need to make students uncomfortable if we want them to learn, and some of the students talked about how they like to get "in the face" of their peers and challenge them to get involved in activism; meanwhile, talking about faith results in such a fear that they report reluctance to even discuss it with friends and colleagues.

One student offered an example of an instance where personal faith was a topic for class discussion. Early in the class, each student had to share a faith statement; a student who was an atheist found himself ostracized by the class and eventually left the course. Without knowing the student, we can speculate that much more was probably at work, but the student who shared the example spoke about the daily discomfort of this student's silence and how, even though she felt bad about his eventual withdrawal, the tension decreased in the classroom afterward. Concerns about how personal faith might offend or marginalize is worthy of consideration at a college and in a society where persons who are not Christian feel marginalized in many ways. If we openly place faith in the classroom, do we create or encourage a more hostile environment for persons from other traditions? Again, in relation to this issue, faculty stated a reluctance to risk such a reaction and felt unprepared to handle it.

Fear of Judgment

Students and faculty also reported a concern that a proclamation of their personal faith might result in a challenge. The student who spoke about the experience of the atheist in a class also noted that the environment was

uncomfortable even for her as a Christian, since the faith statements resulted, directly in class or informally outside of class, in questions from other
students. Other students also spoke about their fears of being challenged or
judged, even specifically remarking about their anxiety that the entire campus might hear about it. Faculty also felt fear of being openly challenged in
class or being judged by students or colleagues who might hear about it later.
Although faculty were concerned for themselves, their most prominent concern was that the classroom discussion would become unmanageable and
that students would be harmed. Again, faculty felt out of their element and
unprepared to respond effectively to the situation.

Faith as Personal

Faith as intensely personal was the most prominent theme in my discussions
with faculty and students. Almost universally, the personal nature of faith
was principal in the conversation and in each concern discussed. Faculty and
students noted that they rarely discussed their faith with others. Similarly to
me, they spoke of religious affiliation and church attendance quite freely, but
only addressed personal issues of faith directly with persons with whom they
were very close. Placing these discussions in a public context, particularly at
a small college where students and faculty know that information finds its
way quickly across campus, creates a great deal of anxiety among students
and faculty. Further, both groups also felt unease about the difficulty in articulating their faith and believed that actions were a better indicator of their
faith. For me, my largest concern is not having the answer for a student in
crisis. My faith seems to serve me well at this particular moment in my life,
but my understanding of faith has evolved and changed to meet the needs of
my present situation. I might be effective at speaking to a student about the
overall nature of a faith journey, but I certainly feel unprepared to help them
find an answer, and doing so seems intrusive in some ways.

   All these concerns were heightened for untenured faculty. Fear of sanctions
or reprisals was not directly mentioned, but junior faculty repeatedly mentioned a generalized fear about how they might be perceived in the larger

community. Even so, senior faculty shared the same concerns, and those fears prevent them from integrating faith into class discussions even on issues of social justice or in service-learning courses where they believe those discussions are important.

Faith in relation to service-learning or social justice creates quite a complex paradox. Almost universally, faculty and students feel that faith discussion is important to understanding the self in relation to the course material and the world, fulfilling the mission of the college, and life beyond college. In spite of this, faculty do not believe that their classrooms, even if engaged with service-learning or social justice issues, are the best places for these discussions; instead, they feel that other departments and organizations on campus are more naturally equipped and trained to deal with these issues. Consequently, faculty and students leave this decidedly important work to others who seem more qualified. I am grateful for those who directly guide students on issues of faith and value the work that they do with our students and their support of the mission statement, but I must admit that I feel guilty when I realize that I have, at least subconsciously, expected others to take responsibility for this issue of student growth. In view of the overwhelming concerns expressed by faculty and students on this issue, those people and places directly identified with issues of faith will need to continue to uphold this area in the future; however, methods do exist for even the most reticent faculty member to integrate faith discussions into the classroom.

Faith in the Classroom Revisited

In discussing methods with my colleagues who do discuss faith openly with students, I found a similar degree of discomfort, but also a background and experience that I do not possess. For instance, one colleague had attended divinity school before earning an advanced degree in a scientific field, and another had focused her dissertation on the role of spirituality in multicultural school settings. These experiences did not make them experts, but did give them some confidence in their ability to handle faith as a topic with students. The most obvious method for the rest of us might be to just *do it* despite our anxieties, but this might not be the right choice for everyone. Charging into the classroom with faith discussions might even be offensive to those who are professionals and trained in doing so, in the same way I am offended when others claim to teach public speaking without having a background in the theory and practice of teaching rhetoric and might also have similar negative outcomes.

Instead of all of us becoming religion professors or pastors, I suggest a more muted approach. Some might argue that this is an evasion of discomfort, but I believe it to be a better response to the situation. The best method would mitigate the concerns of faculty and students while achieving what we hope to achieve from discussing faith in relation to social justice and service-learning.

A couple of my colleagues argued that living their faith was more important as a model than as a topic for classroom discussion. One even noted the Biblical admonition against talking about faith and the requirement instead to live faith. These colleagues clearly indicated in their comments that they live their faith openly and publicly in their dealings with colleagues and students; they contended that their students know them as persons of faith because it was and should be apparent in their acts, in their relationships with students, in their relationships with the world, and in their commitments to social justice. As a result, they noted that students sought them out individually to have discussions about faith and life and that those discussions were infinitely more valuable than a class discussion. Further, they found the idea of disclosing their faith in class and talking about it at least mildly offensive and a possibly empty gesture unless one actively modeled living it. Personally, I have found that students do see me as a person of faith and a few have sought me out to discuss these issues individually, but, considering the large numbers of students who talk to me about any number of personal issues, only a very small percentage talk with me about faith issues. Living faith provides an excellent model, but I do wonder how many students would attribute their positive experiences with those professors as faith related. (I do know that negative experiences are attributed to lack of faith, e.g., "He's evil.") Operating from this assumption may cause us to miss a valuable teaching moment.

First, we must move beyond our compartmentalized view of faith. Identity plays a valuable role in effective teaching. Palmer (1998) writes in *The Courage to Teach*, "Good teaching cannot be reduced to technique; good teaching comes from the identity and integrity of the teacher" (p. 5). Cavazos (2001) expands on this, contending that it is our lived experiences that are the foundation of teaching: She writes, "The educational knowledge teachers possess about what it means to teach and to learn is embedded within their stories. The knowledge becomes most visible and tangible when teachers have the opportunity to communicate with others" (p. 144). Cavazos specifically targets the need to share our stories with other teachers, but certainly the same is true of our need to share with our students. Those stories include our identity as persons of faith, if our faith is lived in teaching and reflected in our interest in service-learning and social justice issues. To do this, we must be able to move beyond our training and society's beliefs about faith in the classroom. Marsden (1992) argues that we must recognize that "religious perspectives, if responsibly held and civilly presented, are as academically respectable as any other perspectives" (p. 7). Further, Lewis contends that to enact social change "you need to talk about religion. Most of us as activists or educators are very nervous about that. It's just not something we're willing to tackle. . . . [I] decided that it would be neat to do something where you open it up and say, 'Okay, I want to know how your faith relates to your politics and to your community development work'" (as cited in Stanton, Giles & Cruz, 1999, p. 222). Lewis speaks of transforming the educational process and pushing beyond our fears by directly engaging the ways faith intersects with service-learning and social justice.

Expanding our definition of faith might help ease discomfort. A conception of a monolithic, unchanging faith is not necessarily helpful in guiding students who come to college from a variety of faith backgrounds. I certainly would not support the idea of a faculty member proselytizing or offering a particular faith as the right one. An understanding of faith based in making meaning seems much less threatening in the classroom and much more helpful to college students, who as Parks (1986) notes are struggling to make meaning of the world around them. In my field of rhetorical theory, much of the material focuses on the ways in which we as humans use language to understand and construct the world around us. Discussions of faith in that larger context fit not only into rhetorical theory, but also into philosophy, literature, history, political science, and countless other disciplines. Opening up these general discussions of meaning can lead to productive discussions or reflections at the individual level.

Further, we must trust ourselves as educators to facilitate a productive discussion. Contentious issues in our fields or in society sometimes result in uncomfortable class discussions, but we as educators have an obligation to confront those issues, and most of us do with success. (For more information on learning how to conduct effective class discussions, see Brookfield & Preskill, 1999.) Faith is an issue that we agree is vital to student development, at least at a church-related college where it is included in the mission statement. This work can be done in courses other than religion by finding ways to address these issues. The approach must be for each faculty member to do what is comfortable. That said, much is to be gained by individually and in class pushing ourselves in this area of faith exploration. If faith is compartmentalized in our lives, then exploring it individually or in a class discussion could result in some valuable insights for our students and ourselves. Palmer (1998) claims, "The more familiar we are with our inner terrain, the more sure-footed our teaching—and living—becomes" (p. 5). In the same vein, examining the ways in which the world constructs and constricts faith in public endeavors allows students to think about how they will negotiate this in their daily lives and in the world beyond college. As noted earlier, these discussions need not be specific to a particular faith tradition to be useful; a general discussion of the difficulties and intersections of faith in public life would be germane to a variety of faith traditions. In such a discussion, students could share their own observations and trials without testimonials or proselytizing.

Similarly, general discussions of spiritual issues can be useful in helping students think about faith in their lives. In my courses, I usually spend some time on vocation and sabbath without invoking a specific faith tradition. In fact, I have students, particularly in senior-level courses, actively contemplate their lives beyond Gustavus in relation to these issues. Students write a proposal for how they will live what they have learned in the world, particularly in relation to social justice issues. By the time they are seniors, they should have identified at least one social justice issue to which they would like to devote themselves. In class we spend an entire day discussing our obligations to use what we have learned and how we can specifically use our knowledge and skills to make a difference. I hope that these discussions inspire, support, and motivate students to make a concerted effort to engage themselves with issues and organizations that they find important.

In the past semester, I attempted to follow my own advice and integrate discussions of faith into the classroom. I chose a course in rhetorical theory and one in service-learning in communication studies. From the student evaluations, students clearly received and incorporated issues of service and social justice. In the written evaluations and in the final class oral evaluation, students spoke eagerly and animatedly about their obligations to work and act in their communities and their ability to make a difference in the world. I sat down with a small group of students at the end of both courses, and they echoed that the class led them to reflect on commitment, activism, and their place in the world, but not faith, and many felt that class should not involve faith. I was aware that my own reticence on these issues kept me from direct exploration of faith, and I will endeavor next time I teach this class to be more direct. Still, these two classes, more than any others I have taught, seemed to understand and truly take time to reflect on their place in the world, on their communities, on their obligations, and on how to undertake action in the world. Many other variables are at play, but I do wonder if my rather poor attempt to integrate meaning and faith into the discussions had some role in the results. Only further semesters of pushing my own and my students' comfort zones will tell, but I am very heartened by the responses and actions of my students.

Faith discussions in a service-learning or social justice context defy simple solutions. Faculty and students report significant apprehension regarding the issue, and yet, faith is central to the mission statement at this church-related college; faith is an essential component in the lives of a significant number of students, and issues of identity and faith are crucial to service-learning and social justice. This chasm of belief and action will not be easily resolved, but ways to mitigate fears and obstructions do exist. Making a move in this direction will benefit students and faculty. Rhoades (1997), in writing of the gap between faith and scholarship, notes, "Rarely do we truly get the chance to integrate these selves that are so important to who we are as scholars, as people" (p. 233), and he urges us to incorporate both in our lives as educators. Being true to what motivates us to teach, to incorporate service-learning and social justice issues into our courses, and to act in the world and in our work in the academy can lead to a more authentic relationship with students, our colleagues, and ourselves.

References

Brookfield, S. D., & Preskill, S. (1999). *Discussion as a way of teaching: Tools and techniques for democratic classrooms.* San Francisco, CA: Jossey-Bass.

Cavazos, L. (2001). Connected conversations: Forms and functions of teacher talk. In C. M. Clark (Ed.), *Talking shop: Authentic conversation and teacher learning* (pp. 137–171). New York, NY: Teachers College Press.

DeVitis, J. L., Johns, R. W., & Simpson, D. J. (Eds.). (1998). *To serve and learn: The spirit of community in liberal education.* New York, NY: Peter Lang.

Gill, M. (1988, Spring). Successful self disclosure. *The Speech Communication Teacher, 2*(3), 7, 16.

Goldstein, G. S., & Benassi, V. A. (1994). The relation between teacher self-disclosure and student classroom participation. *Teaching of Psychology, 21*(4), 212–217.

Goldstein, G. S., & Benassi, V. A. (1996). Students' perceptions of excellent lecturers and discussion leaders. *Journal on Excellence in College Teaching, 7*(2), 81–97.

Goldstein, G. S., & Benassi, V. A. (1997). Teacher self-disclosure and student classroom participation: A reply to Wambach and Brothen. *Teaching of Psychology, 24*(4), 263–265.

Hartlep, K. L., & Forsyth, G. A. (2000). The effect of self-reference on learning and retention. *Teaching of Psychology, 27*(4), 269–271.

Lisman, C. D. (1998). *Toward a civil society: Civic literacy and service learning.* Westport, CT: Bergin & Garvey.

Marsden, G. M. (1992). Introduction. In G. M. Marsden & B. J. Longfield (Eds.), *The secularization of the academy* (pp. 3–8). New York, NY: Oxford University Press.

Palmer, P. J. (1998). *The courage to teach: Exploring the inner landscape of a teacher's life.* San Francisco, CA: Jossey-Bass.

Parks, S. D. (1986). *The critical years: The young adult search for a faith to live by.* San Francisco, CA: Harper & Row.

Pascarella, E. T., & Terenzini, P. T. (1991). *How college affects students: Findings and insights from twenty years of research.* San Francisco, CA: Jossey-Bass.

Pearce, K. (2000, Spring). *What the field of Communication informs us about class discussions.* Retrieved February 27, 2006, from The Faculty Network web site: http://web.bryant.edu/~facdev/Web%20Sites/newsletter/spring00/kpearce.htm

Rhoades, R. A. (1997). *Community service and higher learning: Explorations of the caring self.* Albany, NY: State University of New York Press.

Sloan, D. (1994). *Faith and knowledge: Mainline Protestantism and American higher education.* Louisville, KY: Westminster John Knox Press.

Stanton, T. K., Giles, D. E., Jr., & Cruz, N. I. (1999). *Service-learning: A movement's pioneers reflect on its origins, practice, and future.* San Francisco, CA: Jossey-Bass.

11

SPEAKING TRUTH TO POWER

Nadarajan Sethuraju

When I came from Singapore in the late 1980s to attend college in Louisiana, I was taken aback by the degree to which Americans categorized individuals into discrete racial groups. In Singapore, not only is there less emphasis on racial identity in general, there is also greater acceptance of the multiracial nature of Singaporeans. In Louisiana, people were always trying to figure out whether I was black or white so they could place me in a racial category that they understood. During the second week of school I walked into the cafeteria and had no idea where I should sit. One side was occupied by black students, and the other by white students. Neither side felt like "my" side. Some of the other international students decided that they were white enough to go to the white side because they had lighter skin, but my skin is not light. I realized that many of my international friends had the same kind of preconceived notions about what "white" and "black" meant that many Americans have, and these preconceptions did not fit with my experience growing up in a multiracial, multifaith environment like Singapore.

During my time in Louisiana I experienced all kinds of discrimination, from dating relationships to being called names and having water and beer cans thrown at me, to being held at gunpoint three times by three different white groups. This experience was a definite awakening. I knew I needed to learn more about racial issues in the U.S. to understand racial dynamics and to see how or where I fit in. I spent the next decade expanding my understanding of racial and cultural identity by working in social service agencies, reading as much as I could, visiting or living in a variety of communities throughout the U.S., working in college diversity centers, teaching classes, and ultimately getting a doctorate in sociology. To this day, I am still working to understand issues of diversity.

I have always been moved and motivated by the examples of Martin Luther King, Jr. and Mahatma Gandhi. Both men were inspired by their religious convictions, and both were firm believers that it is our connection to each other as human beings that can motivate us to work for social justice. My goal is to help resolve issues of racial and cultural conflict. I don't want King or Gandhi to have died in vain.

The Gustavus Context

As associate dean for multicultural programs at Gustavus Adolphus College I oversee a diversity center that houses several programs intended to help students and faculty gain a deeper understanding of cultural diversity. The heart of the mission of the diversity center is to "infuse an acceptance and appreciation for difference that is morally and socially just into college life." As a relatively small liberal arts college with about 2,600 students, Gustavus provides an environment in which students can become deeply involved in diversity initiatives if they choose to do so. Its diversity center is charged with a twofold task: to help the community learn about and celebrate diversity, and to increase the minority community on campus. From a sociological perspective, anyone who is defined as "majority" has power and resources, and consequently privilege. The purpose of all diversity programming is to educate and build awareness about issues of power and privilege.

I have chosen to do this work in a college environment (rather than the corporate world, for instance) because I was raised by my parents to believe that education is the solution to injustice. Education is also a stepping-stone to a more nuanced, broader understanding of our world. At a liberal arts college like Gustavus we have an obligation to broaden students' perspectives. My role in an educational institution is to be an educator, but in the kind of work I do it is important that this education engage students by being entertaining and instructive. I think it was Aristotle who said that art must be didactic and entertaining. My goal is to create programming that meets Aristotle's expectations and highlights the subtle privileges and oppression that are experienced on our campus.

Many Gustavus students come from privileged backgrounds. Although more than 80% of our students receive some kind of financial assistance, the vast majority of our students still come from middle-class backgrounds in which college attendance was assumed and expected. Our students are also overwhelmingly white and Christian. They will be the future leaders and decision-makers of our world; this makes it even more vital that diversity programs help them to be more conscious of privilege, oppression, and what one can do to correct inequities.

At Gustavus, we define *diversity* broadly out of the recognition that race is only one aspect of our social identity. Issues of race, religion, sexual orientation, disability, ethnicity, gender, and class are all strands on which we work. We need to make sure nobody is a minority on this campus, that nobody's voice is undermined, whether it's someone who is black, gay, female, or disabled. All must be and will be heard on this campus.

We have a variety of student organizations that are similar to those of other colleges and universities and that are roughly formed around, for lack of a better word, "isms." For instance, Queers and Allies works to raise awareness about GLBT (Gay, Lesbian, Bisexual, Transgender) issues and provides a supportive environment for GLBT students and their allies. Members of the Asian Cultures Club (ACC) help the larger community understand the variety of traditions and cultures among those of Asian descent. A significant number of our students of color are Hmong, and ACC has particular interest in connecting the campus to the parents, especially refugee Hmong parents. This group works actively to maintain those connections and celebrate the success of the children of these refugees. Other groups educate the community about disability issues or issues for women.

The Indigenous Student Organization was formed in 2002 and has helped coordinate two very successful on-campus powwows. The history of our region includes a significant American Indian presence, yet few Indian students choose to enroll at Gustavus. When I first came to Gustavus, I wondered what happened to the Dakotah community that had lived in this area, and why their faces and voices were absent from our campus. Along with several interested faculty and students, I began to explore what we needed to do to make our campus a welcoming place for the Dakotah community.

Establishing the powwow in collaboration with Dakotah elders has been a way to cultivate their presence and acknowledge our regional history.

Another recent initiative has been to invite the campus community to participate in fasting during Ramadan. Although there are only a handful of Muslim students on campus (currently there are seven), the purpose of diversity work is to meet the needs of minority group students and also to provide educational challenges to the dominant cultural group. Ramadan fasting had always been particularly difficult for Muslim students here because there was little institutional acknowledgement of their needs, and there was no critical mass of Muslim students who could provide support for each other. As a college of the Evangelical Lutheran Church in America (ELCA), we pride ourselves on trying to understand all religions, yet many individuals here— including faculty—were ignorant about the different branches of Islam. The diversity center sponsored a series of dinners following sunset during Ramadan and invited the entire community—whether they had fasted or not—to join us for the meal. We also offered educational programs on Muslim practice in several parts of the world, including Kenya, Morocco, Malaysia, and India. These events became an opportunity for interfaith dialogue. Many non-Muslim students fasted for a day to see how it felt. It was fulfilling for Muslim students to have that shared experience and support. Though the numbers of Muslim students hasn't increased, more students are now interested in and informed about Islam and its traditions.

At Gustavus all organizations are open to all students. The Pan-African Student Organization (PASO), for instance, has several white students involved, as well as other students who do not identify themselves as black. It is a college policy that all groups which receive funding from the student senate must be open to anyone, but practically speaking, at a college like ours where there is not a critical mass of students of color, student organizations cannot function without support from other racial communities. Students of color from various racial groups must work together, and white students must be cultivated as allies in our diversity work. It is important to educate whites so that responsibility for justice is not placed only on the shoulders of the minority population.

Doing Diversity Work Within the Context
of a Specifically Lutheran College

Like any college or university, Gustavus has its cherished traditions that have shaped the identity of the institution. These traditions help give Gustavus its unique character and are important links with the history of the college. But tradition is a two-edged sword. It can be an institution's sustaining strength, but it can also be an impediment to change. In defining ourselves as a Swedish Lutheran college, we anchor ourselves deeply in the origins of our college, but we also put a lot of rings around the college and the perception can be that we are saying, "If you are *this*, you can enter this doorway, but not if you are *that*." On this campus, one of the things we hope to do is empower our students to continuously question the day-to-day operation of the campus and why things are done the way they are.

One of our long-standing traditions is morning chapel. The time for chapel at 10:00 a.m. is a respected event during which no meetings or class-es are held to allow anyone the opportunity to attend chapel. Chapel is not mandatory, but the chapel building itself is at the physical heart of the cam-pus (and descriptions of the campus often note this fact). The chaplains' office promotes ecumenism and invites a wide range of people to give hom-ilies. The chapel program also engages with diversity through recognition of particular holidays or events of note, such as Black History Month, Coming Out Week, and Ramadan. Yet many students of color who come from reli-gious traditions that are not Lutheran are not comfortable going to chapel. They are not familiar with the type of service they will see, the type of prayers they will say, the type of music they will hear, or the type of readings that will be done. This unfamiliarity may make them unwilling to enter chapel because it is so different. All who come to chapel can note the strong presence of Christian symbols and practices in such things as the cross and Bible, and even the lighting of candles and the way people move up and down to the podium. For non-Christian students this may consequently be an uncomfortable place. And some students may be of a particular Christian denomination with a more fundamentalist leaning than the ecumenical chapel we have.

One way to honor the tradition of chapel at Gustavus is to broaden the definition of what chapel time could be. Chapel could become not just a physical place, but an idea. When people gather in chapel, they are there to worship and listen to the message of a homilist. They gather as a community of chapel-goers, and they leave chapel with (hopefully) new thoughts. Another way to provide a chapel space is to move "chapel" out of the chapel to other areas on campus where those who come could have an opportunity to learn about other faith perspectives, or discuss issues from a Muslim or Hindu or Jewish perspective. Chapel does not have to be defined by the space, but rather by who is there and what they are talking about. Chapel does not have to have physical constructs to it.

This approach gives us an opportunity to be among different groups of people and not expect to see the same friends sitting in the same pew at the same time. Some of our students are very proud that they have attended daily chapel without missing once since their first year at Gustavus. This was a commitment they made that they honored, yet many other students use chapel time aimlessly. As an educational institution we have the opportunity to make the entire campus a place of worship during "chapel time" rather than to institutionalize one credo and one way of thinking or one place of worship, even if that is the way it "has always been done here."

Another tradition at Gustavus is that the president of the college must be Lutheran. In fact, it is written in our bylaws. The president is both the symbolic and actual leader of the institution. Requiring that the president be Lutheran makes it more likely that, given the Lutheran demographics in the U.S., this person will be white (see the Evangelical Lutheran Church in America's web site for the demographics of the church: http://www.elca.org/re/fyifacts.html). If an institution is committed to recruiting for diversity—as Gustavus says it is—and to enhancing the climate for diversity on campus—as it says it is—the religious or racial identity of the president should never be taken for granted. This is the kind of dominant cultural privilege that must continually be questioned.

Many of our students have traditionally come from Lutheran congregations in our region. There have always been efforts to recruit students of color from other parts of the U.S., and these efforts have had mixed success.

A critical mass of students of color is essential if we are to consider ourselves a truly diverse campus. Research on diversity indicates that all students benefit from diversity, educationally and interpersonally (Smith, 1997). Along with recruitment of students of color we must diversify our workforce at all levels. It is important that all students are able to have teachers who come from different racial and cultural traditions, but it is also important that students see all kinds of diversity in the faces of office secretaries, janitorial staff, and administrative vice presidents. Many years ago the college decided to stop hiring only staff who were Lutheran. In the same way, it is no longer appropriate to hire staff only because they are white.

Gustavus has the wherewithal to be a campus that is outstanding in its diversity work. The presence of a diversity center and the support given to diversity programming are evidence that the voices of students of color are valued and the importance of education for diversity is acknowledged. Many individuals have worked hard to create a welcoming campus climate and to diversify the faculty. The college also works hard to make an impact in the lives of people in the larger Saint Peter community, especially residents who are poor or minority in our area. We need to keep working on all these fronts. We must reach out to the community around us and make this campus accessible to everyone, whether they come to school here or not. We must ensure that the increasing number of Somali and Hispanic residents around us can feel comfortable being part of this campus.

Service-Learning and Social Justice

Service-learning has become a buzzword in educational institutions, especially liberal arts institutions. It is seen as a vehicle for people to do something outside of their learning community so that they feel fulfilled. As part of their education we are impressing on our students that it is important for them to go out and serve the community while they are learning. We must make sure the learning that is happening outside the academic arena is valuable and has a lasting effect and is not simply done because students need to get a degree or jump through another hoop. I become concerned that too many of our students see the service requirement as a hoop to jump through rather than a personal commitment. Asking students to reflect on their service provides opportunities for us to continue to deepen students' engagement, but reflection must be done very well to be effective.

Currently, we offer a wonderful program in India where students study for a semester and learn about issues there. But when I talk to many of our students, they are unfamiliar with the rich American Indian history right in our region, and most have never heard of the mass hanging of 38 Dakotah in 1865, the last mass execution of its size in U.S. history. I encourage people to go to India to learn, but let us not forget we have a lot more to learn and a lot more social justice work that needs to be done right here in our own backyard. Understanding diversity cannot simply happen in classrooms or study abroad programs. Experiencing diversity can be the greatest learning opportunity, but we can experience it right here. We don't always need to go overseas to understand prejudices and classism and caste systems. It is important to recognize that the U.S. is one of the most diverse countries, and globalization is happening here and we have to figure out how to incorporate that into the learning process. Diversity, social justice, and service-learning go hand-in-hand, because engagement in the community offers the kind of exposure to our neighbors that is going to prepare us to function in a global world.

One of the professors in the geography department has been building a relationship with the new refugee community, the Somali and Sudanese people, who have essentially been thrown out of their country in the course of various political and ethnic clashes. They are here and they are really struggling. This professor has listened closely to their concerns and helped them organize many community events. He has taught a class about their refugee experience, and his students have done service projects within this community. Another faculty member organized a community garden that enables a wide range of members of the community to work together as they grow flowers and vegetables. These are the types of initiatives that we as an institution need to say are important, and we are committed to pursuing them. That means every faculty member is going to be asked to be involved in this process. We have a growing Hispanic population in the southwest Minnesota region, many of whom are working here; they are the invisible workers. So, it is important that we do our social justice work here. International travel is important, and I myself have benefited from it. I am an advocate for the international travel that faculty members in the Service Learning for Social Justice program have been able to do, and I participated in one year of the program myself. But we don't need to go to Cuba or Guatemala to do social justice work.

Spirituality and Social Justice

I grew up in Singapore with a Hindu background, but nevertheless was exposed to a lot of Zen and Buddhist teachings and Islam right in front of me every day, listening to the daily call to prayer of the muezzin. I came away from that experience with the view that every religion has ideas about releasing ourselves from all the burdens around us. We can all reach heaven or nirvana, and all these religions talk about the concept of spirituality. *Spirituality* is a connection between the physical human being and the omnipresence of what some call God or the spirit. I think that connection can only be made if each one of us is able to relate to one another. As Martin Luther King, Jr. reminded us, we have learned to fly the great skies, and we have crossed the great physical barriers from mountains to oceans, but the simple matter of connecting as human beings is something we are still struggling with. There is a definite need for a spiritual awakening in terms of connecting to one another as human beings. Despite all the struggles between the Hindus and the Muslims and the Christians, Gandhi stood fast because he was looking beyond the physical forms of relationships, which are the result of faith or belief systems. He considered everybody as human beings, and that spirit brought him close to many houses of worship. He worshipped in temples, in mosques, in a Buddhist worship service. He was able to cross those barriers and connect with other human beings. That to me is what spirituality is all about.

In the U.S., and certainly at Gustavus, most of us live in a very privileged way. That privilege should not allow us to take things for granted. Rather, it should be a sounding board to ask ourselves, "Why am I privileged, what gives me this privilege, and how can I make this privilege available to others?" I think spirituality should not be something that defines our relationship with God. It should be—forgive me for sounding so unchristian—not a relationship between oneself and an omnipresent God, but rather our relationship with another human being. Spirituality is about building relationships. We need to affirm each other's identity and learn about each other, and that learning will help us build a community which in turn will create the kind of leadership that will take us past the challenge of the color line that W.E.B. Dubois described. We have not yet crossed that barrier, but I'm hoping that we will.

The kind of privilege we need to realize is that we live in a society here at Gustavus that is safe, that affords us opportunities to educate ourselves. But once I realize my privilege, I need to make sure that I work so that my fellow brothers and sisters who don't have the same kind of opportunity can achieve it. We must not take our privilege for granted. It's when we take our privilege for granted and do not even recognize we are in that state, that we are no longer spiritual beings. I think it has less to do with God or religion and more to do with human relations and the need to build those human relations. That kind of spirituality is what I'm hoping we can teach students in this work that I do as well as through academic courses and service-learning opportunities.

Challenges to Doing This Work

It can be extremely frustrating when students walk away from diversity programs with less knowledge or awareness than you want them to have, no matter how hard you push and try. At Gustavus, international students are well received, yet most domestic students don't know where in the world the international students even come from, and they often don't bother to try to find out. We tend to promote diversity as a kind of entertainment experience where you get to eat the food and listen to the music, but without being pushed into deeper understanding. We too easily lump all international students together, but then expect them to come up to the stage and sing and dance during international night. Getting people to look at diversity beyond entertainment has been a challenge.

It is even a challenge for international students and students of color themselves to recognize that doing diversity work is not just about the entertainment of others. Given the developmental stages that college students are moving through, it is understandable that many students find it easier to scratch the surface of cultural diversity than to really explore their own experiences with oppression or privilege. And "Minnesota nice," a peculiarly conflict-avoidant tendency in the upper Midwest, ensures that we avoid confrontation whenever possible.

Another challenge in doing this work is to balance the needs of minority group students to have their own separate, safe space and the goal of making every on-campus space welcoming to all students. In the past, the diversity center was seen as more of a place for students of color to retreat to than as a place that welcomed all members of the community and had an educational mission to fulfill. As more white students have come into the center and become involved in diversity-related student groups, some students of color have been upset. Likewise, not all students of color were initially willing to work in coalition with Queers and Allies, and vice versa. In response to one student of color who told me she liked to have the office remain a private space so that students of color could vent with each other (in truth, she used the word "bitch"), I said, "You can bitch about this campus, but now tell me what you want to do about it." A broader awareness of diversity issues is essential for the entire community. We have tried to take the concerns of minority group students and make them public rather than maintain a silo perspective.

On a campus such as ours, which is predominantly white and located in a rural area, people tend to think of diversity as a component that should not emphasize race very much. There is a desire to promote diversity as a way to educate the white majority students, simply educate them about the importance of diversity. So there has been real resistance to the idea of increasing the critical mass of minority faculty, staff, and students on this campus. Some members of the community dislike the idea of affirmative action and do not understand why it might be essential at a place like ours. Other members of the community are uncomfortable with the idea that we are noticing race at all. After a black male transferred to another college, one administrator said to me, "It bothers me that you said we have lost a black male. As far as

I am concerned, we have lost a student." Until we are willing to recognize that in every sense of the word we have lost a black male, we will fail in our efforts to be a truly multicultural college. The desire to be color blind is very powerful on our campus, and it hampers diversity initiatives.

Another example of this color-blind tendency is to assume that institutional practices must be absolutely the same for all students if the practices are to be absolutely fair. When students' grades fall, they are placed on probation and eventually they are suspended if the grades don't improve. I encourage every student of color to appeal their suspension, despite being told by one administrator that this is poor advice, because the student is unlikely to be successful in the appeal and it is a waste of their time. But I want students to understand that they have the right to make this appeal. And I want the college officials to understand that if a Hmong student is appealing a grade, for instance, we cannot evaluate him or her solely on the basis of the grade. There is much about their life we do not understand. First generation college students need a different approach than the standard probationary approach. And some Hmong students in particular, who come from very traditional families, may be balancing extensive family obligations with the demands of their school work. In general, all students (as well as faculty) of color are expected to just blend in and "be more like us."

On the other side of the equation, it can be the case that members of the community become too invested in diversity initiatives and in fact take a kind of missionary approach to diversity work. I believe this is part of a broader liberal problem. When the majority of us define ourselves as liberals, we tend to think we have accepted everything at face value. But when it comes to integrating a consciousness of diversity into our community, then it becomes a question of this is the way we have done it in the past, the way we've always done it, and why should we change this? We are a bunch of good people. One of the best examples of this tendency was the installation of our current president. He was installed in the chapel in a public ceremony conducted by an ELCA bishop. His hiring was a bold move for a number of reasons, and he came with a demonstrated commitment to and effectiveness in enhancing diversity initiatives in his prior position. But observing who was on the stage was a reminder of who we actually are symbolically. Almost every person on that stage was white and male. I made a comment about the symbolism of this to a colleague with whom I was sitting. This person said, "but they're trying." And I said yes, after 150 years of trying we're still trying. A liberal mindset says "As long as we are trying, we're okay. We don't really want to change any aspects of our traditions." It's difficult to address this mindset, because it seems to call into question a person's goodness. And once you question that goodness, there is a resistance. Not only do they not want to hear that they might not be as good as they think they are, they also really don't want things to change if that means discomfort or uncertainty.

Recommendations and Strategies

There are several ways to work more effectively to ensure that diversity initiatives are as successful as possible on a campus. All efforts require persistence and the collaboration of all members of the community. These recommendations emerge from my experience working at colleges in more than one kind of setting.

- Make sure student programs are as active as possible. Hold many events and activities and give students a lot of responsibility for organizing these. When students are deeply involved they have a great deal of commitment and enthusiasm. Find money wherever you can if you don't have a robust budget. The student senate at Gustavus has provided a lot of money for diversity programming, though members of the senate have had to be educated about the fact that a few events are simply not enough and not all diversity organizations are the same.

- Maintain an open-door policy. Ask faculty to bring their students to your office to meet as a class. Host regular open houses. Ask student groups to meet in your center.

- Reach out to faculty in as many ways as possible. Ask them what kind of projects they are having their students do in class, and provide ideas of how they can highlight diversity issues.

- Offer to be a guest speaker in as many classes as you can manage.

- Involve yourself in curriculum initiatives so that diversity is constantly on the table. For instance, at Gustavus we have First Term Seminar (FTS) classes. I serve as a resource for FTS faculty, and I offer to visit every FTS class in the fall. In this way I try to ensure that all first-year students will have some opportunity to learn about diversity initiatives on campus, and will learn who I am and where they can find me.

- Go to events on campus, including those that may not be directly affiliated with your diversity center. For instance, I have reached out to the Greek organizations on campus and created linkages between Greek programs and the diversity center. Training for residence hall assistants provides another avenue to make sure diversity concerns are discussed by those who will be working with students.

- In 2004 we invited tutors from the writing center to hold tutorial sessions in the diversity center several times a week. Typically these sessions are only held in the writing center itself, which is housed in one of our academic buildings. Any student could attend a tutorial session in the diversity center, and this provided yet another opportunity for students to interact academically and socially.

- Provide opportunities for faculty to interact with minority student groups. My office sponsors what we call a "Chat-n-Chew," in which faculty are provided with funds to buy and cook a meal in their homes for a small number of minority students. This provides an invaluable experience for the students and builds a relationship with a faculty member outside of the classroom.

- Reach out to those groups on campus who may feel left out. For instance, some more conservative Christian student groups feel marginalized. But if we are to be a truly diverse institution, all voices must be heard at the table.

- Work hard to maintain a good relationship with other faculty. Without them, it is hard to do this job well. Faculty can work miracles for a diversity center by including in their syllabi campus events that focus on diversity, or by working in collaboration with our office. Whether you like or dislike specific faculty members is beside the point. Leave that at the doorstep. Build a relationship with all faculty, even those who are resistant to your programs. These people don't have to be your friends, but they do have to be your colleagues. I believe in these folks. I believe they will be engaged in things we are doing if we approach them with students' best interests in mind.

- Learn to cherish the students. A college is not really about the faculty. It's not just about the staff. The college is really about the students, and if the students are getting it, you have done your job.

Anyone who is doing this job must remember that we should not think of ourselves as *fighting* for diversity or justice. Instead we should just *believe* in it across the board. Both King and Gandhi encountered a lot of resistance, but they simply used their belief in justice to question every aspect of the systems they were in. We always have to be ready to stand up and question. Just because a system has always been in place doesn't mean it isn't without problems.

Institutions of higher education must take on the charge of working for justice for all. Beverly Daniel Tatum (2000) writes about what she calls the "ABC component" (affirm, build, cultivate). She says it is critical for colleges to affirm everyone's identity. From there, we go on to build a community. Finally, we have to cultivate the kind of leadership that will function in the coming years to realize the dreams of Dr. King because we are not there yet. So we have to affirm people's identity and from there build a community that in turn will cultivate leadership that is going to take into consideration everybody's interests. Everyone's interests are going to be on the table, not one person's interest or one person's privilege. What diversity really means is that when everybody's interests are on the table, then we are going to get a community that is built around diversity. That's the kind of work we need in terms of social justice, spirituality, and service-learning. At Gustavus we have the potential to do this, because we are a small enough community and if it can be done anywhere, it can be done here. We have the wherewithal, we have the support, we have the hearts of many people here. We have a community around us that is definitely becoming more diverse than one would have expected 30 years ago or even 20 or 10 years ago. I think everything is ripe right now. We need to take advantage of this moment.

Acknowledgements

I'd like to acknowledge Kate Wittenstein and Carolyn O'Grady for their assistance with this chapter.

References

Smith, D. G. (1997). *Diversity works: The emerging picture of how students benefit.* Washington, DC: Association of American Colleges and Universities.

Tatum, B. D. (2000). The ABC approach to creating climates of engagement on diverse campuses. *Liberal Education 86*(4), 22–29.

12
SERVICE-LEARNING FOR SOCIAL JUSTICE: MOVING FACULTY FROM PERSONAL TO PEDAGOGICAL COMMITMENT THROUGH FACULTY DEVELOPMENT

Elizabeth R. Baer

I beg you
do something
learn a dance step
something to justify your existence
something that gives you the right
to be dressed in your skin in your body hair
learn to walk and to laugh
because it would be too senseless
after all
for so many to have died
while you live
doing nothing with your life.

—Charlotte Delbo, "Useless Knowledge"

The author of the epigram I have chosen, Charlotte Delbo, is a survivor of Auschwitz who included this plaintive verse in her 1995 memoir. Her call to action is particularly galvanizing and one I have thought of often in connection with service-learning. In what follows, I tell the story of a faculty development program I created, with the ideas and assistance of many other people, at Gustavus Adolphus College in 2002. The program, Service-Learning for Social Justice, is a yearlong experience that includes reading seminars on social justice issues, pedagogical seminars on service-learning, and an international study tour to a country where the group examines local social justice issues. In 2002 the study tour went to Northern Ireland, in 2003 to Guatemala, and in 2004 to Cuba. Politics permitting, another group will travel to Namibia in 2006. I describe the genesis of the program; how it emerged from my personal and professional experiences; how it has been organized, funded, and evaluated; and its symbiotic relationship with the spirit of service at Gustavus Adolphus College.

Coming to Service-Learning: A Personal Account

Perhaps it was growing up Catholic—all the talk by the nuns of the "starving babies in Africa"—that made my later involvement with social justice issues seem natural. In the parochial schools I attended for elementary school and the convent schools I attended for secondary education, issues of morality, equality, and ethics, to say nothing of the discussions of sins—venial and mortal— and our responsibilities as Christians, were as regular a part of the daily fare as our maroon and beige uniforms. Memorizing catechism, coloring saints' pictures, learning to sing Gregorian chants were occasions that encouraged us to think about social justice issues before I had learned that term.

Four years at the premiere Catholic women's college of that era— Manhattanville College in upstate New York—with its required courses in religion and philosophy deepened my understanding and then raised questions. Perhaps, too, it was the service trip to Appalachia I volunteered for during Easter vacation in 1965 as a first-year college student. We took what seemed an interminable bus ride to Berea, Kentucky, to work with a local parish on a variety of tasks. I was somehow chosen as the spokesperson for the group and was taken to the homes of several families so I could speak in detail to groups about the region's needs when I returned to New York. Still engraved on my mind are the stark images of these homes. What struck me forcibly was how barren they were: Unlike my own comfortable home in Massachusetts, these homes had no knickknacks in them, no photographs, no lamps, indeed often no furniture except perhaps a small stove, table and chairs, and, in the corner, rags piled to create a bed of sorts.

I was also influenced by having the radical Berrigan brothers, activist priests in the 1960s, as leaders of my Sodality (a charitable association of Catholic laity). Weekly meetings with Philip or Daniel Berrigan, for which we read some of the emerging texts on poverty and civil rights in America, undoubtedly inflamed my sense of justice and injustice—and certainly coming of age in that explosive era and participating in protests for racial equality and against the Vietnam War also fueled that sense. The rebirth of the women's movement, as I graduated from college, has further shaped my career and my identity.

All these influences made me aware of and committed to social justice through a process not unlike osmosis. One of the reasons I chose to devote 20 years of my career to college administration was the belief, which those 20 years only strengthened, that women's leadership in higher education is too sparse. One of the reasons I refused to put my children in private schools when we lived in Virginia and Maryland was that most of the private schools were originally segregated academies; so, my children attended mediocre public schools and have thrived nonetheless.

Similarly, my literary interests have always run to texts that deal with oppression in some way. Giving birth to my children, one of the most powerful experiences of my life, awakened in me the realization that I had never, in my 10 years of reading literature toward the Ph.D., read a story about a woman giving birth. As someone who relies on texts to refract and mediate my experiences, I recognized that my formal education had focused almost exclusively on texts by white men; I gave myself the gift of 10 years to read women's literature. From writing a dissertation on contemporary women's fiction under the direction of Susan Gubar, one of the most influential feminist literary critics, I went on to study the fiction of women of color, the memoirs of Holocaust survivors, and postcolonial literatures, especially those of India and Northern Ireland. What I find compelling are texts that have served as a cry of protest, as a form of resistance, as an effort at *tikkun olam*, mending the world. What is the power of the book, I urge my students to ask, for making change?

For many years in my classroom, I was content to allow these issues to remain academic. Then, gradually, a change began to occur. While still a chief academic officer, I was invited to participate in a program sponsored by the American Association for Higher Education (AAHE) to teach deans about service-learning. The pilot program was held in Minnesota in recognition of the already deep commitment to human rights that exists in this state. None other than Edward Zlotkowski (1998, 2004), with his apostolic (one might almost say manic) zeal for service-learning, served as our primary instructor. As I recall, we had four sessions and then made a presentation at a conference. I was thus emboldened to incorporate service-learning into a course I had been regularly teaching on the Holocaust. Though the goal of the AAHE program was to get deans to advocate for service-learning on their campuses, I felt I must try it myself before encouraging faculty to move in this direction.

I saw in this pedagogy a possibility for enhancing the emphasis on social justice and civic responsibility in my Holocaust classes. But I was baffled: How could one introduce such a component into a course about the Shoah? Here, Dr. Zlotkowski was of enormous help. He put me in touch with a faculty member at Providence College in Rhode Island and another at Bates College in Maine, both of whom had been pioneers of a sort in creating service-learning components in just such Holocaust courses. Telephone calls to each gave me some paradigms to consider; visits to my family in New England permitted face-to-face meetings with Jane Lunin Perel in the English department at Providence College and Steven Hochstadt, a historian at Bates. Selecting aspects of what each had done in their respective communities, I began to fashion a program for my own students.

I contacted Shalom Home, a residence for elderly Jewish men and women in Minneapolis, an hour's drive away. My 16 students and I spent a morning there, interviewing eight residents. Students worked in pairs to take an oral history of each subject, using techniques I had helped them prepare in advance. Of the eight, two residents were Holocaust survivors; most of the rest had immigrated to the U.S. at some point in their lives; all had experienced anti-Semitism. (Minneapolis, it should be noted, was considered one of the most anti-Semitic cities in the country in the 1940s.) One of the survivors began his story and broke down; unable to continue, he asked the students instead to talk about fishing and baseball with him. The other, who had been a partisan in the Polish woods, talked nonstop for two hours. His testimony was aided by the fact that one of my students spoke Polish; she had been a Rotary scholar in Warsaw as a high school student and was able to put the survivor at ease. Reflecting on our visit back in the classroom, my students realized that they had experienced a powerful lesson in the workings of the memory in these contrasting reactions.

The second part of the service-learning sequence required students, in the final week of the class, to design a way in which they could share what they had learned about racism, homophobia, anti-Semitism, discrimination, and hatred with the college community, the community of St. Peter, or their hometowns. I wanted to instill in them the idea of "giving back," of taking responsibility for passing on the important lessons they had learned. Many chose to develop a unit on the Holocaust for a K–12 class in Saint Peter; several returned to their high schools and taught classes there. A group of three women in the class collaborated to produce dozens of table tents—stiff cardboard folded in half with "Facts About the Holocaust" printed on them, which were then placed for a week on every table in the college dining hall. Appropriately, these table tents contained facts about food in the Holocaust. Finally, two senior art students in the class, perhaps influenced by Art Spiegelman's (1986, 1991) graphic style, created a bold, 14-page booklet, which recapitulated much of what we had learned in the class, and contained maps, definitions, drawings, and recommended reading. Each cover, designed in black and white stripes to suggest the typical *lager* uniform, also carried a felt triangle (different colors were used) and a prisoner number.

No matter what the project, students had to present to their classmates a version of what they did in the community, sharing handouts and results. A 17th-century French philosopher once said, "To teach is to learn twice," and many students identified this aspect of the course as affecting them most profoundly when they completed the course evaluation. The unit undoubtedly gave students tools for continuing their commitment to social justice. It also enabled them to recognize that the problems that led to the Shoah were not unique to Germany 70 years ago, but exist in their own communities now. This rather brutal fact about human nature and our capacity for evil is one of the hardest lessons to learn and to teach in Holocaust courses. The last part of our work took place in April, four months after the class had ended. I brought my students back together to create and conduct the Yom HaShoah service on our campus. At this service of remembrance in our college chapel, a copy of the booklet created by my students was distributed to every participant.

From the Personal to the Pedagogical:
Creating a Faculty Development Program

When I made the decision to become a full-time faculty member again, I was offered an endowed chair by the college president. At Gustavus, being the holder of such a chair carries with it the expectation that one will create a program or a lecture series or in some way give back to the college and community (not unlike the giving back I had required of my students). My experiences with service-learning were still fresh in my mind, and as I began to contemplate what I might do as the Sponberg Chair of Ethics, I conceived of the idea of "ethics in action," rather than another more static or academic pursuit.

I held a number of meetings on and off campus—with Campus Compact and other groups—to explore the strengths our institution already had in service-learning and to identify the needs. I thought a lot about myself as a teacher and scholar. I had political ideas and commitments but my training in a Ph.D, program in English in the 1970s had certainly not encouraged me to think about bringing such views into my classroom or integrating them into my pedagogy. I talked with other faculty, such as a historian teaching a course on social activism who was groping for some way to connect his class to such activism going on now but hadn't a notion of how to begin. Slowly, the possibility of creating a faculty development program began to form in my mind. I had plenty of experience in the value of such programs from my 20 years as a dean. When personal computers emerged on the academic scene in the early 1980s, I had participated in a faculty development program in what we later came to call IT (information technology) proceeding from memorizing vocabulary (e.g., cursor, RAM) to learning the inner workings of computers and finally to mastering WordStar, an early word processing program. Subsequently, I had created and directed faculty development programs on integrating computers into coursework and topics as diverse as feminist literary criticism and economics. Successful faculty development programs, I knew, must be predicated on the premise that faculty are people who love to learn and are, at the same time, inherently conservative, in the sense that they see their role as guardians of their discipline, as conserving traditions of higher education. Given the radical and rapid expansion of knowledge in the 20th century and beyond, having such opportunities for faculty development is imperative, but they must be staged so that they are challenging and affirming. They must also be convenient and efficient, providing faculty with a genuine benefit in exchange for their commitment of time. Finally, such programs must recognize that most faculty have *very* healthy egos; this personality trait enables them to "profess" for 30 or more years to young people, but, mishandled, it can be an obstacle to effective faculty development.

As part of my post-decanal sabbatical, I spent two days observing an experiential education program in the Twin Cities, called the Higher Education Consortium for Urban Affairs (HECUA), in which the students were reading what looked to be a fascinating bibliography on social justice. Suddenly, I longed to read these books and articles, too, in a group of like-minded folks so we could discuss them. I began to put together a faculty development program that would combine such reading with pedagogical workshops on service-learning (one of the campus needs I had identified). I invited a member of the staff at HECUA to collaborate with me, and she suggested we incorporate into the program an international study tour to a country with serious social justice issues. HECUA has sites in several likely places such as Northern Ireland and Bangladesh. This seemed perfect—it would give faculty a sample of experiential education, introduce them to new approaches to pedagogy, and, as such travel always does, enable them to see conflicts at home more clearly.

Thus, the Service-Learning for Social Justice (SLSJ) program was conceived. It was my good fortune that a constellation of events occurred at Gustavus Adolphus College simultaneously that served, if you will, as midwives for the program. First, the college had just received a generous grant for faculty development from the Bush Foundation. The original proposal for $1,500 provided for stipends for individual faculty to undertake travel, research, or other forms of professional development, allowed me to plug the idea for the SLSJ program into the Bush grant. Thus, in the first year of its existence, the SLSJ program was largely supported by the Bush grant.

But not entirely. Other very significant early and ongoing partners included the newly created Center for Vocational Reflection (sponsored by the Lilly Foundation) and the diversity center, both of which had new leadership, people with strong personal commitments to social justice and service-learning. These individuals provided significant support, moral and monetary. Having consulted also with Professor of Education Carolyn O'Grady, who had published a book on multicultural service-learning, and with the dean's office, which subsequently also offered important support to the program, I circulated an invitation to faculty to apply for participation in the first iteration of the Service-Learning for Social Justice Program. This call for applications listed the following goals for the program:

1) To acquaint faculty with some of the literature and theory of social justice and service-learning as a tool for achieving this.

2) To provide faculty with an opportunity to connect their commitment to social justice and change to their pedagogy.

3) To introduce faculty to community organizations with which they might build partnerships for service-learning courses.

4) To give faculty a retreat-like environment in which to engage with each other and highly experienced moderators from HECUA in discussions and explorations of democracy and civic values.

5) To engage in recursive reflections about the theory and practice of civic engagement for ourselves and our students.

The invitation also provided information about the content of the program, including the weeklong study tour to Northern Ireland scheduled for August 2002, expected outcomes, and the obligations of participants. We asked participants to commit to attending all sessions, writing a final report and evaluation on their experiences, creating a course incorporating service-learning, and to make an ongoing commitment to these new pedagogical approaches. A robust applicant pool quickly developed, and by March a group of 16 faculty and administrators, including some of the framers of the program mentioned above, were accepted for participation. I was genuinely delighted with the diversity of disciplines represented: communication studies, English, education, history, nursing, political science, and Swedish! The director of the Community Service Center, at that point largely devoted to the volunteer community service model, also had applied and been accepted. Space does not permit a full recapitulation of the yearlong program. It encompassed a workshop on service-learning offered in April and predeparture seminars in August, which included readings on social justice and "the Troubles" in Northern Ireland as well as an orientation for the trip itself. In mid-autumn, the group participated in an immersion day in Minneapolis, which engendered reflection and made connections between faculty and various community agencies.

Though evaluations completed by all participants in the Ireland experience were overwhelmingly positive, I decided to issue a call for proposals to various potential partners to arrange the travel portion of the SLSJ program in its second year. This resulted in a new partnership, with the Augsburg College Center for Global Education (an institution also affiliated with the ELCA), which has been providing challenging trips with a social justice theme for out-of-school adults for more than 30 years. The center has well-established links with many countries, and we decided to select a Latin American location because of growing student interest and the evolving Latin American studies program at Gustavus. Ultimately, we chose Guatemala as the destination for August 2003. Again, a group of faculty and administrators was assembled through the application process described above, we again enjoyed Bush Foundation funding, and the group undertook the pedagogical training and predeparture readings. Again, the faculty was diverse, representing the fields of biology, English, economics, education, geography, and theatre; also included were the director of the counseling center, the dean for diversity, the director of the Center for Vocational Reflection, and a staff member from the Community Service Center. Just as with the trip to Northern Ireland where we studied the conflict between the indigenous Irish and the colonizing British, in Guatemala the group considered the plight of the Mayans, the indigenous people, in their struggles with the descendants of the Spanish colonists.

When Gustavus Adolphus College reapplied to the Bush Foundation for a second faculty development grant, the Service-Learning for Social Justice program became a centerpiece of the proposal. Funding was secured for a third and fourth year. During the third cycle, there were 18 people in the

group who completed a successful study tour to Cuba, just prior to the pro-
hibition of such programs by the Bush administration. One of the changes
in composition of the third-year group was the large number of faculty relatively new to the institution; this is heartening, because it indicates a recognition by these young faculty of the importance of teaching social justice and
also their embrace of this aspect of our college's mission.

Making a Difference in the Classroom and the Community

This brings me to the important question that must be posed about any faculty development program: What have the outcomes been? Expected and
unexpected, I would say. Several faculty have incorporated service-learning
components, or immersion days, into their classes, thus making connections
between social justice issues in students' texts and in the larger community,
whether that be the town where the college is located, the nearby urban area
of Minneapolis–St. Paul, or international locations where faculty have subsequently taught classes, such as a political science course in Nicaragua or a
biology course in Tanzania. These were the hoped-for outcomes.

As is inevitable, there were some disappointments, such as faculty who,
despite the written promises we had extracted, failed to attend some components of the program or have not yet incorporated service-learning into a
course. Perhaps it would have been wise to insist that such a class be taught
before the international trip was undertaken, as that clearly was a draw for
some faculty. As no stipend was involved in this program, we did not have
that carrot to withhold until the goals of the program were achieved.

What interests me more, however, are the longer term, often more subtle
influences that an experience like this has on faculty. In what follows, I
reflect on excerpts from the reports faculty wrote at the end of the second
yearlong program, the group that traveled to Guatemala. The changes faculty describe seem to fall into two categories: changes in personal commitment
and changes in pedagogy. Most impressive are the ways in which these two
sea changes are intertwined in the accounts faculty give, demonstrating that
faculty have found ways to share with their students their own experiences

and their personal commitment to social justice and civic engagement. An economist writes:

> What I got out of the experience is a keener understanding of the plight of the people and the huge disparities in the allocation of wealth. Most specifically, after the trip to Guatemala, I find myself not holding the same views on globalization that I held before the trip. I must admit I am struggling. . . . There seems to be no mechanism to assure fair share benefits—social, economic, political, environmental, etc.—for all. What changes are needed to value systems?

From a biologist:

> Upon returning from Guatemala I felt a need to be an agent of change just as my students want to do something when returning from Tanzania. I have begun to think of ways that I can be more intentional about the "re-entry" process with this course.

A direct outcome of this rethinking was that this class brought back from Tanzania dozens of handmade baskets and sold them on our campus for many times the price they paid. The entire profits were then sent back to Tanzania to support a school there with which this professor has developed a collaborative relationship. She also tells of her plan to create a new course on ecojustice and a role-playing exercise on community-based conservation for a tropical system to be used in several courses.

An education professor, who already had some familiarity with service-learning before entering the program, writes:

> My participation in the SLSJ in Guatemala was an experience that enabled me to see the value of grassroots service, to feel the emotion that occurs when one is immersed in a cultural experience, to witness the injustice that occurred,

and to be inspired to work towards social justice. The passion for social justice that I held previously has been reignited and shaped in a more positive way, and this will drive my future decisions regarding service-learning in my courses. . . . I am resolute in adjusting my course work to include the component of "local perspective" or "local control" in . . . service-learning activities I set up now. . . . This perspective shift is the most valuable learning experience I gained.

A geography professor wrote this moving response:

> I understood the goal of our trip to Guatemala as inculcating a deeper, more personal understanding of social injustice in order that we might teach about it more effectively. In this respect, I think it worked remarkably well. At the outset, I believe there is an undeniable virtue in taking relatively sheltered, first-world academics and immersing them in a developing country where the experience with social injustice cannot help but be immediate, tactile, highly visible, and emotionally charged. Just being in Guatemala . . . was a transformative experience. We could not have remained aloof and unaffected even if we had so desired. For me personally, as the mother of young children, seeing the obstacles faced by children there on a daily basis was emotionally overwhelming. . . . Having this experience heightened my already existing commitment to work for social justice both within and outside the classroom.

This professor goes on to recount the success of teaching her World Regional Geography unit on Guatemala with slides she had taken and personal experiences to recount: "I had far more to say and to a significantly more receptive audience." She has also designed a new course, called Consuming Places: Tourism, Nature, and Culture, which looks at the impact of ecotourism on

Central America and uses a case study at the nearby Mall of America, and she has cotaught a similar course in Thailand during a recent January term.

All of these self-assessments speak to systemic changes in individual faculty member's belief systems and long-term approaches to teaching. One of the most passionate and eloquent of these testimonials came from an assistant professor in theatre, who directed a community theatre in Connecticut for 10 years before joining our faculty. I quote from her evaluation at greater length, as her experiences "thickened" her already strong commitment to the role of theatre in the struggle for social justice. She says:

> We learned a great deal about Guatemalan history. . . . With this diversity of perspectives came a far deeper understanding of the human cost of systematic oppression, and the resilience and courage of those who resist oppression. . . . My experiences in Guatemala have affected my teaching in both planned and unplanned ways. As a result of my increased understanding and interest in social justice issues in Latin America, I added a new theatre text to each of my classes. . . . In the world theatre class, our discussion of African playwright, Wole Soyinka's *Death and the King's Horseman* in terms of post-colonial theory prompted me to draw on much that I had learned or seen in Guatemala . . . My most active involvement with service-learning is through my extracurricular work with the Gustavus social justice theatre troupe, "I Am We Are." This group works with techniques of the "Theatre of the Oppressed" developed by Brazilian director Augusto Boal. . . . We are currently discussing ideas for a future show based on stories from Guatemala. . . . Most of the activists and survivors there were eager that their stories be heard. Many insisted that if our group of educators did nothing more than listen to their experiences, and then pass their stories on to others, that their time with us was well spent. This idea was plainly echoed when I worked with student actors and with

student activists from the Gustavus Queers and Allies group in preparation for *The Laramie Project.* [Moises Kaufman's 2001 play about the murder of gay student Matthew Shepard in Wyoming was the first production this professor directed after her return from Guatemala.] Students from Queers and Allies bravely shared their stories with the cast of *Laramie,* helping to educate them for their roles in the play. During the following discussion, an actor asked the Q-and A-speakers what they hoped to gain from our production of *The Laramie Project.* One young man replied, "Just to break the silence. Just that we can talk about this." In so many ways, this is the power of theatre for social justice—to break the silence, dispel the ignorance, and tell the stories that need to be told.

Such an approach to theatre and to civic engagement is exactly what Charlotte Delbo (1995) calls for in the epigram at the beginning of this chapter. No doubt my theatre colleague's emphasis on the crucial importance of story resonates with me as an English professor. It is just such an emphasis that I hope to create in my future efforts in service-learning. In January 2005, with two colleagues who had also participated in the Northern Ireland SLSJ, I took 24 students to Northern Ireland to study "the Troubles." We created three intertwined courses in education, the performing arts, and literature; my course was Swords Into Ploughshares: The Power of the Book in the Irish Troubles. Ireland is a country with a distinguished history of literature. What role, my course asked, has literature played in the conflict over the centuries? We considered questions about the role of literature as resistance, protest, and reconciliation in the present conflict, engendered by England's colonial domination of Ireland for 800 years, and its role in the peace-making process. We engaged students in all three courses in service-learning with a volunteer agency in Derry and at Glencree, a peace and reconciliation centre in the Wicklow mountains. These courses were a direct result of our experience as participants in the first year of the Service-Learning for Social Justice program.

Rules for Radicals: Advice on Getting Started[1]

Though the genesis and focus of the Service-Learning for Social Justice program to a certain extent emerged in a particular context, responded to particular institutional needs, and took advantage of a somewhat unique set of circumstances, much of what we have done could be replicated by other institutions, large and small, public and private. Here are some general guidelines that might prove useful to individual faculty, directors of faculty development, and deans.

Funding

This is the sine qua non of successful faculty development programs. The most expensive part of the SLSJ program is the international trip, and while it would be possible to stage training in service-learning without this component, I believe the prospect of international travel helped recruit faculty to the program and also provided a crucial international dimension to our understanding of social justice issues. At Gustavus, generous funding from the Bush and Lilly foundations made this possible. Existing faculty development and faculty travel funds may make such a venture possible at other institutions, but external funding was necessary at our institution to supplement rather meager annual allotments to individual faculty in these areas. Other line items in our budget included photocopies, refreshments, honoraria, in-state travel, purchase of books, and the cost of the one-day immersion program.

Gaining Support of Gatekeepers

When seeking support from various administrative offices, show them how the proposed program supports the institutional mission, fills a need not being met in any other way, may be worthy of external funding and good publicity for the institution, and will strengthen the academic program. Seek their suggestions and ideas as you plan the faculty development program. Don't be afraid to request monetary support. Assure them that their own staff will not be burdened by details.

Inviting Faculty to the Table

Your program must be provocative and provide meaningful learning opportunities. Schedule sessions at times that do not conflict with other activities
and obligations. Provide materials that save faculty time locating these
resources themselves. Don't hesitate to encourage specific faculty to apply;
sometimes these special invitations encourage a person to consider the
opportunity when he or she otherwise would have ignored the call for applications. Be conscious of designing a program that will appeal to faculty in a
range of disciplines. Consider including administrators in the eligible group
of participants: This throws a bridge across a divide far too wide in many colleges and universities and creates links that can be productive.

Utilizing In-House Expertise

The advantages of identifying and utilizing in-house experts are obvious.
They buy into your program and become a booster of it; they also are likely to provide their services pro bono. In our case, faculty and administrators
with the ability to teach service-learning techniques, faculty with expertise
on social justice, Northern Ireland, Guatemala and indigenous people, and
Cuban poetry and film all made contributions to the seminars provided to
faculty. Since these individuals had been identified as experts, they became
part of a resource network which faculty could contact at any point in the
program or thereafter.

Creating Effective Partnerships

Establishing a partnership with an organization skilled in faculty development
and providing travel is essential to accomplishing your program's goals if you
plan to incorporate an international component. While our first partner had a
fine track record of the latter, they were accustomed to working with student
groups, so making the transition to working with faculty was not always done
well. By contrast, Augsburg College's Center for Global Education has been
arranging social justice experiences for adults for 30 years. They have been
splendid partners, bringing to the relationship a wealth of knowledge and networks around the world and in our local community. But be warned:
Maintaining such relationships is very time-consuming for the coordinator of
the program.

Final Reflections

When speaking about the expected and unexpected outcomes of the Service-Learning for Social Justice program and including responses from participants and my own responses, I have endeavored to demonstrate the impact of the program in heightening consciousness and expanding pedagogy. Other outcomes of the program include a reading group of former participants who are engaging with theoretical and pedagogical texts, and discussion of opening a fair trade store in Saint Peter, which would provide a venue for products of indigenous peoples whom we meet as we teach in far-flung places and a locus for service-learning in many disciplines. When the SLSJ program comes to a close, more than 70 members of our community will have participated—nearly one-third of our faculty. These faculty and administrators will have had an invaluable experience that helps them fulfill our college mission; this inspirational statement pledges that we teach a curriculum that is

> Interdisciplinary and international in perspective . . . fosters the development of values as an integral part of intellectual growth . . . affirms the dignity of all people. . . . It is a community where . . . lives of service are nurtured and students are encouraged to work toward a just and peaceful world. (Gustavus Adolphus College, 2005–2006, p. 1)

As I write this, I am preparing for a meeting with the head of the Sudanese immigrant community in a nearby town. When I teach a course called Women and the Holocaust: Gender, Memory, and Representation in 2006, I intend to engage my students in service-learning with this community, whose relatives and friends in Darfur are experiencing a genocide, though the peacemaking organizations on which we rely are curiously reluctant to use that term to describe the killing, the rapes, the destruction of villages, the deaths in refugee camps, and the racial and postcolonial nature of these attacks. Like many of my colleagues, I would at one time have been reluctant to leave the ivory tower of the academy for such an endeavor; uncertain of my skills, better versed in parody and palimpsest than politics, I was content to rely on talk and texts, rather than activism. Now I can encourage students to see the power of story to bring about change when the tellers and transmitters of that story use it purposefully. This is what Charlotte Delbo (1995) had in mind; I like to think she would call it "Useful Knowledge."

Endnote

1) I am indebted here to Saul D. Alinsky's *Rules for Radicals: A Pragmatic Primer for Realistic Radicals* (Random House, 1971).

References

Delbo, C. (1995). *Auschwitz and after* (R. C. Lamont, Trans.). New Haven, CT: Yale University Press.

Gustavus Adolphus College. (2005–2006). Gustavus Adolphus College academic bulletin 2005–2006). Saint Peter, MN: Author.

Kaufman, M. (2001). *The Laramie project.* New York, NY: Vintage.

Spiegelman, A. (1986). *Maus: A survivor's tale: My father bleeds history.* New York, NY: Pantheon.

Spiegelman, A. (1991). *Maus II: A survivor's tale: And here my troubles began.* New York, NY: Pantheon.

Zlotkowski, E. (1998). *Successful service-learning programs: New models of excellence in higher education.* Bolton, MA: Anker.

Zlotkowski, E. (1997–2004). *Service-learning in the disciplines.* Washington, DC: American Association for Higher Education.

13
DEEP LEARNING AND THE BIG QUESTIONS: REFLECTION IN SERVICE-LEARNING

Chris Johnson

Questions drive learning; good questions fuel deep learning; deep learning propels more and better questions (Dalton, 2001). Whatever else it might entail—which is a great deal—service-learning is about *learning*. It is therefore about asking and being confronted by questions, for which a crucial vehicle in service-learning is reflection. Reflection is the heart, the key, the linchpin to service-learning; without it, deep learning cannot happen.

Much has been written about the academic (i.e., discipline- and course-based) learning that takes place in and through reflection in service-learning (Eyler & Giles, 1999; Furco & Billig, 2002; Jacoby & Associates, 1996; Kendall & Associates, 1990). My assumption is that these kinds of learning generally do not (and, in fact, should not) take place apart from what we might think of as the "big questions:" Who am I, really, and why am I here? What does it mean to be human, and how ought I to live? What's my place in the world, how can I make a difference? What do I really care about, and what does my life stand for? Do my work, my relationships, my priorities—my life—contribute to peace and justice? Whom do I see when I look in the mirror of experience, the mirror of the Other? Service-learning reflection is a crucible in which academic knowledge and these kinds of big questions permeate one another. Service-learning can be (and, rightly, often is) also a matter of questions of the spirit.

What Is Reflection, and Why Do It in Service-Learning?

The English word reflection is derived from the Latin *reflectere*, "to bend back," as a mirror bends back the light, making apparent what is otherwise hidden or mysterious. Reflection in service-learning bends the light of our experiences back into our minds, to consider what the experience was about and what it meant (Reed & Koliba, 1995). Reflection also bends the light of our minds—knowledge and beliefs, concepts and theories—back onto the rich landscape of lived experience, bringing new dimensions of flesh and blood, contexts and commitments, to abstract ideas.

The visual or visional connotations of the word—the image of light bending back as in a mirror—are worth dwelling on for a moment. Course content and the community-based experience illuminate each other and themselves. In reflection the student is simultaneously the medium (the lens or mirror) by which theory and practice shed light on the other, another source of light altogether (by virtue of the vast wealth of knowledge, experiences, and capacities that one brings to the process), and a pool of relative darkness into which new light can shine. A mirror can help us see what is otherwise veiled or hidden, at least to us; what we see only with the aid of a mirror is often readily visible to others. Real learning requires change of some kind, beyond simply the accumulation of knowledge; reflection changes us by opening new windows and doors in how we think, believe, feel, and act.

Among the most important ways this can be true is in the way reflection in service-learning can help us to see ourselves in others, and to see others in ourselves. By providing space, time, tools, and encouragement for students simply to pause and think, reflection opens up the possibility that they can become (more) aware of their fundamental connectedness with other people, their belonging to a common humanity, their shared place in realities larger than themselves. Reflection can help students better attend to details and hence better discern the big picture. In this respect vision is very much a metaphor for knowing, for rather than simply absorbing a cacophonous jumble of meaningless data, we (usually, barring certain physiologic dysfunctions like sensory integration disorder[1]) have the ability to organize it into patterns or structures that impart meaning (Trott, Laurel, & Windeck, 1993). Reflection calls attention to the ways we take in and process information so that it registers as something about which we can have feelings, make judgments, and deliberate about our best response. From finer perception can flow empathy, refined judgment and critical thinking, and more richly informed action.

This dimension of vision, or perhaps the blurring or lack thereof, also has to do with blind spots—instances or patterns of selective hearing or practiced numbness, those failures of perception that plunge us into self-deception about ourselves and the persons and world around us. Returning for a moment to the idea of images reflected in a mirror, consider how disorienting that can be: Consider the understated warning etched into the passenger-side rearview mirror on my car—"Objects in mirror are closer than they appear." The conscious effort that goes into careful reflection helps us not to be deceived by what we might assume at first glance is the case about ourselves or others. What we come to see in reflection, some insight about ourselves and others that penetrates more deeply than our ever-moving, surface-level glimpses make possible, is often closer to home than we might at first realize.

On the other hand, mirrors are famously a symbol of vanity, self-absorption, and narcissism: "Mirror, mirror, on the wall, who is the fairest one of all?" Reflection in service-learning helps remind us that we are not, in fact, the center of the universe, and that ours is not the only perspective that counts. The world needs also to be seen, and we need to learn to view ourselves from the perspective of people who are disenfranchised, from the perspective of the environment and of other creatures with whom we share the planet, and through the eyes of those whose lives are diminished by an unreflectively self-centered way of life. Or, consider how it is that a mirror image of something is *reversed*, such that a written message held up to a mirror, for instance, needs to be decoded. If the self, an "Other," or an experience is the "text," what new insight can I discover when I work to decipher that text in and through reflection (Varlotta, 2000)?

These observations point to the volitional, deliberate nature of how we see and take in the world. To be able to perceive and judge well requires conscious effort and commitment to do so. Perception and judgment are processes of active "looking-for" that are informed, in part, by one's beliefs and assumptions concerning what one can expect to see, what is worth looking for, and so on, all of which can be dealt with in reflection. A person may look for certain kinds of explanations for another's actions, for example, because he or she believes it worthwhile and just to do so, because it contributes to the betterment of individuals and society, and so on. Or (in an unreflective, artificially distanced, self-deceptive way) one might look for what one already knows one will see in, for example, an encounter with someone from a different ethnic background or socioeconomic situation: "Everybody knows that *those people* just are that way." In response to which reflection can say, "Ah, but remember: 'Objects in mirror are closer than they appear.'" Reflection in service-learning can help us to develop habits and capacities of active discernment and looking-for by which we can more clearly see ourselves and our place in the world, and by which we can better appreciate our common humanity and fundamental interconnectedness with others.

The depth and clarity of vision that can come with reflection involve the cultivation of certain skills. Chief among these, and at the heart of practical wisdom, is what philosopher Martha Nussbaum (following Aristotle) calls "perception" (Nussbaum, 1986, 1990). Perception, she says, is "the ability to discern, acutely and responsively, the salient features of one's particular situation," (1990, p. 37). She describes this ability in terms of several interrelated skills and habits, such as *discernment, responsiveness, apprehension,* and *discrimination.* These include the ability to hone and engage all the senses with which one takes in reality in order to pay close and patient attention to details; sharp awareness of what is salient (and how and to what degree) in a particular situation; context-sensitive (re)formulation and application of general rules and principles that have been learned and tested through experience; and fine emotional sensitivity.

These perceptual skills and habits—discrimination, attention to detail, imagination, emotional sensitivity—have as their primary object of attention the salient particularities of human existence. These include the anticipated and looked-for explanations of a person's actions and/or character; new and perhaps nonrepeatable details of each situation and the life stories of the persons involved; the context of these relevant details; and the uniqueness of particular persons and relationships, especially love and friendship (Nussbaum, 1990). Good perception discerns the moral salience, for example, of particular features within a situation, and those particular features that make the situation a *moral* one (or a political or economic one—or a situation of whatever type of salience is illuminated in reflection). In either respect, salience may be discerned by virtue of an ability to ask the right questions of a situation. What the right questions are probably cannot be exhaustively fixed in advance, for just as a situation may present something entirely new or nonrepeatable, it may also call for the asking of an entirely new or unanticipated question. (This implies that one question that always ought to be asked is, "What, if anything, is new, unique, or nonrepeatable about this situation, and in what does this newness consist?") As reflection bends back the light of experience and knowledge, it can bring to light what those new questions, those new avenues of thought and discovery, might be.

Another important connotation of reflection in service-learning, suggested by the word's relationship to the bending of light, is pliability, malleability, flexibility (as in "re-*flexion*") of thought, feeling, attitude, and action. Reflection calls upon and can enhance students' ability to be limber in their thinking, to bend ideas in new directions, to transpose concepts, knowledge, and capacities for feeling and action into new, perhaps unfamiliar or unexpected "keys" (to stretch the metaphor a bit). Reflection prods students to engage their fundamentally human capacity to think metaphorically, to recognize the like and unlike between things, to transfer or generalize prior (context-specific) knowledge to new problems or contexts to navigate effectively in an increasingly complex and needful world.[2]

Something of what I mean here is suggested by Nussbaum's (1993) consideration of Aristotle's understanding of justice in response to wrongdoing. Formally, she says, justice for Aristotle is fairness and equality, which entails treating like cases alike and rendering to each what is due, specific applications of which often are able to be captured in rules or legislation (Aristotle, 1985). He recognizes, however, that cases are rarely identical in real life, and determining what elements of *unlikeness* justify what kinds of *unlike treatment* requires *flexibility* in response to particular details, for which general principles and strict legislation will not suffice. What is required is *equity*, a kind of justice that is "superior to and frequently opposed by" (Nussbaum, 1993, pp. 93–94) a strict, legislative justice, which it corrects and completes.

Using the famous analogy of a good architect who knows not to try to measure a complicated structure with a straightedge, but rather with a flexible strip of metal that bends to the shape of the structure, Aristotle argues that particular judgments, "superior in flexibility to the general dictates of law, should bend round to suit the case" (Aristotle, 1985, pp. 1137a30–1138a3). Such an equitable person is inclined to mitigation, and *as such* is a *just* person (Nussbaum, 1993). The equitable or just person, moreover, is characterized by a sympathetic understanding of human things that is rooted in the capacity to perceive particulars and to "judge with" (*suggnômê*) another, at least partially from her or his point of view. That is, in order to "perceive the particular accurately, one must 'judge *with*' the agent who has done the alleged wrong. One must, that is, *see things from that person's point of view*, for only then will one begin to comprehend what obstacles that person faced as he or she acted. . . . Recognizing the burden of these 'human things,' the equitable judge is inclined not to be 'zealous for strict judgment in the direction of the worse,' but to prefer merciful mitigation" (Nussbaum, 1993, pp. 94–95).

My intention here is not to argue with Nussbaum (1993) for mercy and forgiveness in response to wrongdoing per se. Rather, my point is that *pliability of attitude and agility in thinking are associated with careful perception of particulars*, which is one of the things that reflection in service-learning can foster. The emphasis at this point is on what is *possible*, what *might* be, what *could* be, what one *hopes* will be. This capacity for imaginative and creative thinking, feeling, and acting involves clear-sighted apprehension of the past and present and, rather than being constrained by what one finds there, the intellectual and emotional agility to free-associate new combinations, likenesses, and possibilities that are unexperienced and untried. In service-learning reflection, this ability can be coupled with an attitudinal posture of anticipation, flirtation with the possibility of failure as a means of growth, and a desire to push the fringes of the conventional or the comfortable.

Reflection in service-learning, then, bends the light of experience and prior learning back upon and into oneself, helps us to see ourselves in others and others in ourselves, brings to light our capacity for self-deception, enhances our perception of and attention to salient particulars, makes us more limber in thought and attitude, strengthens our capacity to recognize the possible within the actual, and sharpens our vision such that we can better see—and creatively strive for—truth, justice, and hope.

Pedagogy and Best Practices of Reflection

The work of thinkers such as Kolb (1984), Dewey (1933), and Freire (1970/1997) provides much of the pedagogical and philosophical foundation upon which the crucial role of reflection in service-learning rests. Their work has shed light on how learning happens at all and therefore on how the best learning can be fostered. It also emphasizes some of the values that are at stake in learning well, including personal growth, active and informed participation in a democracy, and the cultivation of skills and attitudes that foster social justice.

Building on Dewey (1933), Kolb's (1984) model of experiential learning describes how the interplay of concrete experience, reflective observation of the details of that experience, abstract conceptualization arising from those observations, and active experimentation that applies and tests those concepts in new situations of concrete experience generate deep learning. In service-learning contexts, concrete experience in the community provides the opportunity for active, real-life (what Dewey might recommend as perplexity-inducing, forked-road) engagement with key questions, people, processes, and problems. In reflective observation, students describe, analyze, and rigorously consider the data they encountered in the concrete experience. The task here is to identify the complex web of factors that constitute the situation and shape one's apprehension and interpretation of the experience. Students also attend to the ways in which their involvement affects the situation and try to sort out the foundational or background beliefs, attitudes, values, and intentions they bring to the situation, which predispose them to see and interpret things in certain ways.

At the abstract conceptualization stage of Kolb's (1984) experiential learning spiral, students engage in interpretation and organization of the data by way of the theoretical frameworks they bring to the experience (via the classroom, for example). Here they think critically about the meaning(s) of the experience, the applicability or transferability of prior intellectual (and other) knowledge, and the explanatory effectiveness of specific theories or concepts (often from across multiple academic disciplines and modes of thought). Reflection now begins to push information beyond raw data into something in which students have a stake, something in which they become invested and which they now grasp (or are grasped by). As reflection bridges Kolb's abstract conceptualization and active experimentation stages, theory begins to take on substantive flesh, and possible routes of further inquiry and modes of action begin to suggest themselves. (At the same time, reflective observation still plays a part in that, for example, students can be encouraged to notice what it is that presses most compellingly on their attention and therefore prompts curiosity and possible courses of action.) In active experimentation, students integrate and transform their freshly deepened critical insight, pursue new lines of questioning, and test, build upon, clarify, discard, or act upon their new ideas, insights, and skills, all in ways that inform their ongoing engagement with concrete experience. And so the cycle/spiral goes on.

While reflection is (on the one hand) a normal and ongoing *cognitive process* that is grounded in the very nature of thinking and hence of sound learning, it can be made more explicit and ordered in formal experiential learning contexts by reflection as (on the other hand) a kind of *structured learning activity*. What do we know, then, about *how* to optimize learning through reflection? Hatcher and Bringle (1997), for example, offer these guidelines for maximizing the effectiveness of reflection activities: Reflection activities are most effective when they explicitly link experience to learning objectives, are well structured and guided, occur regularly over time, allow feedback and assessment, and include opportunities for the exploration and clarification of values. In what follows, I draw heavily upon Hatcher and Bringle's work while also expanding upon it.

Reflection activities should explicitly link experience to learning objectives, and so need to be appropriate to the experience and to the objectives. The learning that is sought should be clearly articulated and attended to by the reflection. Learning objectives that specifically include (or at least make room for) big question kinds of knowledge and growth would therefore give rise to reflection activities that allow for and encourage engagement with such questions. One recent study noted that students often experienced learning and growth around "spiritual and ethical values," even when that was not an explicit learning goal (Steinke, Fitch, Waldstein, & Johnson,

2000). Many students who reported this kind of learning, however, also urged their instructors to be more explicit that this kind of growth was among the potential and/or desired learning outcomes, and to craft reflection activities that would better help them to maximize these kinds of learning.

Reflection activities should be structured and guided by the instructor (and/or a supervisor or representative from the community partner, campus student-life staff, or student assistants, as appropriate). Guidance should begin as early as possible with the spelling out of expectations, clear assignments, and criteria for evaluation and assessment of the students' reflective work (if it is to be graded), preferably in the course syllabus or in the student-instructor codevelopment of a learning covenant. Students' ability to draw substantive connections between their experience and the learning objectives is enhanced when their reflection is guided (but not constrained) by focused questions and thought-prompts that lead them to see and explore those connections. Effective guidance and facilitation is itself a set of practices and capacities, postures and attitudes that collectively differ from many forms of conventional teaching, especially in terms of the respective roles of participants and the nature of power and authority in the group. For example, according to Reed and Koliba (1995), an effective facilitator of a group discussion will not play the expert, whose voice and perspective dominates the conversation, but will instead "foster the group's own ability to lead itself" (¶3) by attending to group dynamics, promoting an open and respectful atmosphere, and so on.[3]

Attending to students' varying levels of skill and experience with different modes of reflection is also important and may require the teaching of specific competencies such as close listening, mindful observation, reflective writing, question-asking, and analysis. Reflection activities should also take into account students' "multiple intelligences" (Gardner, 1993) in order to allow students to build upon their strengths and to help them stretch beyond their comfort zones. A written reflection assignment, for example, can also be tailored to help students progress through the stages of Kolb's (1984) experiential learning cycle. The much-used (and perhaps oversimple) "What? So What? Now What?" model,[4] for instance, can help explain to students an assignment for a three-part journal, which includes a description of the experience—Kolb's "reflective observation" stage, analysis of the situation in light of course content —"abstract conceptualization," and exploration of possible courses of action or ways to apply what they've learned to this or other situations—"active experimentation."

To enhance learning and keep students as engaged as possible, a variety of guided content- and context-appropriate reflection activities should occur regularly throughout the term. Frequent, well-guided reflection can help students move through a developmental process (e.g., from acquiring basic knowledge to "dancing" with creative and agile thinking through more advanced concepts, from using simple skills to practicing more sophisticated capacities) and should help them track and take increasing ownership of their own growth over time.

Providing regular opportunities and varied means for reflection also sends a message about the need and importance of simply taking time to pause and reflect. Timely, well-structured reflection as part of a service-learning experience can help students to become intentional about considering the meaning of their actions and the implications of their learning as an integral part of a life well lived. Crafting the safe space for students to explore the relationships between the inner and outer landscapes of their lives and providing (or requiring) the gift of time to think can help students develop the capacities and dispositions of character by which they can live a full life of meaning, passion, and purpose (Palmer, 1990). Deep thinking and effective action require movement and the stillness of contemplation, just as music requires both notes and rests.

In addition to being frequent, varied, and ongoing, well-designed reflection activities include opportunities and mechanisms for substantive feedback and assessment of the students' progress in meeting the learning objectives for the course, how well the service is meeting the needs and expectations of the community partner, and of the instructor's teaching effectiveness. In addition to being a means to measure students' cognitive learning, reflection activities provide an important vehicle for sustained, substantive conversation around weighty issues of self and spirit—with themselves and with others whose voices and perspectives matter.

This can be tricky terrain, to which some teachers will take with more ease than others. As with many aspects of service-learning, engaging with students in reflection around issues of spirituality, moral values, and the like often requires a flexibility in self-understanding on the part of students and teachers and a shifting of typical roles. Tapping into one's ability to be *present* with students as they navigate deep waters and letting them know that you are with them on the journey can be powerful human gifts, and can foster significant learning. "We tend to pay attention only long enough to develop a counterargument," (p. 19) writes Mary Rose O'Reilley (1998):

> We critique the student's or the colleague's ideas; we mentally grade and pigeonhole each other. . . . By contrast, if someone truly listens to me, my spirit begins to expand. . . . One can, I think, *listen someone into existence*, encourage a stronger self to emerge or a new talent to flourish. Good teachers listen this way, as do terrific grandfathers and similar heroes of the spirit. (p. 21)

Service-learning not only links theory and practice, it also weaves together (widely privileged) objective and (often disparaged) subjective ways of knowing. Still, appropriate emotional (and, of course, physical) boundaries need to be maintained, and realistic limitations on one's ability to respond effectively need to be honored.

Another way in which teachers need to be forthright about their abilities to assess student work is in connection with evaluation of modes of reflection that flow from intelligences other than those with which the faculty person is most comfortable (e.g., in determining how to assess a musical or performance piece when one's competencies lie in responding to formal written work). Negotiating clear criteria and processes for evaluation, utilizing various modes of peer assessment, and the like can be helpful in this regard. In assessing the work of a student who chooses to reflect via musical composition and performance, for example (which may be outside one's areas of expertise), it may be helpful to require the student to submit written program notes in order to help the audience (the instructor, the class, the community partner, and/or others) to better understand and appreciate the meaning of the piece. Such an approach still encourages the student to employ his or her strengths but also prods him or her to stretch in other directions.

But even on the relatively safe level of assessing intellectual learning, how can the faculty member really evaluate something that is bound to be so subjective and personal or, as the service-learning detractor's worst-case scenario would have it, so "touchy-feely"? Just as it is important to provide careful guidance to students for what is expected in their reflections (and thereby to help them to steer clear of vacuous and insipid "touchy-feely" tendencies in the first place), it is also important to articulate and utilize clear rubrics for how their reflective work will be evaluated. For example, Bradley (1995) has developed a set of criteria for assessing levels of reflection that can help students to have a clear understanding of how their development as reflective learners should progress. Bradley's criteria illustrate how even big-questions reflection can legitimately be assessed, in that they have to do with demonstrating development toward increasingly sophisticated levels of thinking, reasoning, argumentation, analysis, application and transference of concepts, and communication of ideas.

Hatcher and Bringle (1997) also urge that reflection include the opportunity for students to explore, clarify, and alter their values. Service-learning experiences bring students into contact with thorny real-world issues and perspectives that often challenge their own. Reflection is a crucial means for students to work through paradox and ambiguity, contradiction and complexity, and thus to develop more sophisticated capacities for thoughtful decision-making and deliberate action. As values and convictions are challenged, clarified, altered, or strengthened, patterns of behavior are likely also to be modified, including those having to do with social action, civic engagement, civil literacy, and public responsibility (Moely, McFarland, Miron, Mercer, & Ilustre, 2002). Hatcher and Bringle point to research indicating that "undergraduates who participate in service-learning report an increased desire to serve their community, a deeper sense of personal responsibility to meet community needs, and a deeper level of commitment to community service" (p. 15). While cautioning that service-learning does not necessarily lead to changes in political behaviors or attitudes, compel students to automatically connect their service experiences to an increased sense of civic responsibility, or cause them to become more compassionate or tolerant, they suggest that well-structured reflection can contribute to these kinds of outcomes.

Some practitioners and researchers have also explored ways service-learning can cultivate certain values or character traits (Boss, 1994; Steinke et al., 2000). It is a time-tested insight that in order to become an accomplished craftsperson or artist—a carpenter, say, or a musician—one needs to practice the craft of carpentry or the art of musicianship. Qualities of moral character such as altruism, perceptiveness, compassion, and honesty can be cultivated and nurtured (or conversely, stunted and killed) over time and in the course of living with others in various contexts. Many have also argued that a person can be helped to grow in her or his religious faith or spiritual life through the cultivation of specific habits and practices such as prayer, contemplation, forgiveness, and service. Thinkers in many of the world's religious traditions have long given voice to the connection between action, specifically service to others, and one's growth in the life of faith (Fowler, 1981; Perry, 1968). Service-learning, as a form of experiential learning that immerses students in what we might call "practicing the craft of life," can contribute to students' spiritual and ethical development. The stories of their lives, of who they are and are becoming, now include and have been shaped in part by the experiences and relationships, frustrations and insights they developed while engaged in service-learning. Reflection is an important way that students can actively invest in crafting, understanding, owning, and expressing that narrative, by which their sense of self, fundamental values, motivating commitments, and dispositions to action are bound together in a unified whole.

For example, service-learning can contribute to an understanding of human beings as fundamentally connected to one another in the tapestry of community and social relations. Such an understanding of what it means to be human is itself a dimension of moral character—as is any habit or pattern of belief, perception, emotion, and action—and thus is able to be shaped by experience and reflection upon experience. To see persons as inherently social beings who share responsibility for one another's welfare and for the common good can be a component of a worldview that has been influenced by certain kinds of experiences, as can a construal of persons as inherently isolated, atomistic individuals whose lives, fates, and rights are fundamentally disconnected from those of others (Benhabib, 1987; Dyck, 1994; Sandel, 1982). The service-learning experiences of the students in one study reinforced the former view of the connectedness of persons in a tapestry of mutual responsibility: "We all have a much higher responsibility to serve our community," wrote one student. "I always thought individual works were the most important, however every individual is a part of the community" (Steinke et al., 2000, p. 64).

Students in that study also observed that the helping response evoked by the needs of others often flows from a position of relative abundance and privilege, and from a sense of gratitude. Service-learning can help students to recognize, appreciate, and act on the gifts they have (and may otherwise take for granted), including the opportunity to be in college in the first place and the chance to contribute to the common good because they have the opportunities and resources to do so (Steinke et al., 2000). Simply becoming aware of one's position of relative privilege can be an important insight. Reflection can build upon this awareness by raising further questions about, for example, the systemic causes of injustice, whether and how one's privilege implies certain kinds of obligations to act, and the dangers of paternalism that can come with privilege.

A number of factors may help to optimize these kinds of learning and development, reflective attention which can strengthen courses that include a service-learning component. It is important, for example, simply to be *intentional* (especially via various forms of guided and ongoing reflection) about:

- Growing the seeds of a passion for social justice and other moral commitments that are already present in the character and worldviews of many students. Their impulses to live out their ideals are often deep, and should be honored, even as they may also be strongly challenged by everything from the need to think critically to the overwhelming demands on their time, energies, and loyalties.

- Explicitly articulating that spiritual growth, moral discernment, and social justice are, in fact, among the desired (or at least potential) learning objectives for the course. In many settings, one way of doing this may be to include language in the syllabus that ties the goals of the course to the institution's mission statement. Many colleges and universities proclaim that their reason for being is, for example, to develop in students a capacity and passion for lifelong learning, and to prepare them for fulfilling lives of leadership and service in society. Including (parts of) the mission statement in the syllabus is an effective reminder (to students, teachers, and community partners alike) that this particular class and the experiences and learning connected to it are embedded in a larger, values-driven enterprise.

- Substantively attending to issues of power and privilege, in and out of the classroom, within and between individuals and communities; teachers need to notice, and help students to ask, for example, Who has a voice here, who doesn't, and why?

- Pushing for depth: Students want help in seeking out and analyzing root causes of systemic injustice and in understanding how political and socioeconomic forces work, often with their unwitting participation, to keep people in poverty, for example, or to perpetuate environmental racism.

- Cueing the big questions of self and world, faith and engagement. Many students are ripe for exploring questions of identity, meaning, and purpose in their lives, and are often eager for their teachers and mentors to help them wrestle with these questions. But it simply does not happen as often or as well as it might. Sharon Daloz Parks (2000) argues,

> Many young adults, even those who are regarded as privileged, are often being cheated in a primary way. *They are not being asked big-enough questions.* They are not being invited to entertain the greatest questions of their own lives or their times. (p. 138)

This paucity of opportunity and encouragement to grapple with deep questions of the spirit has profound implications. Sophistication with skills that can help propel young adults up ladders of success (as portrayed by a consumerist, fast-paced, violent society) is too often disconnected from an ability to employ many of those same skills—critical thinking, for example—in questioning what the ladders are made of and upon whose heads they stand. The big questions of meaning and spirit need to be seen as intertwined with others, such as,

> What do I want the future to look like—for me, for others, for my planet? How am I complicit in patterns of injustice? Why is there so much suffering in the world? Why is there a growing gap between the haves and the have-nots? (Parks, 2000, pp. 127–128)

Reflection and Deep Learning: Some Implications

This brings us back to where this chapter began—with the observation that questions drive learning; good questions fuel deep learning, and deep learning propels more and better questions. The questions that emerge in service-learning and can be pursued in well-structured, guided, ongoing, values-clarifying reflection are often big questions, questions of the spirit.

Truthfully, we often don't see much of anything that's extraordinary or unusual. We're "just us," living a normal life as best we can from day to day. But what is that, really? Columnist Ellen Goodman (as cited in De Graf, Wann, & Naylor, 2001) describes our society's idea of "normal life":

> Normal is getting dressed in clothes that you buy for work, driving through traffic in a car that you are still paying for, in order to get to the job you need so you can pay for the clothes, car and house that you leave empty all day in order to afford to live in it. (p. 36)

We often find ourselves caught in the vortex that swirls between abundance and disease, trying to keep up, get by, and move ahead. "Even when our intentions are noble and our efforts sincere," writes Wayne Muller (1999), "even when we dedicate our lives to the service of others—the corrosive pressure of frantic overactivity can nonetheless cause suffering in ourselves and others" (pp. 1–2). As a society we are increasingly burned out, overworked (or, for many, under- or unemployed), consumerist, isolated, disconnected, mistrustful, violent, and environmentally cancerous. We are being increasingly deluded into believing that when it comes to our ultimate sense of identity, wellbeing, worth, and security, we can find them only within our isolated, atomistic selves, our radically individualized versions of Truth, and the "stuff" we strive so frenetically to accumulate. The message is this: "sec U R IT y." That is, when it comes to knowing who you are, what makes your life count, and your own security, the culture says, "You alone Are (U R) It."

But reflection in service-learning can help us to see that the real world calls us out of ourselves and out of our self-deceptions, exposes "normal life" and "sec U R IT y" to be just so futile, fractured, and scrambling up an endless hill, and summons us to more meaningful, life-giving alternatives. Reflection on the big questions opens up the space to consider more humane and truthful ways of being in the world. Instead of being (and teaching our students to be) "normal," we can be intentional about engaging in processes and activities of reflection that:[5]

- Prod us to think of our work, our learning, and the rest of our daily lives as woven together into a larger tapestry of meaning, a way of being in the world that tilts toward justice, purpose, and community. For some, this may take the shape of being mindful of the difference between thinking about questions like "Who am I?" in terms of "what I do for a living," and thinking about them instead in terms of "*Whose* am I, and who am I called to be?"

- Renew a sense of knowing oneself to be "nested" in something greater than oneself, be it community, networks of interdependence, a cause through which one can contribute to the common good, key relationships, a healthy ecosystem, "God," and/or a hopeful future.

- Help us have the courage to pursue the big questions of identity and purpose, of self and security—and to entertain the possibility that these are probably not to be found in ourselves alone, or our work, or our status, or our "stuff."

- Enlarge one's sense of self and of one's capacity to make a difference, and cultivate our students, departments, institutions, households, and communities to be agents of peace and justice in the world.

- Renew a sense of calling to care for the "other" and for the creation, as people who are engaged in the life of the community and who as a matter of disposition and character respond compassionately to suffering, work with others to anticipate and creatively address real community needs, and bring capacities for critical thinking to bear on the designs of the "establishment."

- Help each other to move from awareness to service, from understanding symptoms to addressing causes, from taking thoughtful action to being reflective activists.

- Nurture commitments to and practices of mindfulness, presence, whole-person health, and Sabbath. This can mean a rediscovery of what it might mean, in part, to know that we are nested and graced, and that even our very best, most highly skilled, and well-intentioned efforts won't save us or the planet, or make us most truly who we are.

Reflection is the key to teaching and learning that matters, the kind that takes place in service-learning, because it helps us to map the deep architecture of our lives, the foundational structures or frameworks of belief and value, and the attitudes and actions that hold our lives together. This learning involves an inward and an outward dynamic, a spiraling inward toward the depths of self, meaning, and faith, and outward into an ever-expanding world of community and effective action. Reflection in service-learning illuminates our minds and hearts, and helps us to see ourselves in the midst of finitude, despair, violence, and injustice as able to live meaningful lives of engagement, connection, and hope.

Endnotes

1) I am indebted to personal conversations with Sharon Hill and Kimberly Devine-Johnson concerning various impediments to "normal" appropriation of and response to sense-experience.

2) Since reflection in service-learning helps students exercise and strengthen this crucial capacity of knowing, sense-making, and creative problem solving, it may also be fruitful to consider the various metaphors that are employed in thinking about and engaging in service-learning in the first place—such as, "service is war (on poverty, for example)," "service is business," or text, charity, or citizenship (Taylor, 2002).

3) Reed and Koliba's (1995) *Facilitating Reflection: A Manual for Leaders and Educators* includes helpful guidance on conducting "reflection circles," troubleshooting problems with reflection, and several practical suggestions for reflection activities.

4) A helpful and user-friendly explanation of this model is found in the *Service Reflection Toolkit*, from the Northwest Service Academy (n.d.) in Portland, Oregon. It can also be found on the National Service-Learning Clearinghouse web site: http://www.servicelearning.org

5) My thinking around what follows has been influenced by Rebekah Miles (2001) and by Darrell Jodock and others here at Gustavus who have participated in and helped to shape the various programs and resources of our Center for Vocational Reflection.

References

Aristotle. (1985). *Nicomachean ethics* (T. Irwin, Trans.). Indianapolis, IN: Hackett.

Benhabib, S. (1987). The generalized and the concrete other: The Kohlberg-Gilligan controversy and moral theory. In E. F. Kittay & D. T. Meyers (Eds.), *Women and moral theory* (154–177). Totowa, NJ: Rowman & Littlefield.

Boss, J. A. (1994). The effect of community service work on the moral development of college ethics students. *Journal of Moral Education, 23*(2), 183–198.

Bradley, J. (1995). A model for evaluating student learning in academically based service. In M. Troppe (Ed.), *Connecting cognition and action: Evaluation of student performance in service learning courses.* Denver, CO: Education Commission of the States/Campus Compact.

Dalton, J. C. (2001). Career and calling: Finding a place for the spirit in work and community. In M. A. Jablonski (Ed.), *New directions for student services: No. 95. The implications of student spirituality for student affairs practice* (pp. 17–25). San Francisco, CA: Jossey-Bass.

De Graf, J., Wann, D., & Naylor, T. H. (2001). *Affluenza: The all-consuming epidemic.* San Francisco, CA: Berrett-Koehler.

Dewey, J. (1933). *How we think: A restatement of the relation of reflective thinking to the educative process.* Boston, MA: D. C. Heath.

Dyck, A. J. (1994). *Rethinking rights and responsibilities: The moral bonds of community.* Cleveland, OH: Pilgrim Press.

Eyler, J., & Giles, D. E., Jr. (1999). *Where's the learning in service-learning?* San Francisco, CA: Jossey-Bass.

Fowler, J. W. (1981). *Stages of faith: The psychology of human development and the quest for meaning.* San Francisco, CA: HarperSanFrancisco.

Freire, P. (1997). *Pedagogy of the oppressed,* (Rev. ed.). New York, NY: Continuum. (Original work published 1970)

Furco, A., & Billig, S. H. (Eds.). (2002). *Service-learning: The essence of the pedagogy.* Greenwich, CT: Information Age.

Gardner, H. (1993). *Multiple intelligences: The theory in practice.* New York, NY: BasicBooks.

Hatcher, J. A., & Bringle, R. G. (1997). Reflections: Bridging the gap between service and learning. *Journal of College Teaching 45*(4), 153–156. (Reprinted in *NSEE Quarterly, 1999, 24*(3), 12–16.)

Jacoby, B., & Associates. (1996). *Service-learning in higher education: Concepts and practices.* San Francisco, CA: Jossey-Bass.

Kendall, J. C., & Associates (1990). *Combining service and learning: A resource book for community and public service,* (Vols. 1–3). Raleigh, NC: National Society for Internships and Experiential Education.

Kolb, D. A. (1984). *Experiential learning: Experience as the source of learning and development.* Upper Saddle River, NJ: Prentice Hall.

Miles, R. (2001, October). *That's all a mule can do: Rethinking work and vocation in U.S. culture.* Paper presented at the annual meeting of the Lilly Fellows Program for the Humanities and the Arts, Merrimack, NH.

Moely, B. E., McFarland, M., Miron, D., Mercer, S., & Ilustre, V. (2002, Fall). Changes in college students' attitudes and intentions for civic involvement as a function of service-learning experiences. *Michigan Journal of Community Service-Learning 9*(1), 18–26.

Muller, W. (1999). *Sabbath: Finding rest, renewal, and delight in our busy lives.* New York, NY: Bantam Books.

Northwest Service Academy. (n.d). *Service reflection toolkit.* Retrieved February 27, 2006, from the Students in Service to America web site: http://www.studentsinservicetoamerica.org/ tools_resources/docs/nwtoolkit.pdf

Nussbaum, M. C. (1986). *The fragility of goodness: Luck and ethics in Greek tragedy and philosophy.* New York, NY: Cambridge University Press.

Nussbaum, M. C. (1990). *Love's knowledge: Essays on philosophy and literature.* New York, NY: Oxford University Press.

Nussbaum, M. (1993, Spring). Equity and mercy. *Philosophy and Public Affairs, 22*(2), 83–125.

O'Reilley, M. R. (1998). *Radical presence: Teaching as contemplative practice.* Portsmouth, NH: Boynton/Cook.

Palmer, P. J. (1990). *The active Life: A spirituality of work, creativity, and caring.* San Francisco, CA: Jossey-Bass.

Parks, S. D. (2000). *Big questions, worthy dreams: Mentoring young adults in their search for meaning, purpose, and faith.* San Francisco, CA: Jossey-Bass.

Perry, W. G., Jr. (1968). *Forms of intellectual and ethical development in the college years: A scheme.* New York, NY: Holt, Rinehart & Winston.

Reed, J., & Koliba, C. (1995). *Facilitating reflection: A manual for leaders and educators.* Retrieved February 27, 2006, from the University of Vermont web site: http://www.uvm.edu/ ~dewey/reflection_manual

Sandel, M. J. (1982). *Liberalism and the limits of justice.* New York, NY: Cambridge University Press.

Steinke, P., Fitch, P., Waldstein, F., & Johnson, C. (2000). *Identifying successes in model service-learning courses across Iowa.* Des Moines, IA: Iowa College Foundation.

Taylor, J. (2002, Fall). Metaphors we serve by: Investigating the conceptual metaphors framing national and community service and service-learning. *Michigan Journal of Community Service-Learning, 9*(1), 45–57.

Trott, M. C., Laurel, M. K., & Windeck, S. L. (1993). *SenseAbilities: Understanding sensory integration.* Tuscon, AZ: Therapy Skill Builders.

Varlotta, L. (2000, Fall). Service as text: Making the metaphor meaningful. *Michigan Journal of Community Service-Learning, 7*, 76–8.

14

STUDENT PERSPECTIVES

Callista Brown Isabelle and Lillian Zumberge

Editors' note: College is a time when students often experience profound changes in their understanding of issues they had previously taken for granted. As we talked with our colleagues at Gustavus Adolphus College about the rewards and challenges of helping undergraduates grapple with issues of service, justice, and faith, we became increasingly curious about how graduates of our college might describe their experiences here in learning about these themes. A full-fledged alumni survey was not feasible (though a good direction for future research), but we hoped to glean at least some insight into how—or whether—undergraduate experiences contribute to postgraduate relationships with the issues of faith, service, and justice. We were also frankly curious about whether graduates would think we as teachers had done a "good job" in helping them cultivate and nurture their understanding of service, justice, and faith. Two students who had heard about our project expressed interest in talking more with us about it, and we subsequently asked them to put their reflections in writing. Both of them willingly and energetically took up the chance to think about how these three themes were not only part of their Gustavus experience, but also part of their lives after Gustavus.

Callista Brown Isabelle

It is interesting which conversations I remember from my time at Gustavus, those which in retrospect have quietly yet dramatically changed the course of my life. As a sophomore, I remember hearing a friend describe the sense of exclusion she experienced from members of an evangelical Christian group of which I was a part. She felt the group's rigid theology left little room for questioning and doubt. The doors to open conversation seemed to be tightly closed, and my friend was left on the outside of the group. Realizing that her truth was shared by many, I was struck by my friend's words so deeply that I stopped attending the group meetings and searched for a more open group to call home.

As a junior, I traveled to South Africa with the Gustavus Choir. I remember a brief conversation I had with a woman just as our choir was boarding our tour bus to leave her retreat center. I thanked her for the music she and others had just sung for us, and she reminded me, "There's no such thing as a person who can't sing." Her truth struck me, as we loaded our beautiful velvet robes and polished voices, bound for another concert venue. Over the next years, I felt drawn to help others find their voices and set them free.

Seven years after this experience (having graduated from Gustavus in 2000), I've just completed three years at Yale Divinity School. This stretched me further into ecumenical and multifaith dialogue. I helped to coordinate ecumenical daily worship for the Divinity School Chapel program. I also worked intensely with the Yale Multifaith Council. Christians were the minority in this group, and I learned about the struggles of being Muslim, Jewish, Baha'i, and Pagan at a large university. During my years at Gustavus, I would not have dreamed of such a job. At that time I was trying to find my foothold in Lutheranism after emerging from several years of fundamentalism. I wasn't ready to seek out interfaith dialogue and engage my neighbors of other religions. Surprisingly, a few years later, I loved my work with multifaith university students. My travels to South Africa and Germany while at Gustavus had fueled my desire to ground my religious practice in hospitality toward people of other religions as well.

Only in retrospect can I see how doors opened up at Gustavus that led me to take on such a challenge. While in South Africa with the Gustavus Choir, a Gustavus administrator suggested that I visit a retreat center (Holden Village) for the first time. Someone from Minnesota, at a table in South Africa, gently convinced me to take a plane, bus, and boat to a retreat center in the middle of nowhere. In contrast to the mission trip I took during college, I never considered my time at Holden Village to be service work. I was simply passionate about the hospitality I could provide for village guests. I cooked food, and was fed in return. I learned more from the German,

Japanese, Minnesotan, and Canadian cooks working by my side than I did from all the cookbooks I studied during those years. I needed those years deep in the wilderness, stirring cauldrons of soup, just as much as the retreat center needed a cook. But it was the openness that was cultivated in me at Gustavus, as well as my passion for serving the church in its various expressions, that prepared me for such an unexpected adventure.

In terms of social justice, the move to New Haven also meant living in one of the poorest cities in America. For me, growing up on a farm in Iowa, homeless folks were a distant reality, fairly easy to ignore. Gustavus participates in Hunger and Homelessness Awareness Week, but as a student I mostly kept my distance, choosing not to join the group who voluntarily slept in boxes outside the chapel in an act of solidarity with the poor. Thoughts of homeless, hungry people tugged at my consciousness during those years, but seemed so distant from my reality that I could comfortably ignore those issues.

My years in New Haven challenged me to think about who my neighbors are, to interact with them, and to make myself more vulnerable in the process. During my work in Bridgeport Hospital, I noticed that it was much harder to tell the rich from the poor. Connecticut's richest residents shared hospital rooms with its poorest residents. Hospital gowns and the vulnerability of being sick have a way of transcending the divisions that are more obvious outside hospital walls. Nevertheless, lack of health insurance and family support is still a harsh reality for many patients. Poverty continues to be uncomfortable for me, but in a way that I can no longer ignore. I don't ever want to get comfortable with the growing disparity between rich and poor. My neighbors are no longer "issues" at a distance, but have names, faces, and stories that I am blessed to know—and am praying never to forget.

Learning from service happens for me over time. While some realizations emerge in the moment of interaction with other people, communities, and countries, deeper meaning is made in the ensuing days and years. I can most clearly make connections between my faith and service when I can examine the map of my experiences from a distance. While in South Africa, there was no way to anticipate how one woman's words would inform my sense of musical understanding for years to come. While stirring vats of lentils at Holden Village, there was no way to anticipate how deeply my passion for hospitality would be kindled by simple acts of cooking, sweeping, kneading, and serving. In many ways, Gustavus gave me the tools to begin interpreting this map of experiences. Professors challenged me to think critically and globally. Chapel services awakened my sense of mystery. Mentors encouraged me to pursue further education in new places. International travel oriented my map in a completely new way. Gustavus was a place that fueled my faith and provided room for questions. It is a relatively short stop on the map for most of us. Yet it has also proved to be a sturdy springboard into ventures whose end I cannot see.

Lillian Zumberge

My early exposure to religion was limited. Despite the lack of religious lessons passed down from my parents, I was raised with very specific messages about the importance of service. My mother was always clear to tell her children that the reason she had kids was to raise people who would make the world a better place. My father insisted that we spend each holiday delivering meals and gifts to people less fortunate than we. I remember a methodical lesson on the importance of wrapping donations with the same care and attention to detail as a gift you would give to a relative. This doing of good deeds was never connected, at least verbally, to any sense of faith or religion. It simply was what you did to make the world better for others.

I give this framework to explain that before arriving at college, there was no connection in my mind between being a good person and going to church. My family did celebrate Christian holidays, but also solstice, and we read Thich Nhat Han at the dinner table. But none of this was tied in any way to the Bible.

When I arrived at Gustavus, I joined several high school friends who had come the year before. I did not think about the religious aspect of the school or that the presence of religion would have any bearing on my time there. Like the rest of my life, I assumed it would go on around me and I would go on around it.

My oblivion came to a grinding halt the day someone vandalized my car. My family have always been supporters of the gay community, and sometime earlier I had put a rainbow sticker on my car as a way of showing support for homosexuals. One day in late winter I arrived at my car to find that someone had scrawled all over it in pink lip balm, "F....G FAGGOT." I stood there looking at my car, and then looking around the large student parking lot searching for any sign of the culprit. I was angry and hurt and a little scared. My eyes landed on the center focal point of campus, the chapel spire, and I felt totally alone and not a little betrayed. If religion had played any part in my life directly, it was as a community builder, a glorified pageant of love and ritual. Not a hateful, violent act. I was immediately reminded of my dislike for the popular cliques in high school and their brand of trendy religion, a kind that was meant to reinforce the bond among them with no discernable need to perform "good deeds."

In relating this event to friends I was given a wide range of possible suspects, but surprisingly, the most consistent opinion pointed to someone who was a member of a specific religious group on campus. I was aware that on our campus there were competing views of homosexuality and religion, but I was unaware that something so hostile existed at this nice, friendly place. It is important to note that the perpetrator of my car vandalism was never discovered. What was striking to me, though, was that members of this particular religious group were so consistently the suspects that my friends mentioned. Whether it was true or not, it was the perception that these religious students were the most virulently homophobic that I remember.

It was also during this time that I had my first "verbal damning" at Gustavus. One day in the cafeteria a student asked me if I had accepted Jesus as my personal savior. I had heard this kind of language before, but had never been asked directly and was not expecting it over my Tuesday afternoon lunch. I was eating with a newly made acquaintance, and we had a mutual lack of knowledge about each other. Despite my surprise, I did not struggle to answer because I knew clearly that I had not had a specific moment of accepting Jesus to play such a roll in my life. I answered that I had not done this and that actually, I did not consider myself a particularly religious person. There were further questions about my beliefs about living a good life, which I agreed was important. I countered with my observation that being Christian did not seem to be a clear indication that one was a good person and that I didn't feel it was a necessary component. My lunch partner listened to my response and then, as casually as one would wish me good luck on a test, said that it was all fine and good that I thought I was a good person, but unfortunately I was going to burn in hell for my failure to invite Jesus into my heart. Then he got up and left.

This comment was quite jarring for me. How could the failure to do one thing, among a throng of other things that I would do in my life, be powerful enough to damn me for all eternity? How did this person know this with such cavalier confidence? How does one respond to such a statement? The comment stayed with me and probably served as a cornerstone for my later rejection of all things Christian.

During my second year I made close friends with a group of people who identified themselves as gay, while my first-year friends became increasingly vocal about their Christianity. This was a year of conflict on campus. The umbrella organization for Christian student groups had met and established a list of criteria for what it means to be a "real Christian," one of which was the belief that homosexuality is not an acceptable lifestyle. Although their peers were condemning them based on religion, my gay and lesbian friends were among the most religious people I knew. Nearly all of them were religion majors, "preacher's kids," or preseminary students. The criteria list was published in our campus newspaper, with instructions that individuals who wanted to continue to be members of this umbrella organization would have to sign the list to show their agreement.

This event ultimately culminated in an on-campus conversation between Christian groups and the GLBT (gay, lesbian, bisexual, transgender) group on campus. Moderated by the chaplain, it provided a forum for multiple viewpoints to be expressed regarding these issues. During this entire experience, I was presented with such a complicated picture of what it meant to be religious and to be good. People made various arguments regarding homosexuality and often used the Bible to defend their position. The exact same passage was quoted by opposing sides and interpreted totally differently. Both sides relied heavily on their faith to give them strength during that difficult time, yet somehow that faith could not bring them together. I became more and more acutely aware that my experience of life and specifically this situation was radically different from that of people on either side because I lacked the common denominator of faith. I believed that I was living a good life, standing up for what I thought and helping others, but none of this was based on faith. I believed in spirituality and the presence of a soul but this did not naturally flow into a belief in Jesus as my savior. Student discussions about religion were happening all around me, and some people continued to tell me I would be going to hell. Each time someone asked me if I had accepted Jesus as my personal Lord, my skin crawled. I had nothing against Jesus; from all I had heard he had done great things. Why couldn't I get in touch with this feeling of faith that so many of my friends had wrapped around them?

Compounding this issue was the fact that I had no idea where to go for help in answering these questions. I was not part of the religious community, so I didn't know the outwardly religious adults on campus. My professors had never discussed faith with me, and I was unsure if they would feel comfortable doing so. Looking back, I can see that my spiritual journey was also being stunted by the fact that I was hardly exposed to any non-Christian beliefs at Gustavus. My only choice seemed to become Christian, or to not be Christian.

I decided to meet with the school chaplain. I explained that I had some block about worshiping Jesus. For some reason, that I could not pinpoint, I did not want to feel guilt over this man's death, I did not feel loved by his act of sacrifice, and I didn't feel comfortable handing my life over to his will. The chaplain was the first person that I felt really listened to what I was saying and understood the conflict I was feeling. He turned me on to feminist theology, where I discovered for the very first time that these feelings I had were not just about me being afraid or whiny, but were shared by others. I read some recommended books, and for a while I was buoyed by this newfound sense of solidarity with other women.

My senior year I did my student teaching in an urban high school in Minneapolis. The experience was overwhelming for a variety of reasons. I was struck for the first time by a real awareness of my race and position as a middle-class citizen. Here I was, a white woman from the suburbs, coming to the city to teach children of color about how to behave in order to be successful in my culture. Not too long into this experience I began to feel that I was colonizing my students. My belief in service toward those less fortunate was hitting a roadblock, because I was becoming less sure of exactly what "less fortunate" meant. What was it in me that felt compelled to do this work if it wasn't in some way tied to my own judgment of how people should live? Did I want what was best for these students, or did I want to teach them to behave in a way that would make me more comfortable?

Looking back, I see this as a time in my life when I would have benefited from some guidance and conversation. Perhaps even more difficult was that because I was unaware of the ways in which my personal faith played a role in my choice to be an educator, I struggled to identify a reason to stick with it when the going got tough. At certain points, when I was really struggling, my anxiety and frustration would get the better of me and I would feel defeated.

In the end, I left Gustavus without resolving these issues. I had floundered around with my peers for four years and come out far more confused than at peace. Since graduating in 2001 I have done more exploration into the issue of faith and how it affects my life, my teaching, my relationships. I have yet to find something that really feels right to me. I continue to identify myself as a non-Christian. I am not happy with this definition. I wish I could define myself more by what I am than what I am not.

Am I resentful of my experience at Gustavus? No. It is very likely that had I not gone to such a school I would never have thought at all about how faith played a role in my life. I am grateful for having had the opportunity to hear so many different viewpoints from my friends and peers. Now, having given it a little space, I am much more comfortable discussing religion than many of my friends who went to secular schools. However, I would have really benefited from some more classroom conversations around faith and religion while I was in school, during a time that was so conflicted for my peers and me. As a teacher, I know that students learn so much more from their teachers than from the content of the course.

Editors' note: These two students remind us that the college years are only a fraction of the time most people take for belief development. But for many students it is also the critical and dramatic time in which struggle and confusion create an opening for questions and exploration. This "crisis of faith" period can be essential and helpful because it allows for an instability that opens the door to wonder and clarification.

Faculty and staff comments obviously carry incredible authority and power of influence. Manipulating the classroom environment to balance privilege around these issues is an important task. By the kinds of questions that faculty and staff ask, groundwork is laid for further interrogation and integration.

But it is the entrée into these issues as they collide with each other that creates the context for developing frames of reference, patterning critical questions, interrogating perceptions and bias, and encouraging integration and expansion. These two students remind us that this ongoing work is an important priority in the development of identity.

Perhaps another way to think about it is to distinguish between content and form. In the undergraduate years, much effort is spent assisting students to begin mastery in subject areas while at the same time creating the context for a liberal education. The critical thinking skills necessary to develop a more cohesive worldview are more difficult to label and enable. Yet it is this formative work that helps to give cohesion to the interaction among an individual's perception of faith, the service they complete, and the social justice they champion. Finally, the students' eagerness to engage in conversation about these connections indicates the potential for everyone's continued growth and learning if institutions maintain contact with their graduates. More than inquiring about career or family, asking former students to reflect on their undergraduate years in these terms affords a continuing opportunity for integration.

15

CONCLUSION: WHAT WE KNOW SO FAR

Brian T. Johnson and Carolyn R. O'Grady

When all is said and done, what have we learned about the intersections of faith, service-learning, and social justice? It is clear to us that dialogue on these themes is very challenging for those in the academy. As Brammer asserts in Chapter 10, faculty (and staff and students, for that matter) have well-founded fears about making public their faith commitments (if they are believers) or their choice not to believe (if they are nontheistic). Nevertheless, through our conversations with faculty, students, and staff at our institution, we have come to believe that the best work in service-learning and social justice is done when those involved actively and intentionally explore the ways in which they make meaning of the whole of life (Parks, 2000). As Parks says, human beings, individually or together, "compose a sense of the ultimate character of reality and then stake our lives on that sense of things"(p. 20). The more effective faculty and staff in higher education are at articulating their view of reality and how that view influences their work in service-learning or social justice, the more they can model for students how to reach toward making these connections clear for themselves. If we continue to emphasize a false dichotomy between faith and reason (implying that the faithful cannot be rational or that the scientist can't have spiritual inclinations), the more we perpetuate compartmentalization. Indeed, critical engagement with and interrogation of the role of faith in social justice and service work is an essential enterprise for higher education if we want to develop young adults who bring a thoughtful stance to their activism.

The themes we explore in this volume are relevant not only for church-related colleges, but for all settings in which young adults are encouraged to deepen their understanding of their view of the world. To ignore the ways in which faith, service, and social justice can mutually inform and enhance each other is to ignore fundamental commitments and intersections that shape human existence and, ultimately, to lose any possibility of integration.

Reflections and Suggestions

As we worked on this project, it began to seem as though we were peering into a prism. At times the topic of faith seemed to shine brightly and be most relevant in our research. At other times, social justice shone brightest in our consideration as we explored the ways in which faith perspectives not only enrich, but also oppress. Sometimes the colors in our prism seemed inseparable, and at other times it was difficult to find coherence among them. We end this project with more continuing questions than absolute answers, but we also have a number of suggestions we hope will be helpful to other individuals and institutions seeking more effective ways to explore the intersections of faith, service, and social justice.

Conflicts and Contradictions

Our prism metaphor implies a certain unity of perspective, but in the end it is the multifaceted aspect of the prism that seems most relevant to our work. The themes we have explored in this book are contested topics, particularly the issue of faith in the academy. Certainly many institutions of higher education (such as Wheaton College [Illinois] and the University of Notre Dame, as Loramy Gerstbauer noted in Chapter 7) intentionally maintain a religious identity, and most members of those faculties presumably see no contradiction between personal faith and work in the academy. But how faith is defined and, particularly, how faith should influence social, cultural, and intellectual milieus, are highly contested questions. We have only to look at the current political landscape in the U.S. and other parts of the world to recognize the competing claims for and against a more God-centered notion of the world. Within this debate, institutions of higher education have primarily been viewed as places in which the work of the intellect supersedes theism, with personal faith viewed as either too private or too "fuzzy," or sometimes too narrow, to be part of the academic conversation. In addition, personal faith does sometimes lead to actual anti-intellectualism, with believers abandoning difficult questioning in order to blindly embrace religious dogma (we can easily see this tendency in the forms religious expression sometimes takes in the U.S. and elsewhere).

We ourselves struggle with the implications of our work, as do the contributors to this volume. Part of our struggle can be glimpsed in our alternating between the terms *faith* and *spirituality*, and in our declaration that belief in a God is not required for someone to be considered spiritual. Lisa Heldke and Peg O'Connor point out in Chapter 8 that faith in God is not a prerequisite for living lives of service and justice, and we agree. Some colleagues who read earlier versions of our manuscript bristled when we used terms such as *ultimate meaning* or *transcendence,* because, for them, these words implied value judgments and were mostly obfuscating. As one of our colleagues noted, emphasizing the spiritual can sometimes be an obstacle to the kind of critical thinking that is crucial to consciousness raising and social justice action. And we agree.

And yet, it is clear that religious pluralism in our institutions of higher education is increasing, and that religious or spiritual values permeate the lives of many of our students. To stifle explicit religious dialogue in our classrooms or to dismiss religious belief as irrelevant or anti-intellectual is in contradiction to the reason educational institutions exist at all. We can sometimes allow ourselves to mock or ignore religious belief in a way we would never do if it were race, socioeconomic class, or gender that we were considering as an aspect of an individual's social identity. If we ignore or censure religious views in our students, we cause those believers to withdraw into sectarian groups when our task as educators should be to help students question and explore, as Callista Brown Isabelle and Lillian Zumberge attempted to do while at Gustavus Adolphus College (see Chapter 14). As Nash (2001) advises,

> We must be willing and able to let students know that whenever and wherever issues of religious and spiritual meaning arise for them, we are ready to respond thoughtfully and knowledgeably, just as we would when racial, gender, and sexual-orientation issues arise. We will never arbitrarily rule these questions out of bounds just because they make us nervous, or because we claim to know little about them, or because we ourselves might be harboring stubborn, antireligious stereotypes that embarrass us. (p. 54)

What emerges from the writers in this volume is that faculty and staff are not being asked to become either religion department faculty or chaplains or campus ministers. Rather, faculty and staff are in a unique position to invite students to consider how they are integrating learning into existing frameworks of belief, regardless of religious or nonreligious proclivities. And the extent to which faculty and staff reveal their own commitments has significant and important bearing on the manner in which these issues might be discussed and understood. Nevertheless, issues of power, privilege, and authority make it essential that we carefully consider how to approach the topics of faith and spirituality—whether in a classroom or on a campus—and how these intersect with service-learning and social justice initiatives. How can we explore these intersections most effectively?

Telling Stories

We have learned that the best way to start a dialogue about issues of faith, justice, and service is for individuals to tell their stories about how they understand these concepts. All of us long for a way to make sense of the expected and unexpected events of our lives and establish what Parks (2000) calls "connection, pattern, order, and significance" (p. 14). Our project began because the two of us chose to talk with each other about our teaching dilemmas. From there, our conversation expanded to include three more colleagues. We did not all know each other well, but we felt enough familiarity with each other to agree to discuss faith and spirituality and how our personal understanding of these was related to the work we did on campus. We took turns discussing our individual faith journeys, and our stories included early childhood experiences in addition to what we had come to believe about our spiritual or ethical values as adults. These stories took months to complete and were listened to with great attention and respect. Nash (2001) provides a foundational attitude to take in regard to encountering the religious perspectives of the "other," and that is to ask the question, "What can we learn from each other regarding our differences?" (p. 51). Although we were not close friends at the outset, we believed we could learn something useful from each other's experiences. These conversations in what we called our "spirit group" began with personal stories, developed into conversations about our sense of calling or lack of it, and continued into an analysis of how (or whether) we felt Gustavus as a church-related institution affirmed or negated our sense of our spiritual or moral selves. All of us were engaged in some way with service-learning or social justice initiatives, and all of us hoped for greater integration between our more inward, personal life, and the outward-directed work we were each doing at our institution.

During the course of our two years of meeting, we explored each other's spiritual traditions and practices. Because one of our members reads the Anglican Book of Common Prayer every day, we read parts of it together as a group. Because another of our members meditates regularly, we tried meditating together. When one member of our group was facing the death of her mother, profound questions of existence were explored. We even attended the God at 2000 national conference together at Oregon State University. There was no specific product that was the end goal of our time together, and we did not plan to change our campus climate in any particular way. Rather, the fruit of our time together was that we had found colleagues with whom we could develop a vocabulary for talking about contested topics.

The following questions and activities may be helpful in sharing personal stories that tell about your thoughts regarding faith, service-learning, or social justice:

- What has been your faith or spiritual journey through your life? How is it similar to or different from those with whom you are in conversation? What kinds of "received knowledge" do you carry from your childhood?

- Which teachers have helped you explore your faith or moral values, the way that Mary Solberg attempts to do in her Studies in Religion class (see Chapter 4)? Which teachers have you felt were not receptive to discussions of faith or values in their classroom?

- In what ways, if any, do your personal faith or spiritual beliefs influence the work you do in the academy? How much do you feel your personal faith beliefs *should* influence your work? In what way, if any, do you use spiritual perspectives in the course of your work? (As Jenifer Ward notes in Chapter 9, this was the most important transformational aspect in her teaching.)

- What are the social justice commitments that matter to you and why? What sustains you in your work for social justice?

- How do you understand the meaning of *service*? What service, volunteer, or mission experiences have you had, if any, and what impact have these had on you? How do you respond to Lisa Heldke and Peg O'Connor's critique of the word "service" as ultimately condescending (see Chapter 8)?

- What reading might you share and discuss with others that would inform your discussions about faith, spirituality, service, or social justice?

Campus Climate and Community

When our spirit group seemed to have reached its natural ending point, the two of us continued to think about ways we as educators could help others think critically about issues of faith, service, and justice. We held some student focus groups, and were dismayed to hear how seldom students at our own campus (a church-related institution!) had been encouraged to explore spiritual and faith perspectives in relation to issues of justice or service. And so we began to talk with other faculty, individually and in focus groups. The result is in your hands, but one of the fruits of these conversations is a wealth of advice for examining how well a college or university supports social justice work, service-learning initiatives, or the role of faith and spirituality in these endeavors. Some of that advice is suggested by Elizabeth Baer in her discussion of faculty development (see Chapter 12). We also have the following recommendations:

- Explore the history and context of your institution, the campus narratives surrounding issues of faith, service, and social justice. For instance, Noreen Buhmann and Brian Johnson point out that some of the reason why service has been part of the lingua franca at Gustavus since its inception is because it was so much a part of the vocabulary of the college's founder, Eric Norelius (see Chapter 3). All institutions have stories that reflect a service, justice, or faith orientation, and these can be examined to consider how such narratives shape or inhibit an exploration of the dynamic interplay among them.

At the same time, as Nadarajan Sethuraju reminds us in Chapter 11, it is important to heed the voices of those among us who point to ways in which the institution does not live up to its rhetoric.

• Examine what kinds of programmatic collaborations could be made (or already exist) between offices which focus on issues of service, justice, or faith. For instance, as Noreen Buhmann points out (Chapter 3), a shared position between the Community Service Center and the chaplains' office has provided ways for these two spaces to work together and help students make connections between service and faith. The collaboration between the Service-Learning for Social Justice Working Group and the Center for Vocational Reflection has provided funds and professional development opportunities for many faculty and staff. At Brown University, collaboration between staff in religious life and in the service-learning center has increased opportunities to explore spiritual motivations for engaging in service. Such collaboration can begin simply with two colleagues who are interested in exploring connections, or can become much more formal and official.

• Sometimes it can be easier to initiate a conversation about faith/spirituality, service, or justice when a person from outside the community speaks to these issues first. Consider what kinds of existing public forums can provide a natural avenue for discussions of faith, service, and justice. For instance, at Gustavus there are well established convocations, such as the MayDay! program and the Nobel Conference. Each of these annual events has a specific theme with corresponding speakers who provide critical perspectives on the topic. Our Center for Vocational Reflection has a biannual conference on vocation, during which invited guests provide workshops and talks. Recent speakers at Gustavus have included Krister Stendahl, speaking on religious pluralism; Jodie Williams, discussing her commitment to securing a ban on landmines; Carrie Newcomer, performing her music and discussing the spiritual components of her creativity; and other thinkers such as Sharon Parks, Parker Palmer, and Jim Wallis.

- Gather data on the religious pluralism on your campus and investigate the opportunities students have to practice on campus or to engage in interfaith dialogue. As Florence Amamoto indicates in Chapter 2, our Muslim students do not yet have an official space on campus where they can pray, while many of our Christian students (though not all) are happy to attend daily chapel in the building designed for this at the center of campus. It can be eye-opening for us as faculty and staff to discover exactly what the demographics of students on our campus are, and to consider how students self-report. Does your campus already have an interfaith council? If not, should it?

- Initiate a working group that keeps issues of justice, privilege, power, and authority present in conversations about campus policies, governance, and curriculum. Because Gustavus is a relatively small campus and faculty are deeply engaged in governance, concerns often get raised in our faculty meetings by a variety of individuals. Nevertheless, issues of justice on our campus have been enhanced through the work of such groups as the Committee on the Status of Women, the Social Justice Working Group, and the Women's Studies Program. Often campus policies or practices unintentionally limit equity because they have not been adequately examined or challenged. The goal here is not to exacerbate the already huge tendency for faculty to be vociferous or argumentative (one of our colleagues has noted that getting faculty to work together is not unlike herding cats), but rather to take responsibility for raising concepts of justice, service, and spirituality when appropriate.

- Consider the climate on your campus for raising issues of faith or justice with colleagues or in the classroom. Is it acceptable to be viewed as a religious or spiritual person, or is being overt about one's faith or spiritual practice considered inappropriate and even suspicious? Is activism or social justice work encouraged on your campus, or are such interests considered a distraction from academic pursuits?

Working With Students

More than any other consideration, the way in which we work with students on these issues is the most important. As word of our project began to spread on our campus, we were struck by how many of our colleagues had encountered dilemmas related to discussions of faith, service, or justice with students and were curious about how we had resolved some of these concerns ourselves. In describing their own struggles in this regard, the contributors to this book point the way to several strategies that can be effective in student learning.

- No discussion of contested issues can occur effectively if there has been no groundwork laid to establish some sense of trust in the classroom. Creating course ground rules for discussion can be helpful in reminding participants how constructive conversation can occur.[1] A tone of safety and trust is enhanced when a teacher reveals aspects of his or her own spiritual life or justice commitments.

- Some individuals are uncomfortable with conflict, and so avoid discussions of contested topics. However, it is essential that students have the opportunity to question, challenge, and engage in dialogue about their deepest held beliefs if they are to become critical thinkers. As faculty we must put aside our own discomforts and model ways of engaging in conflict effectively with the goal of fully understanding another person's point of view rather than trying to change their mind.

- Create scenarios that allow students to react to specific situations that are appropriate for the discipline being taught. For instance, in a biology class students can be asked to ponder the potential conflict between deeply held spiritual beliefs about the sanctity of life with the potential good that can come from stem cell research and to consider ways of responding to such a dilemma. In a history class, students can consider the spiritual motivations of some civil rights activists and discuss whether civil disobedience has a moral value. Or, as Mark Bjelland observes in Chapter 5, current philosophies regarding environmental issues and practical concerns for care of the earth are fertile ground for exploring these relationships. Developing scenarios or case stories allows students to interrogate different viewpoints and to become more adept in their personal disclosure on the issues.

- When students return from study abroad experiences, ensure that debriefing sessions provide opportunities for them to discuss the ways in which they were challenged in their crosscultural expectations. For instance, Gustavus students who go to India as part of our study abroad program have usually never before met someone who is Hindu, much less had to confront the possibility that some believers might choose to have faith in multiple gods rather than one. They are often appalled by the caste system, and find many of their cultural assumptions challenged. As Gaston Alzate reminds us in Chapter 6, challenging these assumptions will inevitably produce conflict and create a template for them to critically assess their biased perception. They need assistance, such as Chris Johnson's recommendations about best practices in reflection, for making sense of their experience and integrating it with their previous ways of thinking about faith or justice (see Chapter 13).

- Invite speakers from other spiritual or religious traditions into your classroom, or activists within your discipline, to provide students with additional role models for engaged thinking.

- Challenge students' assumptions about service or volunteer work as something that they do "to" another. Rather, help them understand the importance of reciprocity and long-term relationships in the service-learning experience, and help them understand the internal strengths of an individual or community which has requested service support. Ask students how (or whether) their service project has challenged their existing belief systems.

- Utilize language that leaves room for a variety of perspectives and reminds students of the complexity of issues such as faith and justice. Mary Solberg's use of "lived contradiction" is a helpful reminder that when we take faith, service, and social justice very seriously, we should not find them to be simplistic or easy concepts (see Chapter 4).

- Include readings for your class that raise issues of religious or spiritual values in your discipline, or that address some of the ethical or social justice challenges in your field. The entire course does not need to be revised; simply starting with one article is a good beginning.

- Find opportunities to comment on current national or campus events that reveal the spiritual issues embedded within them.

- Have lunch with colleagues with whom you can discuss the meaning that teaching has for you and what it means to you to be authentic as a teacher. Share teaching dilemmas and insights.

- Those who work in students affairs have many opportunities to encourage conversation among students about contested topics. Facilitated conversations in dorms about faith, service, and justice can often be spaces where students feel freer to participate in dialogue and ask questions. A unique program called Legends, Cookies, & Cocoa, initiated by a staff member of our counseling center, invited individual faculty and staff to spend an evening in conversation with students in a dorm meeting room. The invited guest would read or tell a story, myth, poem, legend, or allegory and then relate it to experiences in his or her own life. This opened up opportunities for students to hear how adult mentors make meaning of the events in their own lives and provided role models for thinking and talking about important life values.[2]

Collaboration and Revision

These are only a few of the possibilities for working on ways to integrate faith, social justice, and service in higher education. Each chapter of this book provides some insight into what has or has not been effective for our colleagues in our context at Gustavus. Works by other authors listed throughout our references provide additional resources and perspectives. The most crucial thing we have learned in this process is that working on these concepts in isolation is disheartening and ineffective. Our research has convinced us that exploring the relationship between spirituality, service, and justice is a practice in which faculty and students can engage together, and that it can lead toward what Sleeter calls "a shared project of a just community" (as cited in Thompson, 2002, p. 78).

Our collaboration has been a complicated metaphor for the nature of this work. As a faculty member and a chaplain, we have had to consistently work at language, create safety and trust to discuss our differences, interrogate our assumptions, and now at the end of this book, explore how we ourselves are integrating these subjects, not only as individuals writing a book together, but in critical companionship with faculty, staff, and students.

What have we come to realize?

When we began this study, we were motivated by experiences of disconnect. Carolyn wondered how to work with students when issues of faith were raised in the classroom, while Brian wondered why he was cautious to raise issues of faith when working with faculty. How might we react to these situations differently now?

Carolyn: When Lucy says that she has prayed for guidance and that God wants her to return and help "those people" in Costa Rica, I would now have the experience of this research to help squelch the internal anxiety I expect would immediately arise. I would know that Lucy, like most college students, is still in process in regard to her spiritual development and has an uncritical understanding of her faith, and I would try to remember that Lucy, like all my undergraduate students, needs careful mentoring on her way to adulthood. I commonly ask students to "say more" when they make a comment that seems unclear or based on assumption. I would ask Lucy to say more about why she is so sure she understands God's message to her. I would say something like, "Exploring one's spiritual or religious values is an important dimension to thinking about whether the vocation of teaching is for you. Let's take a moment and consider how your deepest beliefs might be influencing the choices you are making for a career." I would ask students to turn to the person next to them and say something about this topic (also a common activity in my classes). After five or so minutes of allowing students to talk in pairs, I would ask if anyone would like to share their thoughts on how their spiritual values might be influencing their consideration of teaching as a career. I would be intentional about using the word spiritual rather than reli-

gious to signal a broader, not necessarily Christian, understanding of faith per-spectives.3 And then I would have to "wing it" based on what (or whether) students shared about their thoughts. Perhaps I would try to introduce some more critical perspectives on the type of missionary work Lucy suggests for herself by asking the kinds of questions suggested by Van Engen (2000), such as: What has the U.S. done to help or harm the country you have just visited? Are you aware of organizations that support injustice and poverty in that country? What aspects of the work you wish to do there could be done just as well or more effectively by citizens of that country themselves? I might end the class by asking students to write a short reaction essay, due at the next class, in which they reflect either on how their spiritual, religious, or moral beliefs relate to the topics we are discussing in class, or on their reaction to the discussion in today's class. Of course, all this assumes that I have kept my wits about me and am not having one of those bad-awful-horrible teaching days where nothing goes well.

Brian: *In planning the reflection sessions for students involved in the Hunger and Homelessness Sleepout, I would ask invited faculty speakers to meet with me before the event. I would point out that I expect students to come to the event with a variety of motivations for doing this activity and that these might include religious and political perspectives. I would suggest that the faculty speakers and I cofacilitate the reflection sessions to provide multiple adult role models of activism for students to consider. I would have planned my own session, just in case, to make sure the issues were addressed. I would have created an exercise where students could read brief descriptions of the work of people like Mary Jo Copeland, Oscar Romero, or Brother Roger of Taizé—models of activism and faith. I would ask the students to discuss any parallels they see between these peo-ple's lives and their own.*

Our revised scenarios don't ensure that we won't feel a sense of disconnect again, nor do they guarantee that students, because of those single events, will have been able to adequately integrate their concepts of service, justice, and faith. And yet, we have expanded our thinking while working collaboratively on this book and are even more committed to helping our students develop over time into thoughtful and committed individuals with their own faith or spiritual perspectives, understandings of service, and hopes for justice.

Endnotes

1) The ground rules Carolyn suggests in her classes, in addition to those offered by the students themselves, include:
   • Speak from your own experience and do not "assume" the experience of others
   • Listen hard
   • No put-downs
   • Maintain confidentiality (what is said in the room stays in the room)

2) The model for this program, called Passages, was developed by Tom Balastreri.

3) When Lucy once met with me in my office to discuss something I can't now remember, she made a point of telling me that she could tell by the way I spoke that I wasn't a Christian. While some students might find it alienating that I use language that attempts to broaden the discussion, I expect other students find it reassuring. At the very least, it is a more authentic approach on my part since, indeed, I am not Christian.

References

Nash, R. J. (2001). *Religious pluralism in the academy: Opening the dialogue.* New York, NY: Peter Lang.

Parks, S. D. (2000). *Big questions, worthy dreams: Mentoring young adults in their search for meaning, purpose, and faith.* San Francisco, CA: Jossey-Bass.

Thompson, D. A. (2002, Spring). Transforming connections: Service learning as a practice of solidarity in the feminist/womanist ethics course. *Hamline Review,* 78–84.

Van Engen, J. A. (2000, January/February). The cost of short-term missions. *The Other Side* *36*(1), 20–23.

INDEX